David MacDill

The Mosaic Authorship Of The Pentateuch

Defended against the views and arguments of Voltaire, Paine, Colenso, Reuss, Graf,

Keunen and Wellhausen

David MacDill

The Mosaic Authorship Of The Pentateuch
Defended against the views and arguments of Voltaire, Paine, Colenso, Reuss, Graf, Keunen and Wellhausen

ISBN/EAN: 9783744681087

Printed in Europe, USA, Canada, Australia, Japan

Cover: Foto ©ninafisch / pixelio.de

More available books at **www.hansebooks.com**

THE MOSAIC AUTHORSHIP

OF THE

PENTATEUCH

DEFENDED AGAINST THE VIEWS AND ARGUMENTS OF VOLTAIRE, PAINE, COLENSO, REUSS, GRAF, KUENEN, AND WELLHAUSEN

BY

D. MacDILL, D.D., LL.D.

Professor of Apologetics in the Theological Seminary Xenia, Ohio

DAYTON, OHIO
W. J. SHUEY, PUBLISHER
1896

PREFACE

THE following treatise consists, in part, of lectures delivered to the students of the Xenia Theological Seminary. Some things appropriate only to the theological class-room have been omitted, and additions have been made.

In discussing points that have been much discussed before, and keeping in view the wants of theological students as well as of readers in general, it is necessary, of course, in some cases to say what has already been said by others.

I am indebted to many authors, which will be readily perceived by the learned reader.

It has been thought proper, in quoting from French and German authors, to accompany the quotations with an English translation. Not being acquainted with the Dutch language, I have used Wicksteed's translation of Kuenen's "Hexateuch."

D. MACDILL.

XENIA THEOLOGICAL SEMINARY, August 1, 1896.

CONTENTS

		PAGE
PREFACE		iii

PART I

PRELIMINARY

| CHAPTER I. | THE POINTS IN DISPUTE, | 9 |
| CHAPTER II. | HISTORY OF THE DISCUSSION, | 13 |

PART II

OBJECTIONS CONSIDERED

CHAPTER I.	OBJECTIONS IN GENERAL,	27
CHAPTER II.	CLAIMED IMPROPRIETIES,	30
CHAPTER III.	CLAIMED ANACHRONISMS,	35
CHAPTER IV.	CLAIMED ALLOTOPISMS,	57
CHAPTER V.	CLAIMED CONTRADICTIONS,	63
CHAPTER VI.	CLAIMED DIFFICULTIES,	72
CHAPTER VII.	IMAGININGS,	93
CHAPTER VIII.	PLURALITY OF AUTHORS,	103

PART III

INTERNAL EVIDENCE

CHAPTER I.	ADAPTATION,	119
CHAPTER II.	DEUTERONOMY PRESUPPOSES OTHER PENTATEUCHAL BOOKS,	123
CHAPTER III.	STYLE,	129
CHAPTER IV.	JOURNALISTIC FORM,	132
CHAPTER V.	ACQUAINTANCE WITH EGYPT,	136
CHAPTER VI.	SCIENTIFIC ACCURACY,	143
CHAPTER VII.	HISTORICAL INTEGRITY,	152
CHAPTER VIII.	EXACTNESS,	161
CHAPTER IX.	THE LEGISLATION,	178
CHAPTER X.	ARGUMENT FROM SILENCE,	190
CHAPTER XI.	EGYPTIAN WORDS AND NAMES,	193

PART IV

EXTERNAL EVIDENCE

CHAPTER I.	THE BOOK OF JOSHUA,	197
CHAPTER II.	HISTORICAL BOOKS AFTER JOSHUA,	208
CHAPTER III.	THE PSALMS,	221
CHAPTER IV.	THE PROPHECIES,	225
CHAPTER V.	THE HISTORICAL ARGUMENT,	229
CHAPTER VI.	TESTIMONY OF CHRIST AND THE APOSTLES,	248
CHAPTER VII.	CONSEQUENCES,	257

PART I
PRELIMINARY

PART I

PRELIMINARY

CHAPTER I

THE POINTS IN DISPUTE

I. The Points Advocated by the Analytic Critics.

THE non-Mosaic origin of the Pentateuch, as contended for at the present time, involves many points and propositions, which may be stated as follows:

1. The whole discussion, as carried on by the leading analytic critics, is permeated by the doctrine of evolution. Their aim and effort are to show, by means of this doctrine, that God Almighty had nothing to do in the production of the Pentateuch or any other portion of the Bible, just as the atheistic evolutionists have been endeavoring to eliminate from the minds of men all belief in the theistic origin and government of the universe.

2. Since, according to the theory of development and growth, the Pentateuch cannot be the production of a single mind, nor of one age, there naturally emerges the hypothesis that it is made up of documents written by different authors, who lived in different ages. These documents and their authors are represented by the letters D, E, J, P, and Q. The critics further suppose that these original documents were combined and dovetailed together by writers acting as editors, compilers, and revisers. These are designated by the letters d, e, j, R, P^1, P^2, P^3, etc. A tabular presentation of the letters which represent the supposed authors, editors, compilers, revisers, and redactors of the Pentateuch, looks a good deal like a complicated algebraic equation, or a binomial raised to the fifth power. An American follower of the analytic critics actually presents the following formula:

$$\text{Hexateuch} = \frac{(J+E)}{Rje} + \frac{D}{Rd} + \frac{(P^1+P^2+P^3)}{R}$$

In this fractional equation the denominators represent compilers and editors.[1]

3. In regard to the times in which the supposed authors, compilers, and redactors lived and wrote, these critics hold, or rather suppose, as follows: that J lived in the ninth century B.C.;[2] E in the eighth century B.C.;[3] D in the seventh,[4] probably during the reign of King Manasseh; and P in the fifth.[5] The times of the other writers are scarcely even conjectured, the most of the critics not venturing to propose an hypothesis concerning them.

4. In regard to the times in which the Pentateuchal books, as we have them, were produced, the views of the analysts are as follows: They hold that Deuteronomy, written as they claim by an unknown author, whom they call D, is the book that was found by Hilkiah in the temple, in the time of King Josiah.[6] They suppose that J and E, original documents by unknown and nameless authors, were amalgamated, by another unknown and nameless author, so as to form one book, JE, at some unknown time, either before or after the book of the law was found in the temple. They claim that Deuteronomy is the oldest book of the Pentateuch, the other four books, as we have them, having originated during the exile, or after it.

5. If the origin of the Pentateuchal laws is to be accounted for by the doctrine of evolution, they, too, must have come into existence at different times. The hypothesis of the analysts is that there are three groups of laws, which they designate as the book of the covenant, the law of holiness, and the Deuteronomic legislation; and that these constitute, as it were, three distinct strata deposited in different ages.

6. In the advocacy of these points and propositions, critics are led by logical necessity to introduce many subsidiary hypotheses and subordinate propositions. Much is made of supposed discrepancies and contradictions, both in the historical and in the legislative portions of the Pentateuch. And not only is the historical integrity of the Pentateuch impeached in order to show

---

[1] Bacon's *Genesis of Genesis*, p. 66.
[2] Kautzsch-Socin, *Die Heilige Schrift des Alten Testaments, Erklärung*, p. xiv.
[3] *Abriss*, p. 156.
[4] *Erklärung*, p. xiv.
[5] *Abriss*, p. 188.
[6] II. Kings 22: 8-11; II. Chr. 34: 15-19.

that Moses did not write it, but also the trustworthiness of other scriptures is impeached, because they bear testimony to the early existence of the Pentateuchal laws and books. The denial of the early existence of the Levitical ritual and legislation involves the conclusion that the Mosaic tabernacle never existed at all. Hence the necessity for the hypothesis that the tabernacle, with its whole history, as embraced in the Pentateuch and other parts of the Bible, is but the idea of the temple of Solomon projected back into the past by the Jewish imagination. Another hypothesis necessitated by the rejection of the Mosaic authorship of the Pentateuch is, that the formulæ, "The Lord said unto Moses," and "God spake unto Moses, saying," are a *legal fiction*, gotten up as an expedient to impart the name and authority of Moses to laws enacted long after his time.

Such, in the main, are the views and hypotheses which the analytic critics propose and maintain in regard to the authorship of the Pentateuch.

II. *The Traditional View.*

The traditional view, as it is often called, may be stated as follows:

1. That Moses is the author of the Pentateuch substantially as we have it. It is not denied that Moses may have employed amanuenses, nor that these may have sometimes employed their own style of thought and language. But the acceptance and approval of what they wrote, by Moses, as his own, would make the whole Mosaic.

2. That the last eight verses of the last chapter of Deuteronomy, probably the whole chapter, and possibly some brief passages found scattered through the Pentateuchal books (equivalent to modern editorial and marginal notes) were written by Ezra or some other duly qualified and authorized person. Such additions by a post-Mosaic hand do not destroy the integrity of the work. The traditional theory is that Moses wrote the Pentateuch *substantially* as we have it.

3. Some of the conservative critics are willing to concede that several documents are embodied in the Pentateuch. On antecedent grounds we incline to think this probable. At least we do not repel the suggestion that there may be several original documents combined in Genesis. Who more likely to have such documents and to utilize them than Moses, who was

learned in all the wisdom of the Egyptians? He may have had in his possession family registers and other memorials brought by Abraham from Ur of the Chaldees. He may have had access in Egypt to old documents, which he carried in memory and afterward reproduced with omissions, additions, and other emendations, according to the wisdom and inspiration which God vouchsafed to him. He may have obtained ancient narratives and songs or other traditional lore from his father-in-law, who was priest (or prince) of Midian, a statesman, and a worshiper of the true God.

We do not believe that the analysts have proved the existence of the documents which they denominate J, E, and P, but the evidence they adduce for this is much more respectable than for most of their other hypotheses.

4. That there are errors in the Pentateuch, as we have it, is admitted on all hands. There is no faultless copy of it, nor of any other portion of the Bible. Errors, however, in modern copies and in the ancient manuscripts do not prove that there were errors in the original autographs of the biblical authors.

5. The question of plenary inspiration is not involved in this discussion. This doctrine is not necessary to the defense of the Mosaic authorship of the Pentateuch. Indeed, much of the reasoning on the other side derives all its plausibility from the doctrine of plenary inspiration and its corollaries, the infallibility and inerrancy of the Scriptures. The analytic critics argue thus: There are errors in the Pentateuch; therefore, Moses did not write it. Were it not for the inerrancy of Moses as a biblical writer, the battering-ram of these critics would often swing without anything to strike. It is very remarkable that even the most skeptical critics, in their argumentation, assume as their major premise that Moses was plenarily inspired, or was in some other way secured, as an author and legislator, against self-inconsistency and all other errors.

CHAPTER II

HISTORY OF THE DISCUSSION

Up to the time of Voltaire there were only sporadic cases of the rejection of the Mosaic authorship of the Pentateuch. It is true that pretty long lists of authors are given in treatises of the analytic critics, in such a way (we do not say intentionally) as to make the impression that they all held to the non-Mosaic authorship of the Pentateuch. Thus the names of Aben-Ezra, Carlstadt, Spinoza, Masius, Peyrere, Astruc, Hobbes, Clericus, and others are classed as pioneers or adherents of the analytic criticism. Yet the majority of them adhered to the traditional belief in regard to the authorship of the Pentateuch. Aben-Ezra and Masius claimed only that some things in the Pentateuch were written by a later hand, which a majority of the most conservative biblical critics admit. Peyrere and Clericus gave up their anti-Mosaic opinions or doubts, and returned to the traditional belief. Astruc, who has sometimes been called the father of the analytic criticism, always defended, or professed to defend, the traditional belief. There are in the list three well-attested anti-Mosaic critics, the rash and eccentric Carlstadt and the two infidels Spinoza and Hobbes.

As to the origination of the analytic criticism, which has for its main objective point the non-Mosaic authorship of the Pentateuch, rival claims have been set up. This honor, if honor it is, has been given to Astruc, Reuss, Graf, De Wette, and others. Wellhausen, who, since the death of Kuenen, is probably the ablest of the destructive critics, writes as follows:

"Die Hypothese, die man nach Graf zu benennen pflegt, stammt nicht von ihm, sondern von seinem Lehrer Eduard Reuss. Am richtigsten wäre sie aber zu benennen nach Leopold George und Wilhelm Vatke; denn sie haben dieselbe zuerst literarisch vertreten, unabhängig von Reuss und unabhängig von einander. Ihrerseits sind alle diese Männer von Martin Lebrecht de Wette ausgegangen, dem epochemachenden

Eröffner der historischen Kritik auf diesem Gebiete. Zu einer festen Position ist freilich de Wette nicht gelangt, aber er hat zuerst deutlich die Kluft empfunden und nachgewiesen, welche sich zwischen dem angeblichen Ausgangspunkte der israelitischen Geschichte und ihr selber aufthut." [1] ("The hypothesis, which is named after Graf, proceeds not from him, but from his teacher, Edward Reuss. It would be more correct to name it after Leopold George and Wilhelm Vatke; because they have been the first to give it literary treatment, independently of Reuss and independently of each other. But all these men have gone out from Martin Lebrecht de Wette, the epoch-making pioneer of historical criticism in this field. To be sure, he did not reach a firm position, but he was the first to find and to point out the chasm which opens between the pretended starting-point of the Israelitish history and that history itself.")

It is thus seen that Wellhausen is disposed to ascribe the paternity of what he recognizes as biblical criticism to Graf rather than to Astruc; to Reuss rather than to Graf; to George and Vatke rather than to Reuss; and to De Wette rather than to George and Vatke. The truth is, however, that nearly a century before De Wette, Voltaire had set forth in his various writings nearly all the points embraced in the analytic criticism, and also most of the arguments employed by the critics in maintaining them. These points are as follows:

1. That Moses was not the author of the Pentateuch.
2. That Deuteronomy is the book that was found in the temple in the time of King Josiah.
3. That the first four books of the Pentateuch were composed by Ezra, or by some other post-exilic writer.
4. That the Book of Joshua had a similar origin.
5. That the books of the Hexateuch were compiled from several documents written by as many different authors, who made many mistakes and often contradict one another.
6. That the Law came after the Prophets.
7. That most of the laws that are ascribed to Moses did not originate until long after his time.
8. That the Pentateuchal laws and worship were the result, not of legislative enactment, nor of divine appointment, but of gradual development and growth.
9. That the Mosaic tabernacle never really existed, and that

[1] Wellhausen, *Prolegomena*, p. 4.

the history of it and references to it in the Pentateuch and elsewhere are false.

10. That the books of Kings, Chronicles, and Esther, as well as the Hexateuch, are historically untrustworthy.

11. That nearly all the Psalms are of post-exilic origin, and that King David wrote but very few of them.

12. That Solomon was not the author of the Song of Songs, nor of Ecclesiastes; nor Isaiah of the last twenty-seven chapters of the book that is ascribed to him, nor of all the thirty-nine chapters which precede.

13. The Scriptures abound in anachronisms, contradictions, interpolations, redactions, alterations, and almost all kinds of errors.

14. That neither the testimony of the apostles, nor even that of our Lord Jesus Christ, in regard to the authorship of the Old Testament books is to be accepted as trustworthy.

Nearly all the points embraced in this summary are presented in the writings of Voltaire. Indeed, he presents more of the many points embraced in "the higher criticism" than any of its distinguished advocates of the present age. The only critics who equal him in the fullness and minuteness of presentation are those that undertake to give a summarized view of the whole. He is by no means consistent with himself; but for this very reason he is a better exponent of the analytic criticism, setting forth, as he does, the divergent opinions of the various classes of its advocates, from the professedly evangelical sort up to the rationalists and infidels.

Voltaire expressed his critical views timidly and cautiously at first, but afterward more boldly and openly. In his "Traité sur Tolérance," he refers to certain passages in the Pentateuch, which, he says, had been claimed as mentioning things that occurred after Moses, and which, therefore, could not be from him. He then remarks as follows: "One replies to these objections that these passages are notes added long afterward by the copyists."[1] He then alludes to the opinion held at one time by Leclerc, as being held by some other theologians, but he speaks of them as "a small number of sectaries, whose curiosity sounds these depths." Then, with the semblance of piety and reverence, he makes the following declaration: "When the wise and the ignorant, princes and shepherds, shall appear, after

---

[1] *Traité sur Tolérance, Mélanges*, p. 452.

this short life, before the Master of eternity, each one of us then will wish to have been just, humane, compassionate, generous; no one will boast to have known precisely in what year the Pentateuch was written, and to have distinguished the text from the notes which were in use by the scribes."[1]

It is evident that Voltaire held the opinions which he ostensibly condemns. The fact that he introduces these matters in marginal notes in his "Treatise on Toleration," with which they have no logical connection, reveals his desire and intention to discredit the Mosaic authorship of the Pentateuch. His real sentiments are more fully presented in his "Dictionnaire Philosophique." But even here he at first represents himself as an advocate of traditional views. He begins the first section of his article on Moses by declaring that "philosophy, researches into antiquity, the spirit of discussion and of criticism, have been pushed so far that at length many learned men have doubted whether there ever was a Moses." He remarks that the infidels claim that it is improbable that a man ever existed whose whole life was a continual prodigy; that it is declared in the Jewish books that no copy of the Pentateuch was known until the time of King Josiah; that the prophets make no reference to the Pentateuch, and that Solomon proceeded contrary to the express law of Moses in adorning the temple. He then declares that "according to these infidels, the books attributed to Moses were written among the Babylonians during the captivity, or immediately after it." After referring to Bolingbroke as reasoning against the Mosaic authorship of the Pentateuch, and after quoting the testimony of Christ and the New Testament in favor of it, he affirms that "it is necessary that we should submit our reason, as many men have done." He closes with the very pious remark that "it is our consolation to have the church with us in maintaining the Mosaic authorship of the Pentateuch," in opposition to philosophy, research, discussion, and criticism.

In the second section of the article on Moses, in the "Dictionnaire Philosophique," the author again treats of the authorship of the Pentateuch, and in the pretended character of a believer in the traditional view. He represents the opponents of this view as presenting the following arguments: That the Scripture itself affirms that the first known copy of the Pentateuch

---

[1] *Traité sur Tolérance, Mélanges,* p. 452.

was found in the temple one thousand one hundred and sixty-seven years after the time of Moses, according to the Hebrew computation; that the book was not known until after the exile; that events are mentioned in it that did not occur until long after the time of Moses; that Leviticus and Deuteronomy are contradictory; that the book is not quoted by the prophets, nor in the Psalms, nor in any of the books attributed to Solomon; that the Pentateuch itself does not claim to be the work of Moses; that if Moses was the author he would not have laid down rules for Jewish kings when there were none, nor were likely to be any; that there were not wealth and mechanical skill enough among the Israelites to construct the tabernacle in the wilderness.

The author represents the advocates of the traditional view as replying to the above reasoning as follows: That the ways of God are not as the ways of men; that God proves, leads, and abandons his people by a wisdom which is unknown to us; that the Jews themselves for more than two thousand years have believed that Moses was the author of these books; that the church, which has succeeded the synagogue, and which, like it, is infallible, has decided the points of controversy; and that the learned ought to be silent when the church speaks.

In regard to the above, we remark as follows:

1. The presentation of arguments at the close of this second section of the article on Moses in favor of the traditional view is in accord with the declaration that "the kisses of an enemy are deceitful." The closing remark that the church, infallible like the synagogue, has decided the question, and that therefore the one duty is silence and submission, is, of course, sarcastic, and is intended to decry the opinion which the author pretends to be upholding.

2. The author claims that he is presenting the objections urged by others against the Mosaic authorship of the Pentateuch, but the most of them were originated by himself. He would gladly have fathered them on preceding authors, but was obliged to content himself with declaring in a general way that these are the objections of the learned.

3. In claiming that it is the learned, the scholars ("les savants"), who urge these objections, Voltaire set the example, which has been followed by later analysts. These in many cases are not backward to claim that all or nearly all biblical learning

and scholarship are with them, and that those who do not accept their views are unlearned and prejudiced.

In the third section of the article on Moses, the critic throws off the mask and makes the following straightforward declaration: "In regard to the books attributed to Moses, the most common rules of criticism do not permit the belief that he is their author." He then proceeds in an equally straightforward way to state his reasons for this declaration. They are as follows:

1. That names of towns, as Jair and Dan, that were unknown in the time of Moses, are mentioned in the Pentateuch.

2. That "the book of the wars of the Lord" is referred to, though it did not exist until after the time of Moses.

3. That the iron bedstead of Og, king of Bashan, is mentioned as existing long after the time of Moses.

4. That cities are spoken of as beyond ("au delà") Jordan that were on this side ("en deçà") Jordan, viewed from the point at which Moses was at the supposed time of writing.

5. That sixty great and fortified cities that did not exist in the time of Moses are mentioned in the Pentateuch.

6. That the Pentateuch is filled with accounts of miracles.

7. That the accounts of prodigies and of God's strange and supernatural dealings with the Israelites in Egypt and in the desert, the ten plagues, the crossing of the Red Sea, the destruction of the Egyptian army, etc., are revolting to reason, and cannot have been written by Moses.

After stating these reasons, he proceeds to decry the general contents of the Pentateuch, and closes this third section of his article on Moses with these words: "It is very pardonable in human reason to see in such history only the barbarous rudeness of a savage people of the primitive times. Man, whatever he may do, cannot reason otherwise; but if God indeed is the author of the Pentateuch, it is necessary to submit without reasoning."[1]

Thus in the "Traité sur Tolérance" and the article on Moses in the "Dictionnaire Philosophique," taken together, we have almost all the points and arguments that are set forth by "the higher criticism."

1. Precisely like the analytic critics of to-day, Voltaire was at much pains to prove that Moses did not write the Pentateuch,

---

[1] *Œuvres de Voltaire*, Hachette, Vol. XIX., p. 68.

but at the same time declared that this is a point of no importance. "Whether Ezra or some other author committed this book to writing, is a matter of absolute indifference, since it is inspired."[1] The last part of this declaration does not accord with the views of the leading critics, nor did Voltaire honestly make it.

2. He maintained that there were more than one author of the Pentateuch; that notes, interpolations, and additions were inserted in it; and that parts of it were rewritten by redactors.

3. As to the time when the Pentateuch was written, Voltaire was not consistent with himself. At one time he declares that, "without doubt, it was committed to writing in the time of Saul and Samuel." At another, he speaks of it as "having been written among the Babylonians during the captivity, or immediately after it." At still another time he is quite confident that the Pentateuch is later than the prophecies, Psalms, and the books attributed to Solomon. The more modern analysts have likewise had several hypotheses in regard to the time of the origin of the Pentateuchal books.

4. The notion of development and progress which figures so largely in "the higher criticism" of our times was employed similarly by the French critic.

5. The testimony of Christ and the New Testament to the Mosaic authorship of the Pentateuch was noticed by him, as by the more modern analysts, and, like them, he set it aside as untrustworthy.

6. He employed the same arguments as are now employed by his successors: the account of the finding of the book of the law in King Josiah's time; the *argumentum e silentio*, that is, that the prophecies, the Psalms, and the books attributed to Solomon are silent in regard to the Pentateuch; the neglect of the Pentateuchal books and laws by the Jewish nation; the geographical argument; the philological argument; the difference between the Deuteronomic and the Levitical laws; the rapid increase of the Israelites in Egypt; the impossibility of the erection of the tabernacle in the wilderness for the want of wealth and artistic skill; the improbability and incredibility of the supernatural events which the book records; the claimed anachronisms, discrepancies, contradictions, fictions, and legends, classed as improbabilities, incredibilities, impossibilities, absurd-

---

[1] *Œuvres de Voltaire*, Vol. XIX., p. 61.

ities, and falsities which are charged upon the book by critics in our day. All these were employed by our famous Frenchman. There is scarcely an argument now employed by the analysts that was not employed, or at least suggested, by him. His treatment of the subject of divine inspiration—sometimes admitting it, sometimes denying it, often sneering at it, and all the time saying that it is in no way affected by the question of Mosaic authorship—constitutes him the type and father of the analytic critics in general, some of whom admit the divine inspiration of the Pentateuch and other portions of the Bible, while many of them, and the ablest of them, are as far gone in unbelief as the great infidel critic himself.

In regard to other books of the Bible, the views of Voltaire are in accord with those of the analytics; we might better say, their views are in accord with his. He denies that Solomon was the author of the Song of Songs, Ecclesiastes, or the Proverbs. He denies the trustworthiness of the books of Kings and Chronicles as mere history. In regard to prophecy and the prophets, he propounds the views now held by the most thoroughgoing analysts, but he does this in his usual insidious way. He says: "God forbid that I should wish to compare the Jewish prophecies to all the fortune-tellers who make court to the victorious, and who predict what has happened to them. I remark only that the Jews produced testimonials of their nation in regard to Cyrus one hundred and sixty years before he was in the world." He then quotes from the twenty-fifth chapter of Isaiah in regard to Cyrus, and remarks that some learned men ("quelques savants") cannot believe that God would confer the title of Christ (Voltaire thus translates "anointed") on a profane devotee of the religion of Zoroaster; and that these savants dare to say that these predictions concerning Cyrus were gotten up after the occurrence of the events to which they relate. "These scholars," says he, "appear not to be sufficiently penetrated with esteem for the prophets. Many of them even pretend that it is metaphysically impossible to see clearly the future; that to speak of seeing what is not, is a formal contradiction; that the future is not, and consequently cannot be, seen; that frauds of this kind are innumerable among all the nations; and that it is necessary to distrust entirely ancient history. . . . These learned men do not respect Daniel more than Isaiah." [1]

[1] *Dictionnaire Philosophique*, Article, "Cyrus."

Thus Voltaire was the pioneer critic in regard to "the historical setting" of the prophecies and in denying the reality of all predictive utterances. In these matters he was rather more consistent than some later critics, who deny the Isaianic authorship of the last twenty-seven chapters of Isaiah's prophecy, but find themselves compelled, in logical consistency with their own views and tests, to deny the Isaianic authorship of much that precedes. Thus it is in dispute among them whether the twenty-first chapter of Isaiah refers to a siege of Babylon by the Assyrians in Isaiah's time, or to the siege of Babylon by the Medes and Persians after Isaiah's time. The critics who take the former view admit Isaiah to be the author; those who take the latter view claim that that chapter was written by a post-exilic author. Even Driver, whom Professor Cheyne rebukes for his timidity, conservatism, and concessions to orthodoxy, remarks that more recent writers, among them Kuenen and Dillmann, agree in supposing it to refer to the conquest of Babylon by Cyrus, and hence ascribe it to a prophet living towards the close of the exile.[1] Thus these critics adopt the principle laid down by Voltaire that all the prophets lived after the events which they predict. Even such critics as Driver and Cheyne assume the unreality of all predictive utterances, and employ it as a test to determine the authorship of the Old Testament prophecies, just as did the infidel critic himself.

In regard to the authorship of the books of the New Testament, Voltaire says but little. He treats them, however, as fallible and errant. In both these respects he is at one with the analysts of our age. They began by an attack upon the Old Testament. After a time they withdrew, like repulsed assailants, and made a determined assault upon the authorship and trustworthiness of the books of the New Testament. This movement has in turn been abandoned, and of late the attack upon the Old Testament has been renewed. These critics may be compared to troops failing in their attacks upon a fortified army. They attack the left flank, are repulsed, and swing round upon the right. Not still succeeding, they swing back and renew the attack upon the left. And now the heaviest cannonading is again heard along the line of the Old Testament. Indeed, the forces are now again concentrated against the extreme left of the fortified encampment. The analysts at the present

---

[1] Driver's *Introduction*, pp. 205, 206.

time, like their famous leader, are making the Pentateuch the chief object of attack. Repulsed here a second time, will they again plant their batteries against the New Testament?

Accuracy requires the statement that a few points embraced in "the higher criticism" are not presented in the writings of Voltaire. He does not employ the varied use of the divine names in the Pentateuch as an argument to prove the combination of several documents, by different authors, in the composition of that book. He is silent in regard to the Book of Joshua, and also in regard to the authorship of the Psalms. Nor does he fix the dividing line between Isaiah I. and Isaiah II. precisely at the close of the thirty-ninth chapter. But he presents all the main points of the analytic criticism. No one of the leading critics presents the system so fully as he, though Reuss, Graf, Kuenen, and Wellhausen each presents certain parts of it more elaborately and fully. Indeed, these and other critics have done and are doing little more than to redact the hypotheses and arguments of this founder of the analytic criticism.

The critical analysts, however, do not by any means recognize Voltaire as the founder of their school. Wellhausen does, indeed, say that Voltaire was the first to call in question the possibility of the construction of the tabernacle in the wilderness.[1] But beside this scant reference to him, the analysts ignore him and their indebtedness to him. Nor is it at all strange that they are unwilling to say, "We have Voltaire to our father."

It is true, indeed, that the leaders among them, those who have thought out their hypotheses to their logical conclusions, are thoroughgoing rationalists—veritable infidels; but they prefer not to be recognized as such, at least for the present. Hence the critics are ready to give due, perhaps undue, praise to Aben-Ezra, Astruc, or anybody else that in former times made a suggestion in any way favorable to their system, but are mostly silent in regard to its famous founder.

The views of Voltaire, at the time of their promulgation, attracted a good deal of attention, and about 1771 a book was published in reply, entitled, "Letters of Some Jews to Monsieur Voltaire." This book is characterized by wit and strength. The aim of the writers was to repel the misrepresentations and

[1] "Der Gegensatz ist früh aufgefallen und hat zuerst Voltaire Anlass zu Zweifeln gegeben."—*Prolegomena*, p. 41.

caricatures of Voltaire on the Old Testament and the Jewish race. Yet many of the points and arguments embraced in the analytic criticism are well handled. Voltaire is shown to be a villifier as well as an unfair reasoner. He replied by heaping on the writers sarcasm and abuse, in six letters, published in the "Dictionnaire Philosophique." [1]

The work and influence of Voltaire as a biblical critic, though ungratefully ignored by his successors and followers, have been recognized by the historian Bancroft. In his essay on "German Literature," published about forty years ago, he made the following declaration:

"There is one branch of speculative learning, requiring rare sagacity and deliberation, and cultivated but little except in Germany. It is called the Higher Criticism, and begins its office where historical criticism ends. Thus, as to the poems of Homer, all the evidence which we possess enables us only to establish the essential identity of our printed copies with the edition collated and published by the Alexandrian scholars. But what changes may have taken place in the verse previous to that period? What proof have we that the Alexandrian scholars had an uncorrupted text? The same kind of questions has been raised in theological philology. It is obvious that to ask them of the rash is only to throw open the floodgates of literary doubt. And, in fact, there has been left hardly one eminent author of antiquity who has not been cheated out of part of his fame. Sophocles is made to give up one of his plays; Plato, half of his dialogues; Anacreon, almost all his odes; and the Iliad and the Odyssey are declared to be full of interpolations, the shreds and rags of audacious sophists patched upon the simple and majestic robes of Homer. The too great prevalence of this dangerous method has given to a branch of science an air of skepticism, which was not the object of the writers, and which by no means exists in the people."

Thus wrote Bancroft in 1855 concerning the havoc which "the higher criticism" had made in Grecian literature, by analyzing the works of Homer, Plato, Sophocles, Anacreon, and other authors into patchwork, the shreds and rags of supposed redactors, interpolators, and audacious sophists. Let it be observed that Bancroft remarks, "The same kind of questions has been raised in theological philology." The celebrated historian indi-

[1] Article, "Juifs."

cates the prominence of Voltaire in this work of analysis, both literary and theological, by the following remark: "Voltaire, beginning with skepticism, had proceeded to the work of analysis; and in the general proving to which all things were subjected, a generation seemed resolved on considering what was to be thrown away, and not what was to be retained. The Titans went forth to destroy; and in the overthrow of ancient superstitions, forms of government, and thought, the old world seemed coming to an end."[1]

The dissemination of the analytic views of Voltaire was aided by his politic course and the circumstances of the times. He disavowed hostility to the Bible. He never laid aside the profession and garb of Christianity. He was the nominal head of a religious institution, and held the title of an officer of the church.

Soon after his time there arose in Germany a class of men just like him, nominal members of the church, who called themselves Christians, but were at heart infidels or atheists. The professors in the universities were largely of this class at the time to which we refer. Even the theological professors shared in the prevalent unbelief and irreligion. Thus there was, a hundred years ago and later, in the universities and gymnasia of Germany, a large number of professors who were entirely suited with the biblical criticism of Voltaire; men calling themselves Christians and holding the place of Bible teachers and theological professors, yet having no more faith in the Bible and Christianity than in Homer and the Platonic philosophy; perhaps not so much. To them the views of Voltaire were just the thing. Like him, they could study and discuss the age, authorship, and composition of the books of the Bible, and ignore or scout its doctrines of sin and retribution, atonement and pardon, regeneration and salvation. Like him, they could theorize in a literary way about the Bible as about the pagan authors, attributing to it no more of divine inspiration and authority than to them. It was this class of men, infidel theologians and exegetes, that welcomed Voltaire as a deliverer and gladly accepted the analytic criticism from his hands. Thus what is called "the higher criticism" was originated by the savants of Europe (scholars and philosophers), with Voltaire at their head, more than a hundred years ago.

[1] Bancroft's *Miscellanies*, pp. 118, 198.

PART II

OBJECTIONS CONSIDERED

PART II

OBJECTIONS CONSIDERED

CHAPTER 1

OBJECTIONS IN GENERAL

THE burden of proof rests on the analytic critics, because:

1. There is an antecedent probability in favor of the single authorship of Genesis and of each of the Pentateuchal books. Joint authorship is rare. Almost every book has but one author. A book may have an editor and annotator, who make additions by way of explanations, notes, and references. But even in such cases the book itself is the production of a single mind. Hence, in regard to any book and every book, before examination, and aside from all positive evidence in the case, there is a presumption that it was written by one man.

There is, however, no presumption against two or more books having the same author. Many an author, in both ancient and modern times, has produced many books. And if several books, though anonymous, relate to the same subjects, are ostensibly connected with one another, and are found published together, the presumption is that they have a common authorship. There is, then, an antecedent presumption that Genesis, and every other book of the Pentateuch, is the production of one author. And as these books relate to the same subjects, are ostensibly connected, each succeeding book seeming to be the continuation of the preceding one, and are found published together, the presumption is that they were all produced by one author.

2. Added to this, that Moses wrote the Pentateuch is the *traditional* belief. This was the belief of almost all antiquity, pagan, Christian, and infidel. Even Celsus and Porphyry conceded the Mosaic authorship of the Pentateuch, though Bleek does indeed claim the former as on the other side.[1]

---

[1] *Introduction to the Old Testament*, Vol. 1., p. 5.

3. Still further, the testimony of Christ and his apostles is in favor of the traditional view. This is admitted by all the analytic critics, except some of the less advanced ones, who have not the audacity to assert fallibility and errancy of the Lord Jesus Christ in biblical matters, and hence feel constrained to seek a way out of the difficulty by denying that he recognized Moses as the author of the Pentateuch.

It is thus shown that there is an antecedent presumption that each book of the Pentateuch taken separately, and all the books taken together, had but one author, and that that author was Moses.

In these circumstances, the analytic critics, who maintain that the Pentateuch is the product of many minds, must assume the burden of proof. They must positively disprove its Mosaic authorship or lose the case. They join issue with tradition, with antiquity, and with Christ and the apostles, and they are bound to meet the overwhelming presumption thus created against them by the presentation of evidence that will leave no room for reasonable doubt. Clear and incontestable proofs are demanded by the requirements of the case. The extreme probability, or rather the absolute certainty, that Jesus, the Son of God, made no mistakes and encouraged no errors, must outweigh all the claims of learning and the whole array of critical names which the analysts may present. Such argumentation is of no avail in the case. Nothing but clear and conclusive proof, or rather disproof—disproof of the Mosaic authorship of the Pentateuch, will answer.

But the analytic critics have already presented their case. Their evidence and arguments are in. It is now to be considered whether they have made out their case. Have they disproved the Mosaic authorship of the Pentateuch? Let us weigh their arguments. These come in the form of objections to the traditional belief, and in the main are as follows: Claimed improprieties of thought and speech, which, it is supposed, Moses would have avoided, had he been the author of the Pentateuch; claimed anachronisms, allotopisms, discrepancies, contradictions, and difficulties; historical untrustworthiness; differences in style; the centralization of worship; the neglect and violation of the Pentateuchal laws; the silence of succeeding books in regard to the Pentateuchal books and laws; the finding of the book of the law in the temple, as recorded in the twenty-second chapter of the Second Book of Kings; the character of the Pentateuchal laws as not adapted to a nomadic people, camping in the wilderness, but to an agricultural people, dwelling in fixed habitations.

These are in the main the arguments on which the analysts rely for the overthrowing of the view that Moses wrote the Pentateuch.

CHAPTER II

CLAIMED IMPROPRIETIES

1. ONE of the objections urged against the Mosaic authorship of the Pentateuch is drawn from the fact that it speaks of Moses in the third person. The objectors assume that it is improper for an author to speak of himself in this way, and they further virtually assume that Moses was infallible, or at least that it is incredible that he committed an error of this kind. But for an author to speak of himself in the third person accords with Hebrew, classical, and English usage.

Isaiah[1] and Jeremiah[2] speak of themselves in the third person in the historical portions of their writings. Ezekiel does not invariably employ the first person in speaking of himself.[3] The objectors, of course, deny that Daniel wrote the book that is called by his name, but they must at least admit that the author thought there was no impropriety in Daniel's speaking of himself in the third person; for he is represented as doing so.[4] All the minor prophets speak of themselves in the third person, and nearly all of them in that way exclusively. Such, also, is the style of Ezra,[5] though he also speaks of himself in the first person. Nehemiah sometimes speaks of himself in the third person.[6] Josephus employs this style.[7] The apostles Matthew and John speak of themselves in the third person.[8] It is thus in evidence that it was the prevailing custom among the Hebrew writers to speak of themselves in the third person. It is not surprising that such a man as Thomas Paine should object to the Mosaic authorship of the Pentateuch on the ground that Moses is spoken of in it in the third person,[9] but what shall we say when we find a biblical scholar like Professor W. Robertson

---

[1] Isa. 1:1; 2:1; 7:3; 13:1; 20:2; 37:21; 38:1,4; 39:3-8.
[2] Jer. 1:1,2; 7:1; 11:1; 4:1; 18:1; 20:2,3; 25:1-3; 26:1,2,7,12,24; 28:5, 10-15; 32:1-6; 36:11-21; 38:1-28; 43:1-8; 51:59-61.   [3] Ezek. 1:3.
[4] Dan. 10:1.   [5] Ezra 7:1, 6, 8, 10; 10:1, 6, 10, 16.
[6] Neh. 7:65, 70; 8:9; 10:1.   [7] *Wars of the Jews*, 2:20, *et passim*.
[8] Matt. 9:9; 10:3; John 19:23, 26, 27; 20:2; 21:7, 20-24.
[9] Paine's Works, p. 65. (*Age of Reason.*)

Smith declaring, "One asks for proof that any Hebrew ever wrote of himself in the third person"?[1] After this, what next?

It is well known that many of the classical authors, both Greek and Roman,—Xenophon, Thucydides, Julius Cæsar, and others,—speak of themselves in the third person.

This style of speech is employed also by many of the best English authors. Cowper, Kirk White, Hume, Willis, Holland, and many other distinguished writers speak of themselves in the third person.[2] Professor Sayce often employs this style.[3] Professor Briggs speaks of himself in the third person, though he seems to think that Moses would not do such a thing.[4]

In view of the facts above presented, the objection to the Mosaic authorship of the Pentateuch, drawn from the references in it to Moses as a third person, loses all its force, and indeed it even seems strange that it should be employed at all.

2. A second objection to the Mosaic authorship of the Pentateuch is founded upon those passages which speak approvingly of Moses; such as, "Now the man Moses was very meek, above all the men which were upon the face of the earth";[5] "Moses the man of God";[6] "And there arose not a prophet since in Israel like unto Moses, whom the Lord knew face to face";[7] and some others of similar tone.[8]

This objection is employed by most of the analytic critics from Paine[9] to Wellhausen.[10] They virtually assume that Moses could not have committed any impropriety, at least that of saying about himself such things as are contained in these passages. Indeed, there are two assumptions necessary to the validity of the objection. One is that Moses would not or could not speak commendatorily of himself; and the other assumption is that these passages were not added to the original writing of Moses by an editor or redactor. The analysts very quietly make the former assumption, though they declare Moses to have been a semi-barbarian among barbarians; and they just as quietly make the latter assumption, although they claim that there are interpolations and other additions by revisers and redactors scattered all through the Pentateuch. But let these

---

[1] *Old Testament in the Jewish Church*, p. 321.
[2] See prefaces to their works.
[3] *Hittites*, p. 90; *Fresh Light from the Ancient Monuments*, p. 81.
[4] *Higher Criticism of the Hexateuch*, Pref.; also p. 39.   [5] Num. 12: 3.
[6] Deut. 33: 1.   [7] Deut. 34: 10.   [8] Num. 12: 6, 7; Ex. 33: 11.
[9] *Age of Reason*, pp. 65, 66.   [10] *Prolegomena, Das Problem*, p. 10.

assumptions pass. It is curious to see men who scout plenary inspiration and the inerrancy of Scripture turn round and virtually claim infallibility and inerrancy for Moses, in order to prove that he did not write certain passages in the Pentateuch.

Now, in reply to the objection, we remark as follows:

(1) There was nothing improper in Moses writing all that these passages contain concerning himself. He had proclaimed himself "a man of God." He claimed to have a special commission from the Almighty. He had done mighty deeds and miracles in the name and by the power of Jehovah. He had spoken with God face to face. It was a very small thing to claim to be a man of God and the friend of God, after having been forty days and nights in the divine presence on the mount, and carrying with him back to his people so much of the divine glory shining from his face as to dazzle all beholders.[1] The skeptical objector probably denies all this as being supernatural. But if so, he rejects the history of Moses and with it the entire historical character of the Pentateuch. If the history of Moses is a lie, and if he was not such as he is represented to be, it was, of course, very wrong for him to claim to be a man of God and that God had talked with him face to face as with a friend. In that case, however, he was guilty of something much worse than vanity or immodesty. But if the history of Moses is not to be set aside at the very beginning of the discussion, if "the historical setting" in this case is not to be transformed into a falsehood or a thing of naught by the mere waving of the critic's hand, if the story of the exodus, of the crossing of the Red Sea, and of the giving of the law is to count for anything as history, there was no more impropriety in the claims and professions of Moses than in Michael or Gabriel announcing himself an angel of God. The fallacy in the objector's reasoning is his antecedently assuming that the Pentateuchal history is false.

(2) Such claims as Moses made concerning himself (in case he is the author of the Pentateuch) are presented by others elsewhere in the Scriptures. Daniel reports that the angel Gabriel addressed him in these words: "Thou art greatly beloved," and, "O Daniel, a man greatly beloved."[2] Nehemiah puts on record the fact that he received no salary, but paid into the national treasury one thousand drams of gold, and did not eat the bread of the governor. He then exclaims, "Think upon me, my God,

---

[1] Ex. 34: 28-35.   [2] Dan. 9: 23; 10: 11.

for good, according to all that I have done for this people."[1] When advised to retire into the temple for safety, in a time of danger, he exclaimed, "Should such a man as I flee?"[2] The apostle John records the fact five times that he was "the disciple whom Jesus loved."[3] Renan, one of the destructive critics, brings this charge against the beloved disciple, that "on every page the intention is betrayed of showing that he was the favorite of Jesus."[4] Paul, in comparing himself with the other apostles, hesitated not to say, "I labored more abundantly than they all"; and in what he himself calls "this confidence of boasting," he exclaimed, "In nothing am I behind the very chiefest apostles."[5] Aside from supernatural inspiration, the probability that Moses would or would not make certain declarations is to be determined rather by the usage of other Hebrew authors than by the judgment and assumptions of the theorizing and argumentative critics of modern times.

(3) As to the declaration of Moses that he was the meekest of living men:

(*a*) Meekness, which includes humility, was not considered praiseworthy in ancient times. Until Christianity had leavened the world with its teaching, the meek, humble man was regarded as mean-spirited. Certainly Moses could have gained neither admiration nor respect by declaring himself to be the meekest of men. It required genuine humility and self-denial to be willing to make such a declaration. The critics err in judging of this matter by the more enlightened modern Christian times.

(*b*) It was proper that a record should be made of the meekness of Moses. Formerly he was irascible, hasty, and headstrong, as is shown by his killing the Egyptian and by his repeated refusal to obey God's call to deliver his people.[6] Since these facts were recorded, it was a fitting thing that it should also be recorded that by the grace and discipline of God he afterward became the meekest of men. We can readily believe that he had the divine guidance and approval in making this record for the improvement of mankind.

(*c*) Protestations of humility and meekness are among the things in regard to which taste and custom are continually changing. Daniel Webster, who was not deficient in self-appre-

---

[1] Neh. 5: 14-19.   [2] Neh. 6: 11.
[3] John 13: 23; 19: 26; 20: 2; 21: 7, 20.   [4] *Life of Jesus*, p. 26.
[5] I. Cor. 15: 10; II. Cor. 11: 17; 12: 11.   [6] Ex. 2: 12; 3: 11-22; 4: 1-14.

ciation and self-respect, in his reply to Hayne, declared himself the humblest man in the Senate of the United States—"holding myself to be the humblest of the members here." The gentlemen of the old school—such as Washington and Jefferson—were in the habit of closing their letters with the words, "Your most obedient and humble servant." Professor Driver tries to discard the custom of the employment of the third person to designate oneself, and in his preface, on about three-fourths of the space of the first page, octavo size, he employs the pronoun *I* seventeen times. He does not consistently adhere to this egotism, but sometimes refers to himself in the third person.[1] Kuenen employs "the proud monosyllable" seventy-two times, and other forms of the first person of the pronoun—*me*, *my*, and *myself*—fifteen times in about thirty-nine pages of his introduction to his work on the Hexateuch. All this is largely a matter of taste. We do not say these authors are lacking in modesty, but their egotism appears to some people less becoming than anything that is contained in the Pentateuch. Perhaps, in the coming years, critics will maintain that these authors could not have written the books attributed to them, or that the egotistical passages were by later hands inserted in the books in order to discredit them. Had Moses made as frequent use of the first person of the pronoun as they, perhaps critics would have cited the frequency of its use as indubitable proof that he did not write the Pentateuch.

(4) The declaration that "there arose not a prophet since in Israel like unto Moses, whom the Lord knew face to face,"[2] is admitted on all hands not to have been written by Moses, since it is contained in the passage which gives an account of his death and burial. Dr. Kautzsch's German Bible refers this declaration to Dt, but Driver to the combined authorship of JE. These critics, though differing as to the authorship of it, agree in holding that it was written by another hand than that which mainly wrote the Book of Deuteronomy.[3] That this declaration was written, as itself implies, a good while after the death of Moses, is not incompatible with the Mosaic authorship of Deuteronomy as a whole. Also, the parenthetic clause concerning the meekness of Moses may have been inserted by a hand other than the one which wrote all the rest of the Book of Numbers.

---

[1] *Introduction to the Literature of the Old Testament*, pp. xli., 18, notes.
[2] Deut. 34 : 10.
[3] Kautzsch and his coworkers represent the Deuteronomic author by D, not Dt.

CHAPTER III

CLAIMED ANACHRONISMS

THERE are in the Pentateuch many passages which are claimed by the analytic critics as referring to events that occurred after the time of Moses. They argue, and correctly, too, that a writing must be later than any event mentioned in it.[1] But this argument from claimed anachronisms, as employed by the critics, involves two fallacies. One of these consists in putting particular passages for the entire book in which they are found. The critics virtually reason thus: Moses did not write a certain passage or certain passages; therefore he did not write the Pentateuch. The viciousness of their logic is the more glaring because of their almost invariably assuming that passages which stand in the way of their hypotheses are additions made to the original writing by later hands. Another fallacious proceeding of the critics in their contention about Pentateuchal anachronisms is their employment of the very history which they decry as untrustworthy. In their desire and effort to fix the writing of some passage or book after the occurrence of a particular event, they take that event, as to character, time, and place, just as it is related in the Pentateuch.

But let us examine the passages cited to prove anachronisms.

1. "And the Canaanite was then in the land";[2] "And the Canaanite and the Perizzite dwelt then in the land."[3]

It is implied in these passages that there was a time when the nations mentioned were not in the land, and the analytic critics, Voltaire, Reuss, Kuenen, Wellhausen, and others, claim that this implied time was subsequent to the conquest of Canaan by the Israelites. In this way they endeavor to make out an anachronism and to prove that the Book of Genesis was written long after the time of Moses. But these critics virtually inject the word *still* into these texts, and read, "The Canaanite was then *still* in the land"; "The Canaanite and the Perizzite were then

---

[1] This applies to history, but not to prophetic utterances.
[2] Gen. 12:6.   [3] Gen. 13:7.

still dwelling in the land." Reuss, indeed, translates the first passage thus: "Bien que les Cananéens fussent alors dans ce pays"[1] (although the Canaanites were then in this country)— a fair enough translation. But in a marginal note he remarks, "Que le mot *alors* serait bien étrange dans la bouche de Moïse"[1] ("The word *then* ["alors"] is strange in the mouth of Moses"). Thus Reuss and other analysts read into the passage the idea expressed by the word *still*, or *yet*. But the original Hebrew word means simply *then*, or *at that time*. It is so defined by Gesenius, who refers to one of these passages, and it is so translated elsewhere. The sacred historian merely states that Abram arrived at Moreh and that the Canaanite was at that time in the land; that a strife arose between Abram's herdmen and those of Lot, and that *at that time* the Canaanite and Perizzite were dwelling in the land. The implication is that the Canaanite and Perizzite were already in the land before the arrival of Abram and Lot, and not that these people had disappeared from the country at the time of the conquest. Indeed, as a matter of fact, they continued in the country after the conquest, for it is expressly stated that the Canaanites continued to dwell "in mount Lebanon, from mount Baal-hermon unto the entering in of Hamath"; and that after the conquest "the children of Israel dwelt among the Canaanites, Hittites, and Amorites, and Perizzites, and Hivites, and Jebusites."[2] Our analytic critics, contrary to the plainest historical statements, imagine that there were no Canaanites nor Perizzites in Canaan after the conquest. They appeal to history, which they have already decried as incorrect and untrustworthy, and even that they misquote and misrepresent.

There was a time, however, when there were no Canaanites nor Perizzites in the land. That was a time previous to the immigration of Abraham. On his arrival he found them there. They were there then. As to how long they had been there or how long they remained, the passage gives no information. The anachronism exists only in the imagination of the analysts.

2. An anachronism is claimed also in the references to the city of Hebron. It is mentioned as existing in the time of Abraham. The references to it are as follows: "Then Abram removed his tent, and came and dwelt in the plain of Mamre, which is in Hebron, and built there an altar unto the Lord";[3]

---

[1] *L'Histoire Sainte et la Loi*, Vol. I., p. 342.
[2] Judg. 3: 3, 5.
[3] Gen. 13: 18.

"And Sarah died in Kirjath-arba; the same is Hebron in the land of Caanan";[1] "And after this, Abraham buried Sarah his wife in the cave of the field of Machpelah before Mamre: the same is Hebron in the land of Canaan";[2] "And Jacob came unto Isaac his father unto Mamre, unto the city of Arba, which is Hebron, where Abraham and Isaac sojourned";[3] "And they [the spies] ascended by the south, and came unto Hebron; where Ahiman, Sheshai, and Talmai, the children of Anak, were. (Now Hebron was built seven years before Zoan in Egypt.)";[4] "And the name of Hebron before was Kirjath-arba; which Arba was a great man among the Anakims."[5]

Thus in Joshua the statement is that the former name of Hebron was Kirjath-arba; but it is designated as Hebron in the time of Abraham and in the time of the spies. The inference of some of the critics is that Kirjath-arba was not called Hebron until it was given by Joshua to Caleb, the son of Jephunneh, and that therefore all these references to Kirjath-arba as Hebron must have been written after the conquest and division of Canaan, hence not by Moses. Reuss presents this argument very adroitly. After declaring the Book of Joshua to be utterly untrustworthy, he could not well quote it to prove the incorrectness of Genesis and Numbers. But he translates both the expressions, "the same is Hebron," and "which is Hebron," by the phrase, "anjourd'hui Hébròn" ("at this time Hebron"), putting the words in parentheses. In a marginal note he describes Hebron as "the chief place of the tribe of Judah," not recognizing its existence in the time of Abraham at all.[6] In this way Reuss assumes and insinuates that all the references to Hebron in Genesis were written by an author who lived long after the time of Moses.

We do not object to putting the above-mentioned clauses in parentheses; for they are in their nature parenthetic, and probably the original writer would have enclosed them in parenthetic signs if such signs had been in use in his time. Nor do we object to the suggestion that these clauses were inserted in the original document by a redactor. But our position is that this redactor may have lived in the time of Moses, or may have been Moses himself. For Hebron may have been the original name of the city, to which Kirjath-arba was afterward added, this second name being dropped at the time of the conquest and

---

[1] Gen. 23:2.   [2] Gen. 23:19.   [3] Gen. 35:27.   [4] Num. 13:22.
[5] Josh. 14:15.   [6] *L'Histoire Sainte*, Vol. I., p. 344.

division of Canaan, as related in Joshua.¹ Even Bleek, who cites Genesis 13 : 18 as containing an anachronism, virtually surrenders the point by adopting this suggestion.²

We have now, however, in this matter much more than the suggestion of a possibility. The archæologists have shown that the possible in this case is not only the probable, but the real. They have demonstrated that a century before the exodus Palestine was a province of the Egyptian empire, and that cities and places with which we are so familiar in the Scriptures—Jerusalem, Megiddo, Taanach, Gibeah, Kishon, Hebron, and nearly all the rest—were well known to the officials of the Egyptian government.³ Hebron is one of the places mentioned in the Egyptian monuments. "The spring of Hebron" is mentioned as one of the places in Palestine conquered by Rameses II. It is also found in the inscriptions among the places conquered by Rameses III.⁴ It is generally agreed by Egyptologists that Rameses II. was the Pharaoh of the oppression. It is thus in evidence that in the century preceding the exodus there was in Palestine a town famous for its springs, called Hebron, a place of sufficient importance to be named among the conquests of one of the greatest of the Egyptian kings. There is no anachronism, then, in the references made to this place in Genesis. The writer of Genesis calls it Hebron, though he says that in his time it was also called Kirjath-arba. He intimates, however, that Hebron was the original and better known name, for when he speaks of the time of the building of the town he calls it Hebron, not Kirjath-arba. Whenever he uses the latter name, he informs his readers that he means Hebron.⁵ Now the Egyptian monuments, as above mentioned, prove that in the time of Moses, and before his time, there was a city or town in Canaan called Hebron. The monuments are as yet silent as to Hebron being for a time called also Kirjath-arba. But, as matters are now going, perhaps the next steamer that comes across the Atlantic will bring word that the excavators in Palestine or Egypt have discovered evidence of the double name. In the meantime, this much has already been ascertained, that before the time of Moses the city was known by the name of Hebron, which refutes the charge of anachronism.

¹ Josh. 14 : 15.   ² *Introduction to the Old Testament*, Vol. I., p. 231.
³ Brugsch-Bey, *Egypt Under the Pharaohs*, chs. 8, 11 ; Sayce, *Higher Criticism and the Monuments*, pp. 52, 53, 176, 186.
⁴ Sayce, *idem*, p. 188, note.   ⁵ Gen. 23 : 2 ; 35 : 27.

3. "Pursued them unto Dan."[1]

It is claimed that here "Dan" is employed to designate in the time of Abraham a city that did not receive that name until more than three hundred years after the time of Moses.[2] Voltaire, Paine, Reuss, and other analytic critics so maintain.

The argument of the critical objectors in this case is made up of inconsistencies and assumptions. Though they have much to say about redactions, interpolations, and mistakes, and the resultant uncertainties, in the Pentateuch and elsewhere in the Bible, they nevertheless accept with unwavering confidence the account of the change of the name of Laish to Dan, in the books of Joshua and Judges. They assume that Laish was not formerly called Dan, just as Kirjath-arba was originally called Hebron, the name which it afterward again received. They assume that there was only one city Dan, that is, Laish-Dan, which the Danites took by force, and named after their ancestor. These critical objectors further assume that Dan, as mentioned in Genesis, was a city, though it was not so called, and though Josephus expressly says that it here designates one of the forks of the Jordan, Jor being the name of the other.[3] Totally ignoring the statement of Josephus, the objectors assume that Dan was a city, that there was but one city called Dan, that it was not called Dan before it was captured by the Danites, and that the name "Dan" was not substituted in Genesis by a redactor copyist for "Laish."

4. "And these are the kings that reigned in the land of Edom, before there reigned any king over the children of Israel."[4]

It is maintained that the writer of this passage must have lived after the establishment of the monarchy among the Israelites — at least four hundred years after Moses. Such is the ground taken by Voltaire, Paine, Reuss, and Wellhausen. Paine affirms that this passage proves that Genesis was not written until the time of Saul, and that, as the words "any king" imply more than one, we are brought to the time of David at least. Reuss expresses the same view with disdainful confidence: "Du reste, l'auteur qui a rédigé cette liste n'a pas vécu avant l'époque de David et de Solomon. On devrait enfin ne plus se donner le ridicule de nier cela."[5] ("Finally, the author who reduced this list to writing did not live before the time of David

---

[1] Gen. 14:14. [2] Josh. 19:47; Judg. 18:27-29. [3] *Antiquities*, 1:10:1.
[4] Gen. 36:31. [5] *L'Histoire Sainte*, Vol. I., p. 411.

and of Solomon. People ought no longer to make themselves ridiculous by denying that.")

Notwithstanding the overweening confidence of these critics, there is something to be said on the other side.

(1) Saul was not the first Israelitish king. It is a matter of express and plain record that Abimelech, the son of Gideon, was king in Israel more than two centuries before the time of Saul. The Book of Judges reads as follows: "And all the men of Shechem gathered together, and all the house of Millo, and went and made Abimelech king, by the plain of the pillar."[1] Nor was the authority of Abimelech limited to one city or one tribe; for it is further recorded that Abimelech reigned over Israel three years. It is not, indeed, recorded that he was regularly and permanently established as king, nor that his kingly authority was *universally* acknowledged. But it is recorded that Abimelech reigned over Israel three years.[2] This fills the description in Genesis 36:31: "before there reigned any king over the children of Israel,"—*any* king, regular or irregular, permanent or temporary. Thus, instead of bringing us down to the time of Saul or David, as these critics so confidently assert, this passage does not bring us within two centuries of that time.

(2) Nor does this passage really bring us to a time later than Moses; for there was a king in Israel in the time of Moses— Moses himself. The title of king is expressly given him. "Moses commanded us a law, even the inheritance of the congregation of Jacob. And he was king in Jeshurun, when the heads of the people and the tribes of Israel were gathered together."[3] Moses was recognized as king even beyond the limits of the Hebrew nation. Balaam, the son of Beor, said, "He hath not beheld iniquity in Jacob, neither hath he seen perverseness in Israel: the Lord his God is with him, and the shout of a king is among them."[4] Moses at this time was the head and ruler of the nation, and must be the king to whom Balaam referred.

Moses and after him Joshua were more kingly in character and position than the chiefs or emirs that reigned in Edom before any king reigned in Israel. These Edomite kings, a list of whom is given, were not hereditary rulers, for no one of them was the son of his predecessor, and they lived in different cities. It is evident that they were such kings as Jephthah and Gideon among the Israelites. Reuss virtually admits all this in saying:

[1] Judg. 9:6. [2] Judg. 9:22. [3] Deut. 33:4, 5. [4] Num. 23:21.

"Il ne s'agit pas ici d'une monarchie hereditaire, mais d'une succession de chefs ou emirs (militaires et electifs) places a la tete d'une confederation de tribus. On pourrait comparer cette forme de governement a celle qu'on suppose d'ordinaire aux Israelites du temps des juges, mais á l'egard de ceux lá la critique historique fait ses reserves."[1] ("The reference is not to a hereditary monarchy, but to a succession of chiefs or emirs, military or elective, placed at the head of a confederation of tribes. This form of government may be compared to that which may be regarded as common among the Israelites during the time of the judges, but in regard to the latter the critical historian makes his reservations.") Well, then, the Edomite chiefs or emirs are called kings in our passage, and the corresponding magistrates among the Israelites, called judges, are styled kings also; and among these irregular magistrates must be included Moses, who was the greatest king of them all.

Besides these facts, which indicate that the passage under consideration may have been written in the time of Moses, and even by Moses himself, there are some positive considerations which suggest that the writer must have lived before the establishment of the monarchy. A writer who lived after that event would not be likely to use the word "king" as he does, applying it to the chiefs of the Edomites and to the irregular magistrates of the Israelites called judges. This use of the word points to a time when there were only irregular and temporary magistrates.

Besides, there is reason to believe that the writer of the passage under consideration was contemporary with Hadar, the last mentioned king of the Edomites,[2] for, though the death of each one of his predecessors is mentioned, his is not. Neither is his successor mentioned. Yet the name of his city is given, and his wife's name, and her mother's, and her grandfather's, or, possibly, her grandmother's. A writer disposed to enter thus into particulars would doubtless have recorded the death of Hadar, had he not been still living. This view is confirmed by the fact that the account of the Edomite kings given in Chronicles is the same with that in Genesis, except that in the former the death of Hadar (Hadad) is mentioned.[3] All these facts are accounted for by the view that Hadar was still living when the list of Edomite kings in Genesis was made out, but had died before the writer in Chronicles made a copy of it.

[1] *L'Histoire Sainte*, Vol 1., p. 411. [2] Gen. 36 : 39. [3] I. Chr. 1 : 43-54.

Still further, the word "king" is used in this wide sense in the Book of Judges. The phrase, "when there was no king in Israel," so often employed in that book, refers by way of contrast, not to the subsequent times of the monarchy, but to the preceding times, when Moses, Joshua, and other efficient judges exercised central authority. The expression, "when there was no king in Israel," points to a time when there was a suspension of the national authority through the inefficiency of the judge, or in consequence of there being temporarily no judge at all.

The hypothesis that Moses wrote this passage in the assured belief that, in accordance with divine promise and prophecy, there would be an established line of monarchs in Israel in succeeding times, is not necessary, but is more reasonable than the view of Reuss and others, who make the word "king" in one clause of the verse [1] mean elective military chiefs; and in the other, established hereditary monarchs. Certainly Moses was more of a king than any of the Edomite captains, and he is expressly called a king. Our passage,[1] then, means that there were established and recognized rulers among the Edomites before there were any such among the Israelites, that is, before the time of Moses.

5. Another anachronism is claimed in the use of the name "Moriah" to designate the place where Abraham was directed to offer up Isaac.[2] It is maintained that, according to the chronicler, the name was unknown until the time of David.[3] Voltaire, quoting from Aben-Ezra, sets forth the fact that Moriah is called the mountain of the Lord, as a reason for holding that the Pentateuch was reduced to writing long after the time of Moses.[4] Reuss thinks it very natural that an attempt should be made to give a sort of anticipative consecration to the place on which the temple was built.[5] Both he and Voltaire refer to the chronicler[3] in proof of the claimed anachronism.

We reply: (1) That the analytic critics pronounce the chronicler to be utterly untrustworthy as a historian, but here one of his incidental statements is brought confidently forward to prove a chronological inaccuracy in the Book of Genesis.

(2) The statement in Chronicles shows only that Mount Moriah was chosen as the site of the temple because David had

---

[1] Gen. 36: 31. [2] Gen. 22: 2. [3] II. Chr. 3: 1.
[4] *Traité sur Tolérance, Mélanges*, p. 452. [5] *L'Histoire Sainte*, Vol. 1., p. 300.

sacrificed there, not that the name began to be used in David's time.

(3) It is in evidence that there was a "mount of God"[1] in Palestine long before the time of Moses. In the list of Palestinian cities conquered by Thothmes III. is the name "Har-el" ("mount of God"), which has been identified with the geographical position of Jerusalem, as is shown by Professor Sayce, in his late work.[2] It is thus proved that more than two centuries before the exodus there was a mountain called the mount of God in the region of Jerusalem, corresponding to the Mount Moriah of Genesis.

(4) Even Reuss, after bringing forward this argument apparently with his customary assurance, virtually admits its invalidity, as follows: "Le texte parle de l'une des montagnes de la *terre* de Moriah, et les anciennes versiones n'ont pas toutes un nom prope ici"[3] ("The text speaks of one of the mountains of the *land* of Moriah, and not all the ancient versions have the proper name here").

6. Anachronism is claimed in the reference to "the book of the wars of the Lord."[4]

The objectors urge that this book did not exist until after the time of Moses. Voltaire says, "Comment Moïse auasit-il cité le livre des guerres du Seigneur, quand ces guerres et ce livre perdu lui sont posterieurs?"[5] ("How could Moses quote the wars of the Lord, when these wars and this lost book were subsequent to his time?") Reuss also affirms that the wars of the Lord began only in the last year of the life of Moses, and that materials could not have been furnished for such a book while the Israelites were still far from the Jordan.[6]

The denial of the existence of this book in the time of Moses, on the ground that the wars of the Lord had not yet taken place, furnishes another remarkable example of the ignoring of Jewish history. There were many wars of the Lord before the Israelites came to the Jordan.

(1) There was the war at the Red Sea, where the Lord did all the fighting, and where, after the war was over, the Israelites sang songs in honor of the conqueror: "The Lord is a man of war";[7] "Sing ye to the Lord, for he hath triumphed gloriously;

---

[1] Gen. 22:14.   [2] *Higher Criticism and the Monuments*, pp. 186, 187.
[3] *L'Histoire Sainte*, Vol. I., p. 370.   [4] Num. 21:14.
[5] *Dictionnaire Philosophique*, Vol. IV., p. 65.
[6] *L'Histoire Sainte*, Vol. I., Int., p. 128.   [7] Ex. 15:3.

the horse and his rider hath he thrown into the sea."[1] Here was material for the book of the wars of the Lord.

(2) Then there was the war of the Amalekites, which took place in less than three months after the exodus. Joshua led the Israelites in battle, while Moses sat on the top of the hill with the rod of God in his hand, Aaron and Hur staying up his hands until Amalek was discomfited.[2] Here was more material for the book of the wars of the Lord. "And the Lord said unto Moses, Write this for a memorial in a book, and rehearse it in the ears of Joshua."[3]

(3) Next came the war of Hormah, where a southern tribe of Canaanites made an attack on the Israelites and captured some of them. The tide of war at first was against the Israelites, but they made vows in order to gain the victory, and in the end destroyed their assailants and their cities.[4]

(4) The fourth war was with Sihon, king of the Amorites, who made an attack on the Israelites. But they smote him and his people, and took their cities and lands.[5]

(5) After this Og, the king of Bashan, and all his people went out to Edrei to battle against Israel. But they smote him and his people, and took possession of his country.[6]

(6) The sixth war was with the Midianites. In accordance with the direction of Moses, twelve thousand Hebrew warriors went against them, slew all the males, took thirty-two thousand captives, burnt all the cities and castles, captured six hundred and seventy-five thousand sheep, seventy-two thousand beeves, and sixty-one thousand asses.[7]

All these wars took place before the death of Moses, and yet some critics declare that there were not materials sufficient for the making up of the book of the wars of the Lord. It is true that some of these wars took place near the close of the life of Moses; but he may have revised his writings near the close of his life and inserted this reference to the war-book. Perhaps Moses was the author of it. It appears that he was divinely recognized as the most suitable person to write such a book.[3] At all events, it is shown that the wars of the Lord began before the Israelites were fairly out of Egypt, and that a book of the wars was begun in less than three months after the exodus. Within these three months, forty years before the death of Moses, two famous

---

[1] Ex. 15 : 21. [2] Ex. 17 : 8-13. [3] Ex. 17 : 14. [4] Num. 21 : 1-3.
[5] Num. 21 : 21-31. [6] Num. 21 : 33-35. [7] Num. 31 : 1-47.

CLAIMED ANACHRONISMS 45

wars — the Egyptian and Amalekite — had been finished, and were already celebrated in song and history. Four other wars were waged and finished before Moses died. The contention, then, of Voltaire, Reuss, and other critics that a book of the wars of the Lord could have been written only after the death of Moses is shown to be groundless.

7. A similar argument has been drawn from the references to the Book of Jasher.[1] It is claimed that inasmuch as this is quoted in Joshua, and yet contains some of the compositions of David,[2] the Book of Joshua must have been written after the time of David.[3] And as the analytic critics unite in thought the Book of Joshua with the five preceding books, and call the whole the Hexateuch, they thus derive an argument to prove that the Pentateuch was not written till long after the time of Moses. But even if it be admitted that the reference in Samuel indicates that the Book of Jasher contained some of David's compositions, which is by no means certain, it does not follow that it did not exist in the time of Joshua, because the book, though existing in Joshua's time, may have afterward contained songs written by David. A collection of national songs was sure to receive additions from age to age. The Book of Psalms was formed in this way. The mode of argumentation adopted by these anti-Mosaic critics would lead to the conclusion that the Davidic psalms were written after the exile. The Book of Jasher, then, may have existed in the time of Joshua and of Moses, and have had additions made to it in the time of David. The mention of this book, therefore, in times previous to David does not prove anachronism.

8. "And the children of Israel did eat manna forty years, until they came to a land inhabited; they did eat manna until they came unto the borders of the land of Canaan."[4]

Inasmuch as it is stated in the Book of Joshua that the manna ceased after the Israelites crossed the Jordan,[5] and since Moses died before that event, it is maintained that the writer of the above passage must have lived after the crossing of the Jordan and after the death of Moses. This is one of the arguments that Voltaire appears to have overlooked; but Paine, Reuss, and other critics make use of it. Reuss's presentation of it is as follows:

"Ce n'est là qu'un premier sujet de douter. Dès le début il

---

[1] Josh. 10:13. [2] II. Sam. 1:17-27. [3] Reuss, *L'Histoire Sainte*, Vol. I., p. 128.
[4] Ex. 16:35. [5] Josh. 5:12.

est parlé de choses qui n'arrivent qu'ò la fin du voyage. Exodus 16: 35, nous lisons que les Israelites se sont nourris de manne jusqu'à ce qu'ils fussent arrivés dans leur nouvelle patrie. In effet, Joshua 5: 12 affirme que la pluie de manne cessa cinq jours aprés le passage du Jordain,. c'esta-dire au plus tot six semaines aprés la mort de Moïse (Deut. 34: 8; Josh. 1: 11; 2: 32; 4: 19). Mais le texte de l'Exode parle au passé défini, et non au futur." [1] ("We have here only a prime subject of doubt. At the very start, things are mentioned that happened only at the close of the journeying. In Exodus 16: 35 we read that the Israelites are fed by manna until they have come into their new country. It is, in effect, affirmed (Josh. 5: 12) that the rain of manna ceased five days after the passage of the Jordan, that is to say, more than six weeks after the death of Moses. But the text of Exodus speaks of the past definite, not of the future.")

The argumentation of Reuss is not conclusive:

(1) It is no proof of inaccuracy or of untrustworthiness that things which took place at the close of the journeying are mentioned in Exodus. In history, especially in Bible history, events are not always related in their chronological order; nor does a departure from chronological order create doubt or suspicion, except in the minds of analytic critics and skeptics.

(2) Moses may have written the Book of Exodus at the beginning of the wandering, and inserted this passage [2] near the close of his life on a final review. There is nothing improper in an author's redacting his own writings.

(3) The passage does not speak of the *cessation* of the manna at all. It states merely that the Israelites ate manna forty years, and that they ate it until they came to an inhabited country— the borders of Canaan. There is not a word about the *cessation* of the manna, nor even of the Israelites' ceasing to eat it. The declaration that the Israelites ate manna until they came to the borders of Canaan may seem to imply that then they ceased, and the objector, of course, supposes that they ceased to eat manna at that time because they could not get it; and he further supposes that their inability to get it resulted from its ceasing to fall. But there is not a word of all this in the text. It affirms merely that the Israelites ate manna until they came to the borders of Canaan; but this does not necessarily imply that then they ceased to eat it. When the Hebrew said, "I will call

---

[1] *L'Histoire Sainte*, Vol. I., Int., p. 127.   [2] Ex. 16: 35.

on God as long as I live," or, "I will call on God until I die," he did not mean that *then* he would cease to call on God. When a man and woman, at marriage, solemnly engage to love one another until death, there is no implied promise that they will cease to love each other when they die.

Though, then, the manna ceased after the crossing of the Jordan and six weeks after the death of Moses, there is nothing in this passage that might not have been written by him. The utter silence of the author of this passage concerning the crossing of the Jordan, the entrance into Canaan, and the actual cessation of the manna suggests that he died before these events took place, and that if he were not Moses, he at least lived in the Mosaic age.

But if our passage does indeed imply that the manna ceased when the Israelites came to the borders of Canaan and before the death of Moses, still there is here no anachronism, but a mere discrepancy between Exodus and Joshua as to time. The objector, of course, here gives the preference to the Book of Joshua, however much he may decry in general its historical accuracy. But, after all, may not the ceasing to *eat* manna have begun as soon as the Israelites reached the border of Canaan, and the manna continued until after the crossing of the Jordan? There is a distinction to be made between the ceasing to *eat* manna and the ceasing of the manna itself. People who had been eating manna nearly forty years would embrace the very first opportunity to procure other food.

9. "The Horims also dwelt in Seir beforetime; but the children of Esau succeeded them, when they had destroyed them from before them, and dwelt in their stead; as Israel did unto the land of his possession, which the Lord gave unto them."[1]

The analytic critics maintain that this passage refers to the conquest of Canaan as an accomplished fact, and therefore could not have been written by Moses. Reuss says, "On remarquera qu'il y est question de la conquête de la Palestine comme d'un fait passé"[2] ("It is to be remarked that the question here is concerning the conquest of Palestine as a past fact"). Kuenen sententiously refers to this passage to show that, according to the historical standpoint of the writer, Canaan was already in the possession of Israel.[3]

According to this view, Moses, who died before the conquest,

---

[1] Deut. 2: 12. [2] *L'Histoire Sainte*, Vol. I., p. 278. [3] *Hexateuch*, pp. 34-36.

cannot be the author of this passage. Our contention, however, is that this passage refers to conquests made before the death of Moses.

(1) The Israelites had conquered the Amorites, taken their land, and dwelt in all their cities and villages.[1]

(2) Next they destroyed Og, the king of Bashan, and his people. The record states that they left none of his sons or of his people alive, and possessed his land.[2]

(3) The subjugation of the Midianites furnishes a third example of conquest and spoliation. Israel made war upon them, killed the men, took the women and children captive, burnt the cities and castles, and seized the cattle, sheep, and goods.[3]

In addition to all these conquests, before the death of Moses all east Palestine had been subdued, and with his consent and by his direction was divided up among the two and a half tribes. During the last two years of Moses' life the south Canaanites,[4] the Amorites, and Midianites were destroyed; King Arad, King Sihon, King Og, and five kings of Midian were slain, their armies annihilated, their cities burned, their goods plundered, and their lands (except those of the Midianites) seized, divided, and held as a permanent possession. In this way was treated the whole transjordanic region. In view of these facts, Moses might well say orally, and afterward in writing, that the Edomites destroyed their predecessors and seized their lands, "as Israel did to the land of his possession, which the Lord gave unto them."

We suggest two changes in the English translation, one of which the original requires, and the other of which it allows. The first is the omission of the article before the word "land" (as there is no article in the original); and the other is the substitution of the present-perfect tense of the verb for the past. The sentence will then read as follows: "As Israel has done to land of his possession." The error of the critics is in understanding "the land of his possession" to mean *all* the land of his possession. The omission of the article in English, as in the original Hebrew, makes more evident the error.

10. Deuteronomy 3: 11, the account of Og's iron bedstead.

The critics claim that though Og, the giant king, was slain in the last year of Moses' life, in this passage his bedstead is

---

[1] Num. 21: 23-31. [2] Num. 21: 33-35. [3] Num. 31: 1-12. [4] Num. 21: 1.

mentioned as a thing of antiquity, and therefore the passage must have been written long after Mosaic times. This is the view presented by Voltaire,[1] Paine,[2] Reuss, Kuenen, and many others. Reuss comments as follows: "A Rabbah on montrait le pretendu lit de fer du géant Og, qui avait eté tué dans l'année méme de la mort de Moïse, et le texte (Deut. 3: 11) fait remarquer comme une chose memorable que ce lit existe encore. En general, tout ce chapitre, ainsi que le précédent, raconte les événements de cette même année comme si c'etaient des faits appartenant á une époque lointaine."[3] ("At Rabbah is shown the pretended iron bedstead of the giant Og, who had been killed in the very year of Moses' death, and the text (Deut. 3: 11) mentions it as a memorable thing that this bedstead still exists. In general, this entire chapter, as also the preceding, relates the events of this same year as if they were facts pertaining to a distant period.") Kuenen oracularly writes, "Og's bed, a relic of antiquity."[4]

The basis of the argument in this case is wholly imaginary. There is not one word in this passage to indicate that the iron bedstead was a very old one, or that Og had been a long time dead. Even the formula "unto this day" is not found here. The only thing mentioned as extraordinary is the size of the bedstead, and even this is adduced merely to prove that Og was truly a giant. For anything that is said in the passage, the bedstead may not have been a year older than when its gigantic owner last lay upon it. Its antiquity is wholly an achievement of the critical imagination. The critics practice eisegesis on the text first, and then proceed to the work of exegesis.

11. "Unto this day."

This phrase is employed very often in the Pentateuch, and is cited by the analysts to prove that many of the passages in which it is found cannot have been written in the time of Moses. They claim that it suggests a period of many years as intervening between the age of Moses and the time in which the passages containing this formula were written. The following passage from Deuteronomy may serve as an example: "Jair the son of Manasseh took all the country of Argob unto the coasts of Geshuri and Maachathi, and called them after his own name, Bashan-havoth-jair, unto this day."[5] It is claimed that the

---

[1] *Dictionnaire Philosophique*, Article "Moses."   [2] *Age of Reason*, p. 75.
[3] *L'Histoire Sainte*, Vol. I., p. 130.   [4] *Hexateuch*, p. 37.   [5] Deut. 3: 14.

formula "unto this day" indicates a long lapse of time previous to the time of the writer, and that, as Moses lived only a short time after the transactions referred to took place, he cannot be the writer of this passage. Many other passages in the Pentateuch contain this phrase, and if it necessarily implies a long lapse of time the most of them must have been written long after the time of Moses.

Now Reuss affirms that "unto this day" always implies antiquity. His words are, "La formule implique toujours la notion de l'antiquité"[1] ("The formula always implies the notion of antiquity"). If the critic had only paid a little attention to the exegesis of the phrase, he certainly would not have made this affirmation. Genesis 19:37, 38: "Moab . . . the father of the Moabites unto this day. . . . Ben-ammi . . . the father of the children of Ammon unto this day." Here present time is indicated, or at least the sacred writer did not mean to say that Moab had been the father of the Moabites for *a long time*, and that Ben-ammi had been *a long time* the father of the Ammonites. Genesis 48:15: "The God which fed me all my life long unto this day." Here "unto this day" means present time, and, though preceding time is indeed referred to, it is expressed by the words "all my life long." Numbers 22:30: "Am not I thine ass, upon which thou hast ridden ever since I was thine unto this day?" The time referred to here is not antiquity, nor a long period, but merely the time since the ass had come into Balaam's possession, at most only a few years, and this is expressed by the words "ever since I was thine," while "unto this day" refers only to present time. It is not necessary to discuss the character of the occurrence here mentioned, nor to inquire whether the ass spoke, if it spoke at all, in the Hebrew language. We have the record in Hebrew, and doubtless the language employed accords with good Hebrew usage. Joshua 22:3: Joshua said unto the two and a half tribes, "Ye have not left your brethren these many days unto this day." The time here referred to is the time in which the Israelites were engaged in conquering Canaan, that is, about seven years, and is here expressed by the words "these many days," while "unto this day," as usual, here means present time. I. Samuel 29:6, 8: Achish said to David, "I have not found evil in thee since the day of thy coming unto me unto this day." David, in his reply,

---

[1] *L'Histoire Sainte*, Int., p. 130.

said: "But what have I done? and what hast thou found in thy servant, so long as I have been with thee unto this day?" Here our formula again means simply *up to the present time*, while the preceding time is indicated by other words. In this case the period designated is only a year and four months, for that was the time David had spent in the land of the Philistines.[1] I. Samuel 12 : 2: Samuel said to his countrymen, "I have walked before you from my childhood unto this day." Here, once more, not antiquity, not a long period, but a single lifetime is meant, and that is expressed by the whole phrase "from my childhood unto this day," which is equivalent to "from my childhood to the present time."

On examination, then, we find (1) that the words "unto this day" do not of themselves imply antiquity, nor a long period, but are often employed when the implied time is brief, the lifetime of a man, the lifetime of an ass, seven years, sixteen months, or a still shorter period; (2) that when any period of time, longer or shorter, is designated, it is not done by the formula "unto this day," but by added words or phrases; and (3) that this formula is precisely equivalent to "unto the present time." Thus, the phrase "from my childhood unto this day" is equivalent to "from my childhood until now."

Kuenen, a man of more sober judgment than Reuss, though perhaps even more dogmatic, sets entirely aside the dictum of the latter quoted above, and virtually concedes the futility of the argument derived from this formula by declaring "that there is nothing in this expression absolutely to preclude the Mosaic date," and by giving up all the passages containing this formula in Genesis and all but three in Deuteronomy[2] as not necessarily referring to times later than Moses.[3] Even in regard to the argument as founded on these three passages, he weakens (a thing very unusual with him), as is indicated by the following declaration: "At any rate, the use of the formula 'even to this day' inclines us to place the writers of the Hexateuch long after the times of Moses and Joshua."[4]

It is not strange that Kuenen, after having given up all but three of the passages containing this formula, should only be *inclined* to rely on these as proving the Pentateuch to have been written long after the time of Moses. One of these passages is

[1] I. Sam. 27 : 7.
[2] Deut. 3 : 14 ; 10 : 8 ; 34 : 6.
[3] *Hexateuch*, p. 36.
[4] *Hexateuch*, p. 34.

Deuteronomy 34:6, where the writer, speaking of the burial of Moses, says, "But no man knoweth of his sepulcher unto this day." As we have shown, so far as this passage itself is concerned, it may have been written within a year or even within a month after the death of Moses. The writer merely states that at the time he wrote no one knew of the sepulcher of Moses, but does not even intimate that Moses had been long dead.

Another passage which Kuenen declines to give up entirely is Deuteronomy 10:8, where it is stated that, at a former time, the tribe of Levi was appointed "to stand before the Lord to minister unto him, and to bless in his name, unto this day." We have an account of this separation of the tribe of Levi in the third chapter of Numbers, nearly forty years before the words recorded in this passage purport to have been spoken by Moses. But, as we have shown, Moses might have used the same phraseology, even though that event had taken place only a year or two before. According to Kuenen's view, the writer of Deuteronomy puts improper phraseology in the mouth of Moses, representing him as using words near the time of the occurrence that could be appropriately employed only long afterward. But the author of Deuteronomy thoroughly understood the Hebrew language, and it is more likely that Kuenen and other critics are mistaken than that he committed a grammatical blunder.

The remaining passage which Kuenen declines to give up is the one with which we set out—Deuteronomy 3:14, "called them after his own name, Bashan-havoth-jair, unto this day." But we have shown that the formula here employed, by itself considered, means merely present time. We have shown also that Kuenen himself admits that "there is nothing in this expression absolutely to preclude the Mosaic date." We have further shown that in some cases the statement made in connection with this formula refers to a very brief period of time, as, for example, the time of David's sojourn in the land of the Philistines. Once more, the writer of our passage appears to have been living at the time Jair called the villages after his own name. No preceding time or event is expressed or implied. Jair named the villages "unto this day," at this time, the time then present. And the words purport to be spoken by Moses. Did the author of Deuteronomy commit a blunder in grammar in representing Moses as using language which was applicable only to events long after their occurrence? To employ the phraseology as an argument to prove that the writer lived long after the Mosaic age is to assume that Moses did not speak the words attributed to him, and that the writer committed the literary blunder of attributing words to him that he could not have spoken without a grammatical error.

12. Joseph's declaration: "For indeed I was stolen away out of the land of the Hebrews."[1]

The analysts maintain that Palestine was not called the land of the Hebrews until after the conquest of Canaan, and therefore Moses could not have written this passage. Kuenen coolly assumes the anachronism without proof. Reuss's presentation of the objection is as follows: "Joseph raconte á Pharaoh qu'il a été enlevé du pays des Hébreux. (Gen. 40: 15.) Comment le pays de Canaan pouvait-il étre nommé ainsi, soit par un individu qui, avec ses onze fréres, était le seul represéntant de la nation des Hébreux, soit par Moïse du temps duqual il n'y avait pas un seul homme de cette race dans le pays?"[2] ("Joseph relates to Pharaoh that he was carried off from the country of the Hebrews. (Gen. 40: 15.) How could the country of Canaan be named thus, either by an individual who, with his eleven brothers, was the sole representative of the nation of the Hebrews, or by Moses, at the time in which there was not a single man of this race in the country?")

This statement is marked by the characteristic inaccuracy of its author.

(1) Joseph related, not to Pharaoh, as Reuss states, but to the chief butler, how he had been taken from the land of the Hebrews.[3]

(2) Reuss errs again in asserting that Joseph, with his eleven brothers, was the sole representative of the Hebrew nation. When he said this, he must have forgotten Jacob, his numerous grandsons, and the whole company of sixty-six persons, including only two of the women, that went down into Egypt.

(3) Our critic makes a mistake, or does worse, in using the word "nation" in this connection. Neither Joseph nor Moses calls Jacob's family a nation. They are simply called Hebrews.

(4) It is an unjustifiable assumption to assert, as our critic does, that if Moses wrote this passage he must have written it when there was not a single man of the Hebrew race in the country. It is possible that Moses revised the Book of Genesis

[1] Gen. 40: 15. [2] *L'Histoire Sainte*, Int., p. 131. [3] Gen. 40: 9, 15, 23.

near the close of his life, and that he inserted this very phrase, "land of the Hebrews," after the two and a half tribes, including more than one hundred thousand able-bodied men, with their wives and children,— in all, more than three hundred thousand persons,— had been permanently settled in Palestine east of the Jordan.[1] Critics, who have so much to say about the revising and touching up of books, ought to allow that an ancient author might revise and retouch his own writings.

(5) In the circumstances, Joseph's calling Canaan the land or country of the Hebrews was both natural and proper. What else would he have called it? Had he called it Canaan or the land of the Canaanites, the Egyptians would have regarded him as a Canaanite. If he had named it Palestine or the country of the Philistines, he would have been regarded as a Philistine. He was a Hebrew. His great-grandfather, a mighty prince,[2] was known as Abraham the Hebrew. This name was transmitted to his descendants. The Pentateuchal history shows that in Egypt they were called, not Israelites nor Jews, but Hebrews. Thus the Egyptians knew them and named them.[3] In speaking, then, of Palestine to an Egyptian it was very natural and proper that Joseph should designate it as the land or country of the Hebrews, or the country in which the Hebrews lived. It seems, however, that Reuss objects to the use of this expression in Joseph's and Moses' time, on the ground that the Hebrews did not own the country until after the conquest. In his note on the passage he says: "Un *pays* des Hébreux n'a existé qu'aprés la conquete. Ni Joseph ni Moïse n'a pu s'exprimer ainsi."[4] ("A country of the Hebrews existed only after the conquest. Neither Joseph nor Moses could have expressed himself thus.") Had Jacob and his sons no country at all? Canaan was theirs because they lived in it, just as people in general call the country in which they live their own, whether they possess any real estate in it or not.

But whether correct or not, it was natural for Joseph to call the land from which he had been carried off the land of the Hebrews, and it was proper for the historian to record accurately his words.

13. Another case of claimed anachronism is the naming of the villages of Jair. The passages on which the claim of

---

[1] Num. 1: 21, 25, 35.   [2] Gen. 23: 6.
[3] Gen. 40: 15; 41: 12; Ex. 1: 15, 16, 19; 2: 6, 7, 11, 13; 7: 16; 9: 1, 13.
[4] *L'Histoire Sainte*, Vol. I., p. 420, note.

anachronism is founded are as follows: "And Jair the son of Manasseh went and took the small towns thereof, and called them Havoth-jair."[1] In the address of Moses, recorded in Deuteronomy, the statement is repeated that Jair took certain towns and districts and "called them after his own name, Bashan-havoth-jair, unto this day."[2] But in Judges we have an account of a man named Jair, a Gileadite, who "judged Israel twenty and two years. And he had thirty sons that rode on thirty ass colts, and they had thirty cities, which are called Havoth-jair unto this day, which are in the land of Gilead."[3]

The contention is that cities that received the name of Havoth-jair in the time of the judges are represented in the Pentateuch as having been thus named in the time of Moses — a clear case of anachronism. Voltaire, speaking of Moses and the Pentateuch, says: "Il n'y a pas d'apparence qu'il eût appelé les endroits dont il parle de noms qui ne leur furent imposés que longtemps après. Il est fait mention dans ce livre des villes de Jair, et tout le monde convient qu'elles ne furent ainsi nommes que long-temps après la mort de Moïse."[4] ("There is no probability that he would call places of which he speaks by names which were given them only long afterward. In this book there is mention of the cities of Jair, and all the world agrees that they were thus named only long after the death of Moses.") Other critics say substantially the same thing.

To this our reply shall be brief, and it is just this, that the passage in Judges does not say *when*, nor *after whom*, the cities mentioned therein were named. It does indeed say that these cities were called Havoth-jair, but that they were thus called after the name of Judge Jair is just what it does not say. Voltaire no doubt saw this fatally weak place in the argument, and endeavored to cover it up with the asseveration that "all the world agrees that they were thus named only long after the death of Moses." His successors in criticism have pursued a similar course. Besides, this is a case of apparent discrepancy between authors, not anachronism; but in such cases some critics may always be depended on to decide against the Pentateuch.

14. Kuenen refers to Numbers 15: 22 to show that to the writer of the passage the sojourn in the wilderness was a closed period of history. But what of it? The sojourn in the wilder-

---

[1] Num. 32: 41. [2] Deut. 3: 14. [3] Judg. 10: 3, 4.
[4] *Dictionnaire Philosophique*, Vol. XIX., p. 65.

ness was indeed a closed period of history to Moses and the Israelites during the whole time covered by the Book of Deuteronomy. We suggest, however, that the words, "while the children of Israel were in the wilderness," may be understood as implying that the writer viewed the sojourn in the wilderness merely as still in progress. So far as this statement is concerned, the author at the time of writing may himself have been sojourning in the wilderness.

15. Deuteronomy 19: 14: "Thou shalt not remove thy neighbor's land-mark, which they of old time have set in thine inheritance, which thou shalt inherit in the land that the Lord thy God giveth thee to possess it."

It is maintained that the words, "they of old time have set in thine inheritance," indicate that at the time of the writing of this passage the boundary marks of the lands in Canaan had been in existence for a long time. The passage, however, is in form a legal enactment, and purports to have been uttered by Moses in prospect of their future settlement in Canaan. If the form of expression betrays a later origin, it must be that the writer erred in the use of words. He tried to put such words into the mouth of Moses as would represent him as legislating, before the conquest, for the Israelites after they should have been permanently settled. But he failed to choose the right words, and, by mistake, represents Moses as talking like a man who lived at a much later period. According to the critics, the writer of this passage committed the error of representing Moses as saying that the settlement in Canaan was still future and as virtually saying at the same time that it had taken place long before.

If there had been a future-perfect tense of the Hebrew verb, probably Moses would have said, "Remove not thy neighbor's land-mark, which they going before thee *shall have* set." But for the absence of the future-perfect tense from the Hebrew language, evidently there would not be even the semblance of a foundation for the argument which the critics draw from this passage.

These are the principal passages and arguments that are adduced by the analysts to prove anachronisms in the Pentateuch, and to disprove its Mosaic authorship.

CHAPTER IV

CLAIMED ALLOTOPISMS

It is claimed that there are in the Pentateuch passages that were written in places where Moses at the time was not, and could not have been. The objector reasons as follows: According to the import of some passages in the Pentateuch, the author at the time of writing was in a certain place or country; but Moses at that particular time was in another place or country; therefore, Moses did not write these passages. Principal Cave calls these geographical arguments *anatropisms*. We prefer to call them *allotopisms*. They are a legitimate mode of reasoning. If an allotopism can be established, it is conclusive, like an alibi in a criminal case in court.

1. An argument of the above kind is founded on the words "beyond Jordan," as found in various passages of Deuteronomy. The rendering in the Authorized Version is generally "on this side," or, "on the other side," but sometimes "beyond." It is maintained by the critics that the rendering ought to be "beyond Jordan," as it generally is in the Revised Version. The argument is as follows: In Deuteronomy Moses and the Israelites are spoken of as being beyond Jordan, when they were east of the Jordan. "These be the words which Moses spake unto all Israel beyond Jordan in the wilderness."[1] Now Moses, at the time he is spoken of as being "beyond Jordan," was in east Palestine. If, then, the writer of this passage speaks from his own geographical standpoint, he was at the time of writing in west Palestine. In that case the writer must have been some other than Moses. The question, then, is, Does the writer use the phrase "beyond Jordan" with reference to his own geographical position at the time of writing? Voltaire assumes that he does: "Comment Moïse aurait-il appelé villes au delà du Jourdan les villes qui á son égard étaient en decà?" ("How could Moses call cities on this side Jordan the cities beyond Jordan?")

[1] Deut. 1:1, R.V.   [2] *Dictionnaire Philosophique*, *Moïse*, Sec. iii.

This objection, and the assumption on which it is based, have often been stated, but never improved, by later critics. They assume that the phrase translated "on this side Jordan" in Deuteronomy, Authorized Version, and "beyond Jordan" in the Revised Version, is employed by the writer to designate the side of Jordan opposite to the place occupied by himself at the time of writing, and that the meaning of the phrase can be determined only by our knowing whether the writer was on the east or west side of the Jordan. A little honest exegesis, however, is sufficient to show that the phrase translated "beyond Jordan" has no reference to the writer's geographical standpoint. It will not be denied that it literally means "at the crossing of Jordan." It might well be rendered *at the side of*, or *beside*, *Jordan*. Instead of relying on this phrase itself, or his own geographical location, to indicate which side of the Jordan is meant, the writer makes his meaning known by additional words or phrases, unless it is made clear by the context; thus: "On this side Jordan [at the crossing of, or beside, Jordan] *in the wilderness, in the plain over against the Red sea, between Paran, and Tophel, and Laban, and Hazeroth, and Dizahab*";[1] "on this side [beside] Jordan, *in the land of Moab*";[2] "on this side [beside] Jordan, *from the river of Arnon unto mount Hermon; (which Hermon the Sidonians call Sirion, and the Amorites call it Shenir*");[3] "which the Lord your God hath given them beyond [beside] Jordan."[4] Here the meaning is indicated by the preceding context, in which the possession of the two and a half tribes is located on the one side of the Jordan, and that of the nine tribes impliedly on the other. "Let me *go over* [cross] and see the good land that is beyond [beside] Jordan, *that goodly mountain, and Lebanon*";[5] "Then Moses severed three cities on this side [beside] Jordan, *toward the sun-rising*";[6] "on this side [beside] Jordan, *in the valley over against Beth-peor, in the land of Sihon king of the Amorites, who dwelt at Heshbon*";[7] "which were on this side [beside] Jordan, *toward the sun-rising*";[8] "and all the plain on this side [beside] Jordan *eastward, even unto the sea of the plain, under the springs of Pisgah*";[9] "Are they not on the other side [beside] Jordan, *by the way where the sun goeth down, in the land of the Canaanites?*"[10]

Thus, in the ten cases in which the author of Deuteronomy

[1] Deut. 1:1. [2] Deut. 1:5. [3] Deut. 3:8, 9. [4] Deut. 3:20. [5] Deut. 3:25.
[6] Deut. 4:41. [7] Deut. 4:46. [8] Deut. 4:47. [9] Deut. 4:49. [10] Deut. 11:30.

employs the phrase which in the English version is sometimes translated "on this side Jordan," and sometimes "beyond Jordan," never once does he depend on the phrase itself, nor upon his own geographical position, to indicate which side of the Jordan is meant, but always on added words or phrases, or on the context. In the one case in which no words or phrases are added to complete the meaning, the context makes it sufficiently plain that it is the western side of Jordan that is referred to.[1]

The same is true of this phrase as used elsewhere. Thus in Numbers: "On this side [beside] Jordan *eastward*";[2] "on this side [beside] Jordan near Jericho *eastward, toward the sun-rising*."[3] The use of this phrase in the Book of Joshua is precisely the same. Taking the rendering of the Revisionists, we have the following: "beyond Jordan toward the sun-rising";[4] "beyond Jordan westward";[5] "beyond Jordan . . . on all the shore of the great sea";[6] "beyond Jordan toward the sunrising";[7] "beyond Jordan westward";[8] "beyond Jordan eastward";[9] "beyond the Jordan at Jericho eastward";[10] "beyond Jordan westward."[11]

It is thus shown that the phrase translated in both the Authorized and Revised versions sometimes "beyond Jordan," and sometimes "on this side Jordan," gives no information as to whether the object to which it is applied was on the east or west side of that river, and hence does not indicate the locality of the writer. In every case it is shown which side of the Jordan is meant by additional words or phrases, as "east," "west," "sunrising," "going down of the sun," "land of Moab," "coasts of the great sea," "in the wilderness over against the Red sea," "from Arnon to Hermon," or by the context.

Further, both Moses and Joshua are represented, while in *east* Palestine, as calling it "beber hayarden" (בְּעֵבֶר הַיַּרְדֵּן).[12]

One of the following conclusions is inevitable: Either (1) this phrase means merely *beside*, and not *beyond;* or (2) Moses and Joshua committed a grammatical blunder very often in the use of it; or (3) the writers of Duteronomy and the Book of Joshua committed a literary blunder in putting this phrase into their mouths; or (4) this phrase is used by both the speakers and

[1] Deut. 3 : 20.   [2] Num. 32 : 19.   [3] Num. 34 : 15.
[4] Josh. 1 . 15, R.V.   [5] Josh. 5 : 1, R.V.   [6] Josh. 9 : 1, R.V.
[7] Josh. 12 : 1, R.V.   [8] Josh. 12 : 7, R.V.   [9] Josh. 18 : 7, R.V.
[10] Josh. 20 : 8, R.V.   [11] Josh. 22 : 7, R.V.   [12] Deut. 3 : 8; Josh. 1 : 14.

the writers as a proper name for east Palestine, like cisalpine Gaul by the ancient Romans. But the second and third hypotheses are inadmissible, and according to either of the other, two the objection to the Mosaic authorship is baseless.

2. Another example of allotopism is found in those passages which refer to the cardinal points of the compass west and south.

In the Pentateuch, *Yam* (יָם), the sea, is put for west, and *Negeb* (נֶגֶב), the desert, for south. But when Moses and the Israelites were in Egypt, at Sinai, and in the wilderness, the Mediterranean was not to the west of them, nor the *Negeb* to the south. It is hence argued that the Pentateuch could not have been written in Egypt, at Sinai, or in the wilderness, and therefore not by Moses.

If, like the analysts, we were disposed to deal in hypotheses, we might suppose that Moses, writing the Pentateuch in the wilderness, designated the points of the compass in accordance with his geographical position and surroundings, and that after he came to eastern Palestine, in revising his books, he adapted his nomenclature of the points of the compass to the modes of thought and speech prevalent in that region. Our analytic advocates could not with self-consistency object to the supposition of such revision and redaction.

But our reply is that it is to be presumed that Moses and the Israelites in Egypt and the wilderness used *Yam* for west and *Negeb* for south, just as their forefathers did in Palestine. The Hebrew was a fully formed language before Jacob went down into Egypt. Abraham brought it with him from Ur of the Chaldees, and he found the Canaanites speaking the same language as himself. Sayce testifies that the old Babylonian and Assyrian languages were as similar to that of the Old Testament as two modern dialects in English are to each other,[1] and that the language of Canaan differed but little from Hebrew.[2] Accordingly, the Hebrews and Canaanites, in their intercourse with each other, had no need of interpreters.[3] The Hebrew was therefore an old and well-established language before the migration to Egypt. The Hebrews took that language with them into Egypt and continued to speak it there. In that language *Yam* means

---

[1] *Fresh Light from the Monuments*, p. 29.
[2] *Races of the Old Testament*, pp. 57, 102.
[3] Gen. 23: 15; Josh. 2: 1-22; 9: 1-27.

west and *Negeb* means south. No doubt, Moses and the Israelites, while in Egypt and the wilderness, expressed themselves in this way, because it was in accordance with well-established Hebrew usage. Julius Cæsar did not cease to speak of transalpine Gaul when he crossed the Alps, nor is it necessary for the modern traveler to cease speaking of the Orient when he reaches India or Japan. In after times the Hebrews did not change their mode of speech when they went out of their own country. The captives in Babylonia continued to use *Yam* for west and *Negeb* for south, as is shown by the One Hundred and Twenty-sixth Psalm and the prophecies of Ezekiel and Daniel. To be consistent, the critics should maintain that Ezekiel and Daniel wrote in Palestine.

Palestine, with *Yam* on the west and the *Negeb* on the south, was not unknown to the Israelites, or at least to Moses, in Egypt. Thothmes III., king of Egypt, conquered Canaan 1600 B.C., a century or more before the exodus.[1] Gibeah, Migdol, Merom, Megiddo, and other towns made familiar by the Pentateuchal history, twenty-five in all, are named in the list of places that submitted to the conqueror. Mention is made of the *Negeb*, or southern district. The Pharaohs kept possession of Canaan until the time of Moses. Rameses II., the Pharaoh of the oppression, had a long struggle with the Hittites for the possession of Canaan. A line of Egyptian fortresses was established as far north as Damascus. Thus a knowledge of Canaan was kept up among the Egyptians in the time of Moses. The tablets give an account of the travels of an Egyptian *mohar* in Palestine, in these times, describing how he went in his chariot to Gebal, Sarepta, Sidon, Hazor, Tabor, Hamath, and other cities; how he had his clothes stolen one night, and how at another time he had a wheel of his chariot broken, and was necessitated to have it repaired at a blacksmith shop.[2]

Thus in the time of Moses there were frequent communications between Egypt and Canaan and adjoining and tributary provinces. Thus, too, there was much to remind Moses of the land of his ancestors and to preserve in him the remembrance and love of his mother tongue, with its idioms and peculiar forms.

The matter, then, stands thus: In the Hebrew language, spoken in Canaan before the time of Abraham, *Yam* designated the west,

---

[1] Wilkinson's *Ancient Egypt*, Vol. I., pp. 399-403.
[2] Sayce's *Fresh Light from the Monuments*, pp. 56-59; *Hittites*, pp. 27-31.

and *Negeb* the south; the Israelites in Egypt continued to use their native language; the Hebrew was the mother tongue of Moses, as well as of the Israelites in general; hence, to him and to them, whether they were in Goshen, or at Sinai, or near to Palestine, or whatever their geographic position might be, *Yam* meant the west, and *Negeb* the south. Hence the use of these words in this sense in the Pentateuch does not indicate the locality of the author at the time of writing.

CHAPTER V

CLAIMED CONTRADICTIONS

It is maintained that there are contradictions in the Pentateuch, and therefore that it is not the production of Moses. The objector assumes that Moses would not contradict himself, and accounts for the supposed contradictions by the hypothesis that the Pentateuch was written by another author, or rather by many other authors.

This was the oft-repeated argument of Voltaire and Paine. It seems to be confidently relied upon by Reuss[1] and Kuenen,[2] who give lists of passages claimed to be contradictory.

1. Kuenen claims that what he calls "the two creation stories," contained in the first and second chapters of Genesis, are contradictory. He says: "The division of the work of creation into six days is entirely unknown to the second story. Moreover, the order of creation is quite different in the second: first, the man is created; then trees and plants; then animals; and, lastly, the woman."[3] In regard to these claims, we remark as follows:

(1) There is a presumption against any such contradiction as Kuenen thinks he finds between these two passages. The author of Genesis, even though he were an uninspired and an ordinary man, was not likely to be guilty of such palpable inconsistency. Even on the hypothesis of two authors, the contradiction is unaccountable and improbable. Why did not the compiler of the two accounts, or some redactor afterward, harmonize them? According to the analytic view, there was, besides the first compiler, a host of writers whose business it was to retouch and improve the Pentateuchal books. Whether, therefore, there was but one author of Genesis or many, the existence of such transparent blemishes as Kuenen claims in that book would be strange and improbable.

(2) Our critic assumes that because the six days' work is not

---

[1] *L'Histoire Sainte*, Int., pp. 39-43. [2] *Hexateuch*, pp. 38-40. [3] *Hexateuch*, pp. 38, 39.

mentioned in the second chapter, therefore it is denied. This is unreasonable. Silence, if it does not give consent, is at least not denial. Otherwise, we might say that Kuenen is contradicted by Reuss in regard to this very matter in hand; for the latter is silent in regard to it, though he makes it his special business to find contradictions in the Pentateuch.

(3) The order of narration in the two chapters is different, but this difference is no contradiction. Authors are not bound to state events in the order of their occurrence. They may treat of the same subject twice or oftener; they are not bound to follow the same order of presentation; and in the second treatment or account they may give particulars not contained in the first. According to our critic's view, if a second witness in court does not repeat all the testimony given by the first, or does not give it in the same order, there is contradiction between them.

(4) Kuenen ignores the common-sense view which has commended itself to readers and students of the Bible in general. That view is that the account contained in the second chapter of Genesis is designed to supplement the account contained in the first by the addition of some particulars. In this second account man is taken as the special subject. His twofold nature is suggested by additional information concerning his creation,[1] and then is set forth the provision that God made for him. Among other things, it is stated that the Lord brought the beasts of the field and the fowls of the air to Adam, that he might name them.[2] Their formation out of the ground is mentioned in this connection, and if it is to be understood that they were formed *immediately* before they were brought to Adam we would be compelled to recognize the passage as conflicting with the first chapter, where the formation of the land animals is assigned to the fifth day and the creation of man to the sixth. But such a construction is not necessary. Owing to the want of the pluperfect tense in the Hebrew language, the perfect is often made to do duty in its place. Hence, the meaning may be presented thus: "And out of the ground the Lord God *had* formed every beast of the field and every fowl of the air." Only the beasts of the *field* are here mentioned, not the beasts of the *earth;* and only the *land* fowls,—the fowls formed out of the *ground*,[3]—not the water fowls, are mentioned. The fact that the animals brought to Adam were formed out of the ground is the thing

[1] Gen. 2:7, 8-25. [2] Gen. 2:19. [3] Gen. 1:20; 2:19.

indicated, not the *time* of their formation. The thought would be expressed in English thus: "The Lord God brought to Adam the beasts and birds which he had formed out of the ground."

(5) Finally, Kuenen deals here only in assumption and assertion.

2. Reuss finds a contradiction in the passages one of which represents Sarah as the daughter-in-law of Terah[1] and the other as his daughter.[2] But there is here certainly no contradiction; for when Sarah married Abram, her father's son, she became the daughter-in-law of her father. Here, also, according to the analytic view, Kuenen contradicts Reuss, for the former is silent in regard to this supposed contradiction.

3. Reuss[3] affirms that the account of Abraham's attempt to deceive Pharaoh[4] is a story told in two other places,[5] with variations. Kuenen decides that the deception, after its first failure, is too improbable psychologically for the same author to ascribe both attempts to Abraham.[6] According to Reuss, we have here, of the same affair, three reports contradicting one another as to persons, times, places, and circumstances. Kuenen holds this view in regard to two of the reports, but is silent in regard to the third.

As a matter of course, the hypothesis that these three accounts, or even two of them, relate to one event involves the notion of contradiction. But this hypothesis is made without just reason. There is nothing improbable in Abraham's doing the same thing twice and in Isaac's doing it once. The "psychological" reason assigned by Kuenen is puerile. It is not incredible that Abraham should resort to an expedient that had failed. Men often do this. They fight and fail, and fight again; they deceive and fail, and try to deceive again. History abounds in examples of this. If future theorists should imitate the course of the critics, the former may, with their hypotheses and fancy, make as great havoc of secular history as the latter are trying to make of the narratives in the Pentateuch. Perhaps some future critic will decide that the accounts of the beheading of Charles II. and Louis XVI. are discordant stories of the same event. Why not? Both the culprits were kings, both had been dethroned, both had been imprisoned, both were tried by irregular courts, both were condemned and executed by their own subjects, and both were

---

[1] Gen. 11 : 31. [2] Gen. 20 : 12. [3] *L'Histoire Sainte*, Int., pp. 40, 41.
[4] Gen. 12 : 10-20. [5] Gen. 20 : 1-18; 26 : 1-11. [6] *Hexateuch*, p. 39.

put to death in the same way. How many points of similarity there are! In the coming ages the man who has a theory to maintain will not find it difficult to persuade himself that all the accounts of the death of these two monarchs are only variant stories of one beheading. Perhaps some skeptical investigator in coming time will pronounce a like judgment on the accounts of the death of Lincoln and Garfield. The similarities are very striking—both Presidents of the United States, both elected by the same political party, both assassinated, both surviving for a time the assassin's attack, both assassinated in Washington, both assassinated in public, the assassin in both cases put to death. The historical skeptic will perhaps talk, like Kuenen, about psychological improbability in the case. He may say: (1) that it is psychologically improbable that the public assassination of a President, followed by the speedy death of the perpetrator, would be very soon repeated; (2) that the improbability is increased by the fact that the first assassination is represented by historians as being perpetrated in the theater, in the presence of hundreds of people, and the second in broad daylight, in the thronged streets of Washington City; (3) that the improbability, amounting to incredibility, is further shown by the fact that it was claimed at the time that the second assassin was insane, which shows that many even then regarded the act as performed by a sane man as incredible.

This is a fair representation of the way that Reuss, Kuenen, and other analysts, by means of hypothesis and fancy, construe two or three Bible narratives as discordant stories of one event, and then infer contradictions as to persons, places, times, and circumstances. It is to be noted that though these critics are keen to observe similarity in these narratives they seem to be blind to the dissimilarities. In this way just conclusions are not likely to be reached.

4. Reuss and Kuenen claim that there are two accounts of the origin of the name "Beer-sheba."[1] Of course, their aim is to prove that they are contradictory, and thus to prove that Moses did not write them both. If there are seeming contradictions in these accounts, they are only seeming ones. It is, indeed, said that Isaac digged the well called Beer-sheba.[2] But it is said that Abraham digged the well and named it. This looks very much like an improbability, if not a contradiction.

[1] Gen. 21: 25-31; 26: 32, 33.   [2] Gen. 26: 15, 18.

For how could Isaac dig a well that had been digged before? The sacred record, however, makes this matter plain, for it is expressly stated that the Philistines stopped all the wells which Abraham digged and that Isaac had digged them again.¹ Nor is there any contradiction in saying that both Abraham and Isaac named one of the wells Beer-sheba. When the well had been filled up by the Philistines, the name ceased. When the well went out of existence, the people had no use for the name. But when Isaac redigged the well, he gave it the name which his father had given it before. The express declaration is that Isaac digged again the wells which the Philistines had stopped and "called their names after the names by which his father had called them."²

5. Reuss and Kuenen hold that we have two discordant accounts of the removal of Joseph to Egypt.³ According to one of these accounts, Joseph was taken by his brothers out of the pit into which they had cast him and was sold by them to Ishmaelites, who took him to Egypt. According to the other account, he was stolen out of the pit by Midianites, while his brothers were eating bread, and was carried to Egypt and sold to Potiphar, an officer of Pharaoh.

One of the main arguments in favor of the hypothesis of two discordant accounts is the fact that Joseph is said to have been sold both to Ishmaelites and Midianites,⁴ and that also Joseph's sale in Egypt is attributed in one place to the Midianites⁵ and in another to the Ishmaelites.⁶ The question to be determined is whether these two names designate two sets of persons or only one.⁷ Now, that the Midianites were Ishmaelites is expressly declared in Judges 8: 2. It is there said of the Midianites, after their defeat by Gideon, "They were Ishmaelites." Reuss states that the Midianites were accounted Ishmaelites, and refers to the passages concerning the sale of Joseph to prove it. In his note on Genesis 25: 1-6 he says: "Ces Midyanites sont ailleurs rangés parmi les descendants d'Ismael (Juges 8: 24, comp. Gen. 38: 28, comp. avec 25 et 39: 1)"⁸ ("These Midianites are elsewhere ranked among the descendants of Ishmael"). Yet he forgets all this, and, in his eagerness to find a contradiction in the account of the sale of Joseph, contradicts himself.⁹

¹ Gen. 26: 15, 18. ² Gen. 26: 18. ³ Gen. 37: 18-36.
⁴ Gen. 37: 27, 28. ⁵ Gen. 37: 36. ⁶ Gen. 39: 1.
⁷ Reuss, *L'Histoire Sainte*, Vol. I., p. 52; Wellhausen, *Composition des Hexateuchs*, pp. 54, 55. ⁸ *L'Histoire Sainte*, Vol. I., p. 379.
⁹ *L'Histoire Sainte*, p. 52.

We are not now discussing the question whether there are two or more narratives dovetailed together in the Book of Genesis, but whether there are contradictions in the account of the sale of Joseph. And we advert to the identification of the Midianites with the Ishmaelites in that account and elsewhere, distinctly admitted by Reuss, as showing the unreality of the claimed contradiction.

As to the claimed contradiction between the two statements that Joseph was stolen[1] and that he was sold,[2] there need be no difficulty, if we only allow to words that latitude of meaning which all mankind gives them. He who takes a man and sells him is a thief and a robber. Those who think that Joseph contradicted himself in speaking at one time of his removal to Egypt as a sale and at another as a theft would do well to reflect a little on the old Deuteronomic law: "If a man be found stealing any of his brethren of the children of Israel, and maketh merchandise of him, or selleth him; then that thief shall die."[3] This fully justifies the variant language of Joseph concerning the stealing and selling of himself by his brethren and the Ishmaelites. Clearly the author of Genesis had more common sense than our critics.

6. Reuss and Kuenen claim that there are contradictory accounts of the change of Jacob's name to "Israel." They quote in proof Genesis 32: 28 and Genesis 35: 10. But do these passages conflict? In the first, the change of name is announced in connection with the wrestling of Jacob with the angel. In the second passage it is mentioned in connection with Jacob's second visit to Bethel. The change itself from "Jacob" to "Israel" could not be made twice, but the change might be *announced* twice or oftener. Reuss himself destroys the objection in his presentation of it. He says: "Le nom d'Israel fut donné á Jacob, d'aprés chap. 32: 28, en suite de la lutte nocturne que le patriarche avait soutenue contre Dieu. Au chap. 35: 10, ce changement de nom est relaté une secondé fois á l'occasion d'une autre rencontre."[4] ("The name of 'Israel' was given to Jacob, according to chapter 32: 28, in consequence of the nocturnal wrestling which Jacob had sustained against God. In chapter 35: 10 this change of name is related a second time, on the occasion of another rencounter.") Observe the statements: The name of "Israel" is *given* on the occasion of the wrestling;

---

[1] Gen. 40: 15.   [2] Gen. 45: 4.   [3] Deut. 24: 7.   [4] *L'Histoire Sainte*, Int., p. 42.

this change of name is *related* a second time. This explodes the objection.

7. Contradictions are claimed in the accounts of Esau's wives, and in the statements concerning the father-in-law of Moses. In Genesis 26:34 ; 28: 9 the names of Esau's wives are given as Judith, Bashemath, and Mahalath. But in Genesis 36: 2, 3 their names are given as Adah, Aholibamah, and Bashemath. The father-in-law of Moses is called Jethro, and also Reuel; he is called also a Midianite,[1] a Kenite,[2] and perhaps by implication a Cushite.[3]

But these passages embracing proper names are a very insecure foundation for charges of contradiction. Copyists were especially liable to make mistakes in the transcription of proper names. Hence, in urging such objections as we are dealing with, the critics are in danger of treating mere clerical errors of transcribers as contradictions of the original writers.

Besides, among the ancient peoples with whom we are specially concerned it was not uncommon for a person to have two or more names. Thus, we have Abram and Abraham, Jacob and Israel, Esau and Edom, Sarai and Sarah, and probably Iscah as a third name.[4] We do verily believe that our critics have some knowledge of these facts. As before shown, Reuss in one place recognizes the fact that the Midianites were accounted as Ishmaelites, though he seems in a short time to have forgotten it. But it may be said, even granting that the father-in-law of Moses had two names,—Reuel and Jethro,—how can we acquit the Pentateuchal record of self-contradiction in calling him, expressly or impliedly, in one place an Ishmaelite, in another a Midianite, in another a Kenite, and in another a Cushite? This can be done very easily by accepting every one of these statements as true, and by believing that Jethro was all these combined in one—an Ishmaelite by descent, a Midianite by nation, a Kenite by tribe, and a Cushite by residence, precisely as Moses was a Shemite by descent, a Hebrew by nation, a Levite by tribe, and an Egyptian by residence.

8. It is claimed that there is a contradiction in the statements made concerning the birth of Benjamin, Jacob's youngest son. One statement is, that he was born when there was "a little way to come to Ephrath," and that Ephrath is Bethlehem, in the land of Canaan.[5] But a little further on in the same chapter

---

[1] Ex. 2: 16-21; 3: 1; 18: 1. [2] Judg. 1: 16; 4: 11. [3] Num. 12: 1.
[4] Gen. 11: 29. [5] Gen. 35: 16-19.

the names of Jacob's twelve sons, including Benjamin, are given, and then this statement is made: "These are the sons of Jacob, which were born to him in Padan-aram."[1] The claimed discrepancy is stated by Reuss as follows: "Au même chapitre, 35: 16, il est dit que Rachel accoucha de son fils Benjamin près de Bét-léhem. Et quelques lignes plus loin, v. 26, il est dit que tous les douze fils de Jacob, énumérés nominativement, Benjamin y compris, étaient nés en Mesopotamie, avant le retour du patriarche en Canaan."[2] ("In the same chapter, 35: 16, it is said that Rachel was delivered of her son Benjamin near to Bethlehem. And some lines further on, verse 26, it is said that all the twelve sons of Jacob, mentioned by name, Benjamin included among them, were born in Mesopotamia, before the return of the patriarch to Canaan.")

By way of reply, we remark:

(1) The statement of Reuss is not accurate. The sacred record does not say that "*all the twelve* sons were born in Mesopotamia." The words "all" and "twelve" are thrust in by the critic as a make-weight in the argument.

(2) The birth of Benjamin took place before the arrival at Hebron, on the journey from Padan-aram.

(3) If the record read in this way: "These are the sons of Jacob, who were all born in Mesopotamia, except Benjamin, who was born on the way to Hebron," the most captious critic could have found no fault. But this exceptional statement is a part of the record. It had been stated just a few lines before that Benjamin was born on the home journey a short distance from Bethlehem, and it was no more necessary to repeat this statement than to state a second time that Jacob's other sons were born in Padan-aram.

9. It is claimed that there are two discordant accounts of the settlement of Esau in Seir. Both Reuss[3] and Kuenen[4] maintain that according to one passage Esau was established in Seir *before*[5] Jacob's return from Mesopotamia, and according to another not till *after*[6] his return. In this latter passage it is indeed stated that the permanent settlement of Esau in Seir was effected after Jacob's return to Canaan; but in the other passages it is not stated that this settlement was effected before. They say nothing about Esau's permanent settlement, or his settlement at

---

[1] Gen. 35: 21-26. [2] *L'Histoire Sainte*, Int., p. 43. [3] *L'Histoire Sainte*, Int., p. 42.
[4] *Hexateuch*, p. 39. [5] Gen. 32: 3; Gen. 33: 16. [6] Gen. 36: 6-8.

all, in Seir. What they state is as follows: (1) Jacob sent messengers to Esau in the land of Seir or Edom;[1] (2) the messengers returned with the information that Esau was approaching with four hundred men;[2] (3) after the interview between the brothers, Esau returned to Seir.[3] These are the facts, and all the facts, stated. They do not prove that Esau had as yet settled at Seir. He may have been there temporarily. The fact that he had under his command four hundred men favors the supposition that he was at this time engaged in a military expedition; but at all events his settlement in Seir is not mentioned, and is a mere inference of our critics, employed to support a theory.

10. There are other passages which the analytic critics claim to be contradictory. These in general are those that are cited by the skeptics in their efforts to disprove the divine inspiration and authority of the Scriptures. Nothing, or at least very little, that is new has been of late presented on this subject. We have considered what we believe to be the most plausible arguments employed by the critics, who have endeavored to fasten the charge of inconsistency and contradiction on the Pentateuch.

[1] Gen. 32: 3.   [2] Gen. 32: 6.   [3] Gen. 33: 16.

CHAPTER VI

CLAIMED DIFFICULTIES

THE analysts often employ against the Mosaic authorship of the Pentateuch argumentation of this sort: That it contains statements that are improbable, or that can scarcely be true, or that are difficult to believe; and that therefore Moses is not their author. Generally, when one of these gentlemen says that some things contained in the Pentateuch can scarcely be true, he has already peremptorily decided in his own mind that they are untrue; and when he says that some things contained in the Pentateuch are difficult to believe, he means that such things are incredible by scholarly and candid minds. Expressions of peremptory disbelief and rejection are withheld for the present as inexpedient, while the effort is being made to infuse doubts or suspicions into the minds of readers.

The claimed improbabilities, incredibilities, and impossibilities which are made the basis of objections to the traditional belief we class together as difficulties, and proceed to consider them.

I. Hebrew Genealogy.

One of the difficulties is in connection with Genesis 46: 12, where Hezron and Hamul are mentioned among the children of Israel that came into Egypt.[1] They are included among the sixty-six souls that came with Jacob into Egypt.[2] Now Hezron and Hamul were the sons of Pharez, the son of Judah, and, as the critics say, it is difficult to believe that Judah could have had two grandsons, sons of Pharez, born before the migration to Egypt. Reuss states the difficulty as follows: "Juda, dont les deux derniere fils pourvaient à peine être nés, a déjà deux petit-fils, issus de l'un d'eux"[3] ("Judah, whose two last sons could hardly have been born, already has two grandsons, from one of them").

The improbability that Judah had two grandsons at the time

[1] Gen. 46: 8-27.   [2] Gen. 46: 26.   [3] *L'Histoire Sainte*, Vol. I., p. 434.

of the migration to Egypt is argued as follows: He was only forty-two years old. For Joseph was thirty years of age when he stood before Pharaoh, and since that time nine years had elapsed, seven of plenty and two of famine; Joseph, then, was thirty-nine years old at the time of the migration. Judah was only about three years older, for he was Leah's fourth son, and born, it is inferred, in the fourth year after Jacob's double marriage.¹ Joseph's birth is recorded next after that of Dinah, who was Leah's seventh child, and born presumably in the seventh year after Jacob's and Leah's marriage.² It is then inferred that Judah, having been born in the fourth year after Jacob's and Leah's marriage, was three years older than Joseph and was forty-two years of age at the time of the migration. And that Hezron and Hamul were not born before that time seems to be proved by the events that occurred in Judah's family. (1) Judah married and had three sons, Er, Onan, and Shelah. (2) Er grows up, marries Tamar, and dies without children. (3) Onan marries Er's widow, Tamar, and dies without children. (4) Shelah was not yet grown, and Tamar waits, expecting to marry him. (5) Tamar, having waited in vain for Shelah to marry her, deceives Judah and has by him two sons, Pharez and Zarah. (6) One of these twin sons grows up, marries, and has two sons, Hezron and Hamul.

All these events are mentioned after the account of the selling of Joseph. Events are not always mentioned, in the Pentateuch and elsewhere in the Bible, in the order of their occurrence. But we concede, notwithstanding, that it is difficult to believe that Hezron and Hamul were born before the migration—so difficult, indeed, that we do not ourselves believe it. Yet the names of these two persons are set down in the genealogical register among those that were born in Canaan and went down to Egypt with Jacob.³ This is one of the difficulties which our critics employ in the effort to show, in the words of Colenso, that "the books of the Pentateuch contain, in their account of the story which they profess to relate, such remarkable contradictions and involve such plain impossibilities that they cannot be regarded as true narratives of actual, historical matters of fact." [4]

Our reply is as follows: In the genealogical registers of the Israelites there are various omissions, exceptions, substitu-

---

[1] Gen. 29: 31-35. [2] Gen. 30: 21-24. [3] Gen. 38: 1-30.
[4] Colenso, *The Pentateuch*, p. 60.

tions, and imputative reckonings which may seem strange to us with our Occidental ideas, but which were in accord with Hebrew ideas and with Hebrew modes of speech, and which, when rightly construed, are accurate and truthful. The counting of Hezron and Hamul, though born afterward in Egypt, among those who migrated with Jacob, is only one of many examples of this sort. The Hebrew genealogical registers abound with them. Our critics seem to need information on this subject, and to be made to know the facts.

1. The genealogical table in question begins as follows: "And these are the names of the children of Israel which came into Egypt, Jacob and his sons: Reuben, Jacob's first-born."[1] Here Jacob is placed among the children of Israel—counted as one of his own sons. He is again counted among the sons of Leah. "These be the sons of Leah, which she bare unto Jacob in Padan-aram, with his daughter Dinah: all the souls of his sons and his daughters were thirty and three."[2] Here Jacob is placed among his sons and daughters—counted as one of his own children. His name, which stands at the head of the list,[1] must be counted in order to make the thirty-three sons and daughters of Leah.

Also, in this register, Serah, the daughter of Asher, is counted among his sons: "And the sons of Asher; Jimnah, and Ishuah, and Isui, and Beriah, and Serah their sister."[3] Serah is here placed among the sons of Asher. She is again placed among the sons of Zilpah: "These are the sons of Zilpah, whom Laban gave to Leah his daughter; and these she bare unto Jacob, even sixteen souls."[4] Here Serah, the granddaughter of Zilpah, is counted among Zilpah's sons, and must be so counted in order to make the number sixteen.

2. In this register many who were actually born in Canaan are counted among those born in Padan-aram. "These be the sons of Leah, which she bare unto Jacob in Padan-aram, with his daughter Dinah; all the souls . . . were thirty and three."[2] Of all these only seven were born in Padan-aram. For Jacob remained there only twenty years and was married at the end of the seventh year. His first-born, Reuben, could then have been only about thirteen years old at the time of the return to Canaan. Hence none of Leah's grandchildren were born in Padan-aram. Yet in the family register they are all, twenty-five in number, set

---

[1] Gen. 46:8.   [2] Gen. 46:15.   [3] Gen. 46:17.   [4] Gen. 46:18.

down as born in that country. Even the two sons of Joseph, who are expressly mentioned as having been born in Egypt, are counted among those that came from Canaan. "All the souls of the house of Jacob, which came into Egypt, were threescore and ten." [1] The sons of Joseph are included among the threescore and ten that came from Palestine into Egypt; for they must be counted to make up that number.

3. Also, some of the sons of Benjamin, born in Egypt, are counted among those that migrated with Jacob. "And the sons of Benjamin were Belah, and Becher, and Ashbel, Gera, and Naaman, Ehi, and Rosh, Muppim, and Huppim, and Ard."[2] Thus Benjamin is represented as having ten sons. Reuss writes, sneeringly, as follows: "All those who have read the history of Joseph in Egypt imagine Benjamin, the cadet of the family, to be a young boy. His name became proverbial for this reason. Ah! well, from chapter 46: 21 we learn that when Jacob went to settle in Egypt, in the second year of the famine, this little Benjamin was the father of ten sons, a number which none of his elder brothers came near attaining."[3] In the light of certain well-known facts the above-quoted piece of criticism is seen to be well nigh ridiculous.

(1) "This little Benjamin," "this young boy," was now about thirty-seven years old.

(2) In this register, and elsewhere in the Bible, grandsons are included among the sons.

(3) As a matter of fact, Gera, Naaman, Muppim, Huppim, and Ard are shown to be grandsons or great-grandsons of Benjamin.[4] Thus the number of his sons is reduced at least to five. It is not difficult to believe that a man thirty-seven years old might have five sons, especially if he lived in a time and place in which a man might have two or more wives. The difficulty, then, does not consist in Benjamin's having an incredible number of children at the time of the migration, but in the fact that his grandsons, although not yet born, are represented, like Judah's, as going with Jacob to Egypt.

(4) These peculiarities of Hebrew genealogy are not confined to the Book of Genesis, but are found in other parts of the Pentateuch. Exodus 1: 5: "And all the souls that came out of the loins of Jacob were seventy souls: for Joseph was in Egypt

---

[1] Gen. 46: 27.   [2] Gen. 46: 21.   [3] *L'Histoire Sainte*, Int., p. 97.
[4] Num. 26: 38-40; I. Chr. 7: 6-12; 8: 1-7.

already." Jacob himself was one of the seventy. He is expressly included in that number.[1] Thus Jacob is represented as among those who "came out of the loins of Jacob." We found him before counted as one of his own children.[2]

4. From this family register of Jacob the names of women are undoubtedly omitted. It contains only two female names—Dinah, who is counted as one of the thirty-three sons of Leah, and Serah, the daughter of Asher, counted as one of the sixteen sons of Zilpah. But were there only two women—one daughter and one granddaughter—among all Jacob's descendants at this time? In the twelve families immediately descended from Jacob, embracing sixty-nine persons, only one girl born? This is one of the things that, some critics would say, are hard to believe. For us, at least, it is easier to believe that in Jacob's company the men and women were about equal in number, and that his daughters and granddaughters, like Jacob's sons' wives, have been omitted from the family register, except Dinah and Serah, who for some special reason (possibly because they became founders of families) were admitted to the rank and rights of sons. In one place Jacob's daughters are referred to in the plural number.[3] That names which we antecedently would expect to find in the Hebrew genealogies are omitted from them, is an undeniable fact. According to the genealogy in Exodus 6: 16-18 we have but four names,—Levi, Kohath, Amram, and Moses,—apparently representing four generations; but in I. Chronicles 7: 23-27 we have, covering the same space of time, the following names: Ephraim, Beriah, Rephah, Telah, Tahan, Laadan, Ammihud, Elishama, Non, and Jehoshua—ten in all, representing ten generations. Here we have positive evidence that in the genealogy of Moses five names and generations are omitted. Besides, as we proceed to show, there are other cases of omissions from genealogical registers.

Ezra, in giving his own descent, omits six names between Azariah and Meraioth.[4] These six omitted names represent six generations.

In the genealogy of Christ many names are omitted. At first Christ is declared to be the son of David, and David the son of Abraham.[5] In this declaration all the names and generations between David and Christ, and also between David and Abraham,

---

[1] Gen. 46: 27. [2] Gen. 46: 8, 15. [3] Gen. 37: 35.
[4] Ezra 7: 3; I. Chr. 6: 7-14. [5] Matt. 1: 1.

are omitted. The gaps, however, are filled up afterward, but not fully. There are three names omitted between Joram and Ozias. "Joram begat Ozias," says the register in Matthew.[1] But this is true only constructively, for, according to the history, Joram (Jehoram) begat Ahaziah, and Ahaziah begat Joash, and Joash begat Amaziah, and Amaziah begat Azariah, called also Uzziah (Ozias).[2] But all this is omitted in the genealogy given in Matthew, and Joram is there said to have begotten Ozias (Azariah), his great-great-grandson. Matthew also omits the name of Jehoiakim from the record. He says, "Josias begat Jechonias and his brethren."[3] But these were Josiah's grandsons. Jehoiakim, their father, was Josiah's son. But Jehoiachin (Jechonias) is substituted for Jehoiakim, just as, above shown, Uzziah (Ozias) is substituted for Ahaziah.

In I. Chronicles 24: 4 twenty-four men living in King David's time are declared constructively to be the grandsons of Aaron, and in I. Chronicles 26: 24 one of the officers of David is declared to be the son of Gershom, the son of Moses, constructively the grandson of Moses.

Such are the facts we have to deal with in these old Hebrew genealogies—omissions, exceptions, substitutions, and imputative reckonings. There is neither sense nor candor in taking one or two of these facts and considering them apart from the class to which they belong and from Hebrew ideas and usages, and founding upon them the charge of impossibility and error.

It is perhaps not possible to explain all the peculiarities and difficulties connected with the Hebrew genealogies, but there is one principle running through the Pentateuch and the Bible which explains many of them, and that is the principle of substitution, representation, vicarious agency. Moses is declared to have spoken to all the congregation of Israel, when he had addressed only their representatives, the elders.[4] David is declared to have killed Uriah with the sword of the children of Ammon.[5] Nebuchadnezzar is declared to have slain the young men of Jerusalem with the sword and to have carried away the vessels and treasures of the temple to Babylon.[6] Levi paid tithes in Abraham to Melchisedec.[7] The legal principle that what a man does through his agent he himself does was fully recognized by the ancient Hebrews. They carried into their

[1] Matt. 1: 8. [2] II. Kings 8: 24; 11: 2; 12: 21; 15: 1. [3] Matt. 1: 11.
[4] Ex. 19: 7-14, 25. [5] II. Sam. 12: 9. [6] II. Chr. 36: 17, 18. [7] Heb. 7: 9, 10.

every-day life the ideas of the responsibilities and liabilities of substitutes, representatives, and agents that are recognized in our civil courts. This fact explains several peculiarities in the Hebrew genealogies. Hezron and Hamul, grandsons of Judah, appear to have been substituted for his sons Er and Onan, who died in Canaan. The two former are therefore placed in the family register among those who went down into Egypt. Hence, too, the grandchildren of Leah are represented as born in Padan-aram. If Jacob ever had a legal residence in Canaan, he lost it by an absence of twenty years and by his living in Padan-aram during that time. But we understand that he never had a legal home and residence in Canaan. Abraham, after a stay of about forty years in that country, declared himself a stranger and sojourner.[1] After a further stay of some years in Canaan he did not still regard it as his home; for in directing Eliezer to go to Padan-aram to procure a wife for Isaac he said, "Thou shalt go unto my country."[2] The only possession he had in Canaan was a burying-place.[3] Neither to him nor to any of the patriarchs did the Lord give in Canaan, aside from Machpelah, as much as a footbreadth of the soil. The grant of Canaan to the Hebrews was all prospective. In the patriarchal age it was theirs indeed, but only in the sense that they sojourned in it.

There were special reasons for regarding Jacob as belonging to Padan-aram. He lived in that country twenty years. He was connected with one of the families of that country, both as an employee and by a double marriage. All his children but one were born there. Padan-aram was then Jacob's home and country. In Canaan he was, like his fathers, a stranger and sojourner; hence Benjamin, though actually born in Canaan, and also his grandchildren born in Canaan, are put down in the family register as born in Padan-aram. This very same thing is done in our times and country. The children born of American parents in foreign lands are counted as born in our own country. All such persons are enrolled as home-born citizens — *registered as born at home*.

Dinah and Serah are placed among the sons and grandsons doubtless because they were accorded the rights of sons. There was no place in the family register for women, and hence, if recognized at all, their names must be placed among those of the men. To be sure, the names Leah, Rachel, Zilpah, and Bilhah

---

[1] Gen. 23: 4.   [2] Gen. 24: 4.   [3] Gen. 23: 4.

are mentioned, but only incidentally, to designate their sons. They are not *counted*.

Finally, though perhaps not all difficulties can be removed, we know enough to repel the charge of contradiction and falsehood.

II. *The Increase of the Israelites in Egypt.*

A second difficulty is found by the skeptical critics in the account of the increase of the Israelites in Egypt. The number of Jacob's company at the time of the migration is said to have been seventy. At the time of the exodus the number of the Israelites is given as about six hundred thousand men, besides a mixed multitude that went up with them.[1] Counting the whole population as about four times more numerous than the able-bodied men, we have two millions as the number of the Israelites at the time of the exodus. It is maintained by the analytic critics that this presupposes an impossible rapidity of increase during the sojourn in Egypt. Voltaire declared it to be an unreasonable supposition that a nation should increase from seventy persons to two millions in two hundred and fifteen years.[2] Colenso, the arithmetical critic, Reuss, and others have urged the same objection.

This objection is based on the hypothesis that the sojourn in Egypt continued only two hundred and fifteen years. If it continued four hundred and thirty years, the objection is without force. The considerations which favor the longer period are as follows:

1. The divine declaration to Abraham, "Know of a surety that thy seed shall be a stranger in a land that is not theirs, and shall serve them; and they shall afflict them four hundred years."[3] These words do not fix the precise duration of the sojourn, but of the oppression. The descendants of Abraham were to be afflicted during a period designated by the round number of four hundred years. This is irreconcilable with the hypothesis that the entire residence in Egypt lasted only two hundred and fifteen years. The Israelites were not oppressed during the first years of their stay in Egypt.

2. The longer period is favored by a further declaration made to Abraham: "But in the fourth generation they shall come hither again."[4] The sojourn in Egypt was to continue during

---

[1] Ex. 12 : 37, 38. [2] *Dictionnaire Philosophique*, Moïse, Sec. iii. [3] Gen. 15 : 13. [4] Gen. 15 : 16.

four generations. But what is the duration of one generation? We are not to judge of the length of time thus designated by the duration of the generation in our times, nor even in the time of Moses. Since this language was addressed to Abraham, its meaning to him is its meaning now. Terah, Abraham's father, lived two hundred and five years, and Abraham himself one hundred and seventy-five years. Isaac was born when Abraham was one hundred years old, and died at the age of one hundred and eighty. Abraham's own generation, counted from his birth to the birth of his son, was a century in duration. Four generations are equivalent, therefore, to four hundred years.

3. Clearly, Stephen understood these predictions as indicating that the Israelites, the posterity of Abraham, should endure oppression in a foreign land four hundred years. "And God spake on this wise, That his seed should sojourn in a strange land; and that they should bring them into bondage, and entreat them evil four hundred years."[1] Here, and in Genesis, the sojourn is spoken of as to be, not in Canaan, but in a foreign land; and it is not Abraham, nor Isaac, nor Jacob, but Abraham's posterity that is to be enslaved and afflicted during four generations and four hundred years, and in a foreign land.

The skeptical critics, of course, contemn all predictive utterances as unreal and fictitious. But aside from their prophetic character, such utterances are valuable as testimonies of Jewish authors and people to the duration of the sojourn and oppression in Egypt.

4. "Now the sojourning of the children of Israel, who dwelt in Egypt, was four hundred and thirty years."[2] The Revised Version reads "which they sojourned in Egypt," instead of "who dwelt in Egypt." Colenso objects to the new rendering, because it clearly makes *all* the sojourning spoken of take place in Egypt, while he thinks that, according to the old rendering, the sojourning may have been partly in Canaan. Colenso, however, admits that the rendering "who dwelt in Egypt" is awkward, and that the original words may be more naturally translated "which they sojourned in Egypt," as in the Revised Version. He admits, too, that this is the rendering of the Vulgate, Chaldaic, Syriac, and Arabic versions. (He might have added the Septuagint,[3] German, Spanish, and French versions.)

[1] Acts 7 : 6.   [2] Ex. 12 : 40.
[3] So far as the phrase under consideration is concerned.

The reason that Colenso assigns for adhering to the confessedly awkward and less natural rendering is that otherwise he must find the Apostle Paul in error, and must also find some mistakes in the genealogy of Moses.[1] Here is an admirable spectacle, indeed. A man who denies plenary inspiration and maintains that the Bible abounds in errors, a man who is engaged in an effort to show that the Pentateuch and the Book of Joshua are historically untrustworthy,—such a one adhering to an awkward translation and rejecting a more natural one, in order that he may not charge mistakes on Paul and the Pentateuch! It is evident, however, that Colenso was unwilling to give up "the awkward" rendering, because, in that case, he would be compelled to admit that the whole sojourn of four hundred and thirty years took place in Egypt, and to give up the argument drawn from the increase of the Israelites against the historical integrity of the Pentateuch.

Reuss, however, who was much superior to Colenso in scholarship, and even perhaps more skeptical, makes no attempt to bend this passage to suit his own views, but translates as follows: "Or, les Israélites avaient séjourné en Égypte pendant quarte cent trente ans, et ce fut au bout de quartre cent trente ans, ce jour-là même, que le peuple de Dieu sortit en corps du pays d'Égypte"[2] ("Now, the Israelites had sojourned in Egypt during four hundred and thirty years, and it was at the end of four hundred and thirty years, on the very day, that the people of God went out as a body from the land of Egypt"). Reuss admits that we have here an express and clear declaration that the Israelites sojourned in Egypt four hundred and thirty years, and his way of setting aside this testimony is by asserting that there was a divergent tradition. Kuenen also admits the representation here to be that the sojourn in Egypt lasted four hundred and thirty years, but claims this to be inconsistent with the exodus in the fourth generation, and talks about the passage as being the work of a redactor.[3] But other analytic critics, as Kautzsch and his colleagues, admit the reading, attributing it to P, without saying anything about a redactor.[4] That we have an express declaration in Exodus 12:40 making the duration of the sojourn four hundred and thirty years, is too plain to be denied by most of the critics.

[1] *Pentateuch and Book of Joshua*, pp. 149, 150.
[2] *L'Histoire Sainte*, Vol. II., pp. 35, 36.   [3] *Hexateuch*, p. 331.
[4] *Heilige Schrift des Alten Testaments*, p. 68.

It is true, indeed, that in the Septuagint Version there is a various reading of the passage, as follows: "Now the sojourning of the children of Israel, which they sojourned in Egypt *and in Canaan*, was four hundred years." The words "*and in Canaan*" are without support, and are not insisted on by any of the critics.

5. The *genealogies* favor the longer period.

We have already adverted to the prophetic declaration that the Israelites should return to Canaan in the fourth generation.[1] We have already shown that, owing to the length of human life in Abraham's time, a generation must have meant to him a period of one hundred years or more. Besides, in immediate connection with the declaration above referred to, it was expressly said that the descendants of Abraham should be afflicted in a foreign land four hundred years. The four generations, then, must cover four centuries.

We are reminded, however, that there are in the genealogy of Moses but three names (Amram, Kohath, and Levi) between him and Jacob, and that therefore Moses and the exodus must have been much less than four hundred and thirty years after the migration to Egypt.[2] But, as we have already pointed out, in the Hebrew genealogies names are frequently omitted, the name of a grandson or of a more distant descendant being substituted for that of the son; and it can be shown beyond a reasonable doubt that names are omitted in the genealogy of Moses.

We have already called attention to the fact that in Chronicles there are ten names given between Jacob and Joshua.[3] As Joshua was by one generation later than Moses, the latter must have been nine generations later than Jacob. It is in vain that the skeptical critics cry out against the trustworthiness of the chronicler in this matter, for similar testimony is given elsewhere. In the Book of Joshua[4] five names are given between Jacob and Zelophehad, the latter of whom died before Moses.[5] This places Zelophehad at six generations after Jacob. Precisely the same names are twice given in the accounts of the descent of Zelophehad contained in the Book of Numbers. Thus we have four witnesses to the fact that there were more than four generations between the migration to Egypt and the exodus. One witness does, indeed, give four genealogical names as inter-

[1] Gen. 15: 16. [2] Ex. 6: 16-20. [3] I. Chr. 7: 22-27. [4] Josh. 17: 3. [5] Num. 27: 3.

vening between these two events,[1] three witnesses give each six such names,[2] and one gives ten.[3] In view of the fact that in the Hebrew genealogical registers names were frequently omitted, the name of grandson, great-grandson, or of a still remoter descendant being substituted for that of the son, it is seen that there is no contradiction between these witnesses, and that the testimony of the one who gives the largest number of intervening names may be accepted without impeaching the veracity or the accuracy of the others. This view is confirmed by the testimony of Genesis, which states that the Israelites were to be oppressed in a foreign land four hundred years,[4] and were to be absent from Canaan during four generations, each of them being of the length of a generation in the time of Abraham.

6. Another consideration in favor of the longer period is the statement of the Apostle Paul, "And this I say, that the covenant, that was confirmed before of God in Christ, the law, which was four hundred and thirty years after, cannot disannul."[5] It is maintained by Colenso that the four hundred and thirty years spoken of by the apostle includes the residence of the patriarchs in Canaan, as well as that of their descendants in Egypt. But the apostle does not allude to the law as given four hundred and thirty years after the covenant was *made* with Abraham. He does not mention the *making* of the covenant at all, but the *confirmation* of it. "The law, which was four hundred and thirty years after." After what? Not after the *making* of the covenant, but after it was *confirmed*.[5] Now the covenant was confirmed several times. The last confirmation before the giving of the law took place just before the descent into Egypt.[6] The four hundred and thirty years mentioned by the apostle, therefore, date from the migration, and designate the duration of the sojourn in Egypt.

7. Josephus in one place[7] (unless we have a false reading) follows the reading or gloss of the Septuagint in Exodus 12 : 40, but in two other places he expressly declares that the Israelites suffered oppression in Egypt four hundred years.[8] In one of these he records this declaration as having been previously made by himself in an oral address, thus virtually reaffirming it. Though, then, our Jewish author does indeed quote the declara-

---

[1] Ex. 6 : 16-20.   [2] Num. 26 : 28-33 ; 27 : 1; Josh. 17 : 3.   [3] I. Chr. 7 : 22-27.
[4] Gen. 15 : 13.   [5] Gal. 3 : 17.   [6] Gen. 46 : 1-3.   [7] *Antiquities*, 2 : 15 : 2.
[8] *Antiquities*, 2 : 9 : 1; *Wars*, 5 : 9 : 4.

tion of the Septuagint in favor of the shorter period, he yet three times contradicts it by affirming that the oppression in Egypt lasted four hundred years. Thus his testimony is decidedly in favor of the longer period of four hundred and thirty years.

We conclude, then, that this was the duration of the sojourn in Egypt.

And this is a complete answer to the objection which the analytic critics draw from the large increase of the Israelites in Egypt. Though numbering at first only seventy persons, they might readily grow into a nation of two millions in four hundred and thirty years. The ratio of increase in that case would not be so great as that of the population of the United States during the last century.

But even on the hypothesis of the shorter period, the increase of the Israelites in Egypt is not by any means incredible. In two hundred and fifteen years there might be six generations, each of the duration of thirty-six years, very nearly. Jacob had twelve sons. These had all together fifty-three sons, or, on the average, four and a half apiece. It is not necessary to assume the ratio of increase in Jacob's immediate family (twelve to one), nor even the half of it, as the standard of increase in succeeding generations. If we assume the average increase to be five to one, which is a fraction above the increase among Jacob's grandsons, provided all the names are given in the family register (which is by no means certain), then in the two hundred and sixteenth year, and in the sixth generation, these fifty-three grandsons would have had a posterity numbering 828,125 males. This number, together with the survivors of the preceding generations, might certainly have furnished six hundred thousand able-bodied men. If the rate of increase in Jacob's immediate family is taken as the standard, then his fifty-three grandsons would have had 1,099,008 male descendants even in the fourth generation. Again, Jacob and his four wives increased from five to seventy persons, male and female, in about fifty years, even on the supposition that he had but one daughter and one granddaughter (which is not probable). The ratio of increase in this case is seventy to five, or fourteen to one, every fifty years. On this basis of calculation, Jacob's company of seventy persons would have increased to 2,689,120 in two hundred years. Thus, even on the hypothesis that the sojourn in Egypt continued only two hundred and fifteen years, the increase of the Israelites to two millions of people was not impossible, and hence is not incredible.

Some of the skeptics confound the improbable with the impossible and the incredible. The impossible is what *cannot* come to pass; the incredible is what *cannot* be believed. Many improbable things not only are possible, but do actually come to pass. Indeed, improbable things are occurring almost continually. It was possible, though antecedently improbable, that the Israelites in Egypt should increase from seventy persons to two millions—from sixty-eight males to six hundred thousand able-bodied men. It is so represented in the sacred record, which declares that God caused the very efforts of the Egyptians to restrict the growth of the Hebrew nation to result in their multiplication.[1] The skeptical critic may, if he chooses, deny the superintending providence of God, but he does so in opposition not only to the consensus of Christian people, but also to the common judgment of mankind.

Besides, the sacred record declares, as the ablest of the analytic critics admit, that the Israelites sojourned four hundred and thirty years in Egypt, and that six or even ten generations intervened between the migration and the exodus. Colenso supposes that the ratio of increase of the males was three to one, and, counting the grandsons of Jacob as fifty-one in number, he finds the males in the fourth generation to number only one thousand three hundred and seventy-seven, instead of six hundred thousand.[2] But if he had based his calculation on the hypothesis of the longer period for the sojourn (four hundred and thirty years) and ten generations of forty-three years' duration each, he would have found the tenth generation to number in males 1,003,833, and, of course, the whole population to be double that number, or about two millions.

The difficulty we are dealing with exists only in the minds of skeptics and analytics.

III. *Number of the First-born.*

The critics found one of their objections to the trustworthiness of the Pentateuch and its Mosaic authorship on the number of the first-born among the Israelites, as compared with the whole population. The number of the first-born males a month old and upward is given as 22,273;[3] the number of able-bodied men

---

[1] Ex. 1 : 12, 20.   [2] *Pentateuch and Book of Joshua*, p. 166.   [3] Num. 3 : 43.

was 603,550;[1] the whole population was more than two millions, and the number of males presumably over one million. There was, then, only one first-born to eighty-eight of the entire population. As the number of the first-born could not be less than the number of families, and also the number of mothers, there must have been eighty-eight persons in every family, on the average, and each mother must have had, on the average, eighty-eight children. This is a statement of the difficulty in the strongest terms. Reuss makes the average family consist of one hundred persons, but brings the number down to fifty-five, and again to twenty-seven.[2] Wellhausen fixes the number at forty.[3] Colenso varies between the numbers forty-two and thirty for each family.

There are several considerations which help to remove the difficulty.

1. One of these is that, in the generation that immediately preceded the numbering, the male children, including the first-born, had been destroyed according to the decree of the Egyptian king. Doubtless in this way marriage and increase, for some time before the exodus, had been checked, if not prevented. Reuss, on account of "the generation which could not contribute to the increase of births," reduces the proportion of the population to the first-born from one hundred and eleven to one, down to fifty-five to one.[4]

2. In many families, perhaps in one-half, the first-born was a girl. It would seem that the oldest son in such cases was not counted as the first-born, for the reason that he did not "open the matrix."[5] Reuss admits the force of this consideration, and on account of it reduces the proportion from fifty-five to twenty-seven.

3. There were some families in which the children were all daughters. In such cases surely no first-born was counted, at least if the father was not a first-born.

4. In some families the first-born had been removed by death before the census was taken. Even Colenso admits the force of this consideration. He supposes that one out of every four among the first-born had died before the numbering, and he reduces in this way the supposed average number in a family to thirty persons.[6]

[1] Num. 1: 46. [2] Note on Num. 3: 43, and Int., p. 87. [3] *Prolegomena*, p. 304.
[4] *L'Histoire Sainte*, Int., p. 87. [5] Num. 3: 12.
[6] *Pentateuch and Book of Joshua*, pp. 144, 145.

5. It is a question whether the first-born of the wife, or only the first-born of the husband, was counted. Polygamy prevailed to some extent among the ancient Hebrews. If a man had several wives, the first child of his first wife, at least if a male, was counted as his first-born. But was the first child of each of his other wives counted as a first-born? If a man had a dozen wives, who all had children, did he have a dozen first-borns? Again, suppose that a man had two wives in succession, marrying the second after the death of the first, and that both had children; had this man, according to law, two first-borns in his family, both of whom he must redeem by the payment of the prescribed sum?

Certainly the law in some places does seem to require the enumeration and redemption of the first-born not of the husband only, but also of each and all of his wives. "Sanctify unto me all the first-born, whatsoever openeth the womb."[1] This, at first view, seems to include all the first-born, male and female, both of the husband and of the wife and of all the wives. Yet it is clear that this law is to be understood with limitations. First-born females were not included. "Number all the first-born of the males."[2] And a few verses farther on, the enumeration is again restricted to the males among the first-born.[3] We understand, too, that the enumeration was again limited to one first-born in a man's family, and was not extended to the children of all the wives. Abraham had three wives and issue by them all, yet he had but one first-born. Jacob had but one first-born among his four sets of children by his four wives. The Hebrew law forbade a man to make the son of a favorite wife his first-born, instead of the real first-born.[4]

We think the evidence preponderates in favor of the view that only one first-born was counted in a man's family, and that the disproportion between the number of the first-born and the whole population is to be correspondingly discounted.

6. In many cases the first-born in his father's family was married and had a first-born son of his own. His father might not have been a first-born or might be dead. His mother, brothers, and sisters might still be living. Was this man counted in the enumeration of the first-born along with his own first-born? Were there two first-borns counted in this man's family? In such cases in Egypt, on the evening of the

[1] Ex. 13:2.   [2] Num. 3:40.   [3] Num. 3:43.   [4] Deut. 21:16.

Passover, did God slay two first-borns in one family, father and son? It seems reasonable to suppose that the first-born, who was himself the head of a family and had a first-born to be counted and redeemed, would be exempt from the enumeration. In that case, then, only unmarried first-borns would be counted, and the enumeration would be limited mainly to the first-borns under twenty or twenty-one years of age.

7. There is reason, we think, to believe that the law in regard to the first-born *was not applied to those who were born before its enactment.*

It was enacted just before the exodus, at the time of the destruction of the first-born in Egypt. In consequence of this event the Lord claimed the first-born among the Israelites as belonging specially to himself.[1] The language of the statute seems to indicate that it was intended to apply only to the cases that should occur after its enactment: "whatsoever openeth the womb," "all that openeth the matrix, being males,"[2] — not those who had already opened the womb, that is, were born before the law was enacted. This law, then, was not *ex post facto* — it was not retroactive.

Now the time intervening between the exodus and the numbering of the first-born was not much more than thirteen months.[3] The number of the first-born (22,273) may seem too large to have been all born within that time.[4] It presupposes 44,546 marriages, one marriage to every forty-four of the population, since about one-half of the first-borns would be females; but the oppression in Egypt, and Pharaoh's decree that all new-born Hebrew male children should be drowned, would certainly very much decrease the marriages during the time more immediately preceding the exodus. The result of deliverance from bondage and from the king's cruel decree would naturally be a vast number of marriages immediately after the exodus. The people had not much to attend to besides courtship and marriage.

8. In the last place, according to the law, *the first-born males above five years of age were not included in the 22,273.* The proof of this proposition is as follows: The Levites were taken by the Lord instead of the first-born. But there were 22,273 first-borns and only 22,000 Levites. The two hundred and seventy-three overplus first-borns were redeemed at the rate of five shekels apiece. It was expressly enacted that the ransom price should

---

[1] Ex. 13: 1-16. [2] Ex. 13: 2, 12, 15. [3] Num. 1: 1. [4] Num. 3: 43.

be "five shekels apiece by the poll, after the shekel of the sanctuary."[1] It is also stated that the whole amount of the redemption money for the two hundred and seventy-three was one thousand three hundred and sixty-five shekels, which is five shekels per head. Now the law expressly declared that this should be the ransom price for a person from a month old to five years old.[2] Since the overplus first-borns were redeemed at the price of five shekels apiece, and since this was the ransom price of a male from one month to five years old, while that for a male from five to twenty was twenty shekels,[3] it follows that the two hundred and seventy-three and the entire twenty-two thousand were not more than five years old. This is corroborated by the view presented above in regard to the law not reaching back beyond the time of its enactment. But, really, no corroboration is needed. The redemption of these first-borns at the rate of five shekels apiece proves that they were not over five years old. If, then, there were more than twenty-two thousand first-borns five years old and under, the whole number of first-born of all ages must have been twelve or fifteen times as many, and the critics are relieved of all difficulty about the disproportion between the number of this class of persons and that of the whole population, and also about the size of the old Hebrew families. This whole difficulty, as presented by them, is founded solely on their own misapprehension.

IV. *Sustenance of the Cattle and Sheep in the Wilderness.*

According to the sacred history, the Israelites took sheep and cattle with them out of Egypt. They had "flocks and herds, even very much cattle."[4] At Rephidim, before they came to Sinai, "the people murmured against Moses, and said, Wherefore is this that thou hast brought us up out of Egypt, to kill us and our children and our cattle with thirst?"[5] The number of the sheep possessed by the Israelites at the exodus is suggested by the observance of the Passover. The number of lambs necessary for two millions of people, one lamb for every ten persons, would be two hundred thousand. The number of sheep would be three or four times greater—six or eight hundred thousand. The cattle were probably also numerous.

How did these flocks and herds subsist in the wilderness? How did the Israelites maintain them? Our critics hold that

---
[1] Num. 3: 46, 47.   [2] Lev. 27: 6.   [3] Lev. 27: 5.   [4] Ex. 12: 38.   [5] Ex. 17: 3.

they were not, and could not be, maintained; that the Israelites had no sheep and cattle at the exodus—at any rate not large numbers of them, or, if they had many sheep and cattle, these perished in the wilderness. They infer that in either case the historical accuracy of the Pentateuch is gone, and that therefore Moses is not the author of it.

In reply to the question how the flocks and herds were maintained in the wilderness, we answer, partly by *natural* and partly by *supernatural* means.

The Pentateuch represents the Sinaitic peninsula as furnishing sustenance for sheep and cattle, and not as being altogether covered with barren rocks and sand. It was a wilderness or desert, indeed; but a wilderness, in Bible phrase, is merely a country uninhabited, or with few inhabitants. It may be either fertile or barren. Anah fed the asses of Zibeon, his father, in the wilderness, but he could not have done so if there had been no grass nor fodder there.[1] Our Saviour fed the five thousand in "a desert place," yet there was "much grass" in it.[2] The first mention made of the wilderness of Sinai is to the effect that Moses used it as a pasture ground for the sheep of his father-in-law. It is stated that "he led the flock to the back side of the desert, and came to the mountain of God, even to Horeb."[3] Doubtless the Israelites, when they came to Sinai and Horeb, found pasturage where Moses had found it before. This is, indeed, implied in the fact that they were forbidden to let their flocks and herds feed before the mount.[4]

Travelers testify that there are vegetation and pasturage in this region. Lepsius speaks of ascending Mount Sinai,[5] and then says, "Here, to my astonishment, between the points into which the summit is divided, I found a small, level valley, plentifully supplied with shrubs and herbs." He describes the Wady Feiran, in the neighborhood of Sinai, as a fertile valley, abounding in trees, herbs, and flowers.[6] Ritter speaks of this valley in the same way, calling it a *garden, park,* and *paradise.* He also speaks of other portions of the peninsula as fertile and productive, though it is in general a barren waste.[7] Professor Palmer testifies that "most of the valleys contain some vegetation," and that "the barest and most stony hillside is seldom entirely destitute of vegetation."[8]

We do not care to push this point any further. We deem it sufficient to show that the representations of the Pentateuch in

---

[1] Gen. 36:24. [2] Matt. 14:15; John 6:10. [3] Ex. 3:1. [4] Ex. 34:3.
[5] Mount Serbal, however. [6] *Letters from Egypt,* etc., pp. 296, 305.
[7] *Geography,* Vol. I., pp. 301, 303. [8] *The Desert of the Exodus,* pp. 33, 34.

regard to vegetation and pasturage in the wilderness are fully sustained by modern travelers and investigators. We do not claim that the flocks and herds of the Israelites were sustained, or could have been sustained, wholly by natural means.

Colenso affirms that "there was no miraculous provision of food for the herds and flocks." He even asserts that "they were left to gather sustenance as they could, in that inhospitable wilderness."[1] Now what the author means is, that according to the representations of the Pentateuch there was no miraculous supply of food for the sheep and the cattle, and that they subsisted wholly by natural means. But does the Pentateuch really or virtually deny that there was any miraculous provision for these animals? Is silence in this case equivalent to a denial? We think that, on the contrary, this silence is to be interpreted, in view of the circumstances, the other way. The Hebrews at this point were under a miraculous dispensation. They were brought out of Egypt by a series of stupendous miracles. They crossed the Red Sea by miracle. The cloud which led them by day, and the fire by night, were miraculous. Their food and drink, the manna and the quails, and the water from the rock were supplied by miracle. Even their clothes and shoes were preserved by miracle and made to last for forty years. And yet are we to assume that every miracle that took place is mentioned, and that silence is virtual denial? It is not mentioned that the sheep and cattle had any miraculous supply of food; therefore, there was none, says the objector. By parity of reasoning he might conclude that the sheep and cattle did not go through the Red Sea as on dry land, but swam through, on the right and left flank of their masters. At Marah the people were about to perish with thirst, and were supplied by miracle, but not a word is said about the sheep and cattle. Did they live without water?[2] At Massah and Meribah the people did indeed complain that not only they and their children, but also their cattle, were perishing with thirst; and when Moses cried to the Lord, and the answer was, "Thou shalt smite the rock, and there shall come water out of it, that the people may drink,"[3] not a word was said about water for the sheep and cattle. These poor animals were compelled to live without water, were they? Is that the way in which we are to understand the record? Mention is indeed made of a miraculous supply of water for the sheep and cattle at

---

[1] *Pentateuch and Book of Joshua,* p. 118.   [2] Ex. 15 : 23-25.   [3] Ex. 17 : 1-6.

Kadesh. God said to Moses, "Thou shalt bring forth to them water out of the rock: so thou shalt give the congregation and their beasts drink."[1] But the objector, to be consistent, ought here to find additional reason for believing that the silence about the beasts in the other cases proves that they lived on without water or else died. Again, the objector ought to say that though there was a miraculous supply of water for the people, at Beer the beasts were suffered to die again.[2]

The truth is, that generally the occurrence of miracles is not affirmed, but suggested. It is not said that the sea was divided miraculously. The record is, that "Moses stretched out his hand over the sea; and the Lord caused the sea to go back by a strong east wind all that night, and made the sea dry land, and the waters were divided."[3] The facts are stated; the miracle is only inferred. Moses, at God's command, smote the rock at Horeb, and the water gushed out.[4] These are the facts; the miracle is suggested. Christ said to the man with the withered hand: "Stretch forth thine hand. And he stretched it forth; and it was restored whole, like as the other."[5] The facts only are stated. That the healing was miraculous is purely an inference. In general, miracles are recorded in this way. Indeed, we may say that in most cases they are not recorded at all, but the facts which suggest them.

Now we have the facts recorded which suggest the miraculous supply of food and water for the sheep and cattle in the desert. The Israelites took their flocks and herds with them. In the wilderness there was not a sufficient supply of food for the multitude of beasts. But they lived; they did not starve. They must, then, have had a supernatural supply of food. In what special way this supernatural supply of food was furnished, we are not informed. God may have caused grass to spring up in the desert. The Lord does sometimes turn a desert into a fruitful land, as well as a fruitful land into barrenness.[6] It seems to us that only those who disbelieve in miracles are likely to have any difficulty in regard to the sustenance of the sheep and cattle in the desert. Such is the real position of Reuss, Graf, Wellhausen, and Kuenen, the ablest and most distinguished champions of the analytic criticism. Why should such men talk or write about the question of food for the sheep and cattle, while they know well that their skepticism in regard to the supernatural and to miracles gives the lie to the whole Pentateuch and to nearly all other parts of the Bible?

[1] Num. 20:8. [2] Num. 21:16. [3] Ex. 14:21. [4] Ex. 17:6.
[5] Matt. 12:13. [6] Ps. 107:34-38.

CHAPTER VII

IMAGININGS

We assign to this class those objections which we regard as resting on purely fanciful grounds. Some of the objections urged against the Mosaic authorship of the Pentateuch involve no unreasonable interpretations, nor are based on palpably incorrect representations; but some of the objections and arguments employed on that side are founded on unmitigated misrepresentations, or fanciful views and interpretations. We therefore call them *imaginings*. Some of these we will notice.

1. Reuss claims that the account of the dismissal and departure of Hagar and Ishmael asserts a self-evident impossibility, and that it is therefore palpably absurd. If he is correct in his representations, Moses did not write this account, for we are quite confident that he did not write nonsense. Our critic construes the account in question to mean that Hagar carried off on her shoulder her son Ishmael, her big boy of fourteen, who, in case of need, might have carried his poor mother.[1] After making this statement he expresses his astonishment by an exclamation-point enclosed in brackets. This is pure imagination. It is neither stated nor implied that Hagar carried Ishmael, but the very opposite. The account shows that Abraham gave bread, a bottle of water, and Ishmael to Hagar, and that he put the bottle of water on her shoulder, but not Ishmael.[2] This view is in accordance with Reuss's own translation, as follows: "Abraham prit du pain et une outre remplie d'eau et donna cela à Hagar, en les mettant sur son epaule, ainsi que le garçon, et la renvoye"[3] ("Abraham took bread and a skin filled with water and gave that to Hagar, putting them on her shoulder, and the child, and sent her away"). According to this rendering, it is not necessary to understand that Abraham put Ishmael, as well as the bread and water-skin, on Hagar's shoulder. The French version reads, "He gave to her also the child."

[1] *L'Histoire Sainte*, Int., p. 96. [2] Gen. 21 : 14. [3] *L'Histoire Sainte*, Vol. I., p. 367.

2. A fanciful argument has been drawn from the military strength of the Israelites to prove the unhistorical character of the Pentateuch. It is claimed that it is not supposable that a nation embracing six hundred thousand able-bodied men would submit to cruel oppression and allow their new-born babes to be drowned without forcible resistance, as the Israelites are said to have done. Voltaire began this kind of argument, and has been followed by Reuss, Colenso, and others. This is another argument that owes all its plausibility and force to imagination. These critics imagine the six hundred thousand able-bodied men to have been brave warriors. They forget that slavery had had its natural effect upon them and had made them cowards. They were so unfit for war that the entrance into Canaan was necessarily postponed forty years, in order that the generation of cowards might die off, and that a generation that had not experienced the debasing effects of slavery might arise. It is related in the history that when the fugitive Israelites saw their late masters, well-trained warriors, advancing with their horses and chariots they became alarmed and cried to the Lord for help. This has been treated by some of the critics as a matter of reproach to the Israelites, or rather to the author of the history, as if such conduct were incredible. But it was natural that when the fugitive slaves saw the embattled hosts of their former lords they should feel and act just as represented. Even if they were armed, they were without military organization, officers, and training. They were no better than a mob. They knew they were helpless, and acted accordingly. The critics, if they were disposed, might learn something from the course pursued by the slave population in the United States during the late Civil War, up to the time when the National Government began to furnish them with arms and officers. In number they were to the Israelites about as two to one. This impeachment of the historical accuracy of the Pentateuch on the ground that it is incredible that the Israelites at the time of the exodus were, as represented, timid and submissive, is one of the fanciful absurdities that have been perpetrated in the name of biblical criticism.

3. Another specimen of this kind of criticism is found in Reuss's attacks on the personal history of Moses. He writes as follows: "Elle présente des difficultés qui sont de nature à étonner ceux qui la lisent dans la supposition que c'est lui-même

qui a é-crit ses mémoires"[1] ("It presents difficulties of a nature to astonish those who read it in the belief that he himself wrote his own memoirs"). Our critic endeavors to make out inconsistency and confusion by arguing as follows: (1) In one passage but one son of Moses is mentioned; in another, two sons are mentioned. (2) These two sons must have been infants at the time of Moses' return from Midian to Egypt, for one ass carried them and their mother; yet how could they still be infants, since Moses had been married forty years? (3) Moses, we are told, had married an Ethiopian woman; but who was she? was this a recent or a former marriage? were Zipporah and this Ethiopian woman the same person?[2]

These are specimens of the difficulties in the history of Moses which are claimed to prove that he did not write it. We reply as follows:

(1) The mention of *one* son does not imply that there were no others. When the birth of Moses is recorded, no allusion is made to other children in his father's family, though Miriam and Aaron were born before him. The marriage of Amram and Jochebed is mentioned, and then it is stated that "the woman conceived, and bare a son," though she had already borne a daughter and a son.[3] Why does not the critic claim inconsistency and confusion here? Carlyle states that Oliver Cromwell, son of Robert and Elizabeth Stewart Cromwell, was born April 25, 1599.[4] In the coming ages, when some man with a very fine critical instinct, or with some favorite hypothesis to defend, reads this declaration, and then a little further on reads that Oliver was the *fifth* child of his parents, and again, further on, reads that they had *ten* children in all, and sees their names in a marginal note, he will perhaps exclaim: "What difficulty and contradiction have we here! This book was not written by Carlyle. We have here two authors and a redactor." The futility of Reuss's criticism is further seen from the fact that the language he cites has reference to the birth of the *first-born* of Moses. How else could the writer do than use the singular number, since it was not a case of twins?

(2) Reuss fails to show that the sons of Moses are represented as infants at the time of the return to Egypt. The fact that one of them had not been circumcised does not prove anything in

---

[1] *L'Histoire Sainte*, Vol. I., p. 82.   [2] *L'Histoire Sainte*, Int., p. 83.
[3] Ex. 2: 1, 2.   [4] *Life and Speeches of Oliver Cromwell*, Vol. I., p. 20.

regard to his age; for it was the unusual delay of the circumcision that produced the difficulty.[1] Nor does the statement that Moses set his wife and sons "upon an ass" prove that his sons were infants. Reuss gets the translation right,—"les fit monter l'ane" ("made them mount the ass"),—but quotes it incorrectly in his argumentation—"*un ane*" ("*an* ass," or "*one* ass"). Though the singular number is employed, there may have been more than one ass. In Hebrew, as in English, the singular is often employed to suggest the plural. Had Noah's ark but one window?[2] Did Jacob's sons take each but one ass and one sack to transport corn from Egypt to Canaan?[3] Did Simeon and Levi, in slaying the men of Shechem with the edge of the sword, use but one weapon?[4] We have such forms of speech in English. When cavalrymen leap into the *saddle*, do they all mount *one* horse? When soldiers in battle rush forward *sword* in *hand*, have they all but *one* hand and *one* sword? When they charge at the point of the *bayonet*, have they but a *single* weapon? When Moses put his family on the ass, he did not necessarily put them all on *one* ass; or if there was but one ass in the case, it does not follow that he set them all on that one ass at the same time.

(3) After all, Gershom and Eliezer may have been small enough to ride with their mother on one ass. In combating this idea Reuss will have it that Moses was married and had a son born to him soon after he fled to Midian. This notion, however, is not in the record. The order of events, as there given, is as follows: Moses' flight to Midian, his dwelling there, his sitting by the well and watering Jethro's sheep, his dwelling with this man, his marriage to one of his daughters, the birth of Gershom.[5] All these events are crowded into the small space of eight verses. Other events, among them the birth of a second son, are also mentioned as occurring before the return to Egypt.[6] How much time intervened between one of these events and another is unknown. Moses may have dwelt ten, twenty, or thirty years in Midian before he sat by the well. He may have dwelt several years with Jethro before he married Zipporah. It is possible that he may not have had a son until years after his marriage. For anything that is contained in the record, Gershom and Eliezer may have been born near the close of the residence in Midian. Esau and Jacob were born twenty years after Isaac's

---

[1] Ex. 4:25.　　[2] Gen. 8:6.　　[3] Gen. 42:27.
[4] Gen. 34:26.　　[5] Ex. 2:15-22.　　[6] Ex. 18:3.

marriage. Isaac was born more than a quarter of a century after Abraham's marriage. From all these considerations it is inferred that the sons of Moses may have been very small boys at the time of the return to Egypt.

(4) The marriage of Moses with an Ethiopian (Cushite)[1] woman is not inconsistent with anything else recorded concerning him. Zipporah may have died, and the Cushite may have been a second wife. Or Moses may have taken a second wife while Zipporah was still living, for polygamy by him is not more improbable than by Abraham and Jacob. Or Zipporah herself may have been the Cushite woman.

4. Another imaginary difficulty is brought forward by Reuss in regard to the size and weight of the tables of stone on which the decalogue was written. He thinks they must have been entirely too large and heavy for Moses to carry. He supposes that the six hundred and twenty Hebrew letters embraced in the decalogue would occupy at least a square meter and a half of surface, each letter occupying twenty-five square centimeters.[2] According to this hypothesis and calculation, the six hundred and twenty letters of the Hebrew decalogue occupied more than sixteen square feet of surface, and each table must have been more than four feet long and two feet wide. Stone tables of such length and breadth, with corresponding thickness, would likely be too heavy for Moses to carry.[3] Reuss calls attention to the fact that Moses was eighty years old ("un octogenaire"), and reminds us that Sinai was a pretty high mountain. He forgets, or disbelieves, the statement that up to the time of Moses' death "his eye was not dim, nor his natural force abated."[3] But we are willing to admit that it certainly would be very difficult for Moses, however strong he might be, to carry two large slabs of stone from the top of Sinai down to the camp of the Israelites, and it would be still harder for him to carry them from the camp up the mountain's side.[4] Why did not our critic think of the last-mentioned difficulty?

But the hypothesis on which the above calculation is based is very fanciful and extravagant. Reuss supposes that twenty-five

[1] Num. 12:1.
[2] "Ce texte se compose de 620 lettres. Avec l'écriture carrée actuelle, ce texte, en ne tenant au cun compte des marges et des interlignes (la séparation des mots n'étant pas d'usage) aurait demandé au moins un mètre carré et demi de superficies, même en ne calculant pour chaque lettre que l'espace minime de 25 cm. carrés."—*L'Histoire Sainte*, Int., p. 66. [3] Deut. 34:7. [4] Ex. 34:4.

square centimeters were necessary for each letter, and twenty-five square centimeters are eight square inches and a fraction. Thus Reuss assigns over eight square inches to each letter, making it more than two and one-half inches long and wide. This is utterly unreasonable. Even the old so-called uncial letters were generally only an inch in length and breadth. But suppose that the letters employed in writing the decalogue occupied each the space of one square inch; then the whole surface occupied by them would be six hundred and twenty square inches, a little less than a surface twenty-five inches long and the same in width. Two tablets, then, each two feet and one inch long and one foot and one-half inch wide, would contain the six hundred and twenty letters of the decalogue. But there is an important fact which Reuss has overlooked or ignored, and that is that the tablets were written on both sides. Such is the express statement: "The tables were written on both their sides; on the one side and on the other were they written."[1] All this explicitness and emphasis of declaration are lost on the critic who is intent on proving the Pentateuch historically untrue. In view of the fact that the tablets were written on both sides, we may reduce our tablets above mentioned to one-half their size, that is, to one foot and one-half inch in length and one foot and one-half inch in width. Tablets so diminutive in size would, of course, be of little thickness and weight. Thus the tablets on which the ten commandments were written need not have been much larger than a schoolboy's slate, though the imagination of the critic has magnified them into slabs as large as tombstones.

5. What Reuss says about the first journey of Jacob's sons to Egypt to buy food is a fine specimen of fanciful criticism. He will have it that, according to the account as found in Genesis, they went into Egypt each having but one sack, and that they returned to Canaan each one having only one sack of grain. He is also quite sure that, according to the account, but one of the asses was fed during the entire journey.[2] The way such conclusions are reached is this: The writer mentions but one sack, therefore he meant there were no others; he refers to the feeding of but one of the asses, therefore he meant that all the rest went altogether without food. Such criticism is not surpassed by anything found in the biblical commentaries of Voltaire. Our famous critic of Strasburg might have drawn some other

---

[1] Ex. 32: 15. [2] *L'Histoire Sainte*, Vol. I., p. 108.

conclusions equally candid and reasonable. He might have affirmed that each man, according to the account, carried his one sack on his shoulder, and took his ass along only for company; for Joseph's order was, "Fill the men's sacks with food, as much as they can carry."[1] He might have claimed that the men, during the first journey to and from Egypt, ate no food at all; for, though mention is made of one of the asses being fed, there is no allusion to any of the men either eating or drinking. He might have claimed that Benjamin, at the second visit, in Joseph's house ate five dinners at one meal; for it is expressly stated that his mess was five times as much as that of any of his brethren, and it is not stated that he did not eat it all. It is wonderful what some of the learned critics can do by means of the argument *e silentio*.

6. Graf, too, has taken a hand in this imaginative criticism. The following is a specimen: "Nach der Num., C. 2, 3, gegebenen Beschreibung soll die Stiftshütte in der Mitte des Lagers stehen (vgl. Ex. 25: 8; Ezra 37: 26, 28), und die Leviten zunächst, dann die zwölf Stämme rings um dieselbe symmetrisch je drei nach der einen der vier Himmelsgegenden sich lagern, und nach ähnlicher Anordnung soll auf dem Marsche das Heiligthum in der Mitte des Zuges gehen, Num. 10: 11 ff; nach den andern Erzählern dagegen steht die Stiftshütte ausserhalb des Lagers und die Bundeslade zieht dem Volke voran. Jahwe spricht mit Mose vom Deckel der im Allerheiligsten stehenden Bundeslade her Ex. 25: 22; 30: 6; 36; Num. 7: 89. . . . Nach den andern Erzählern tritt Jahwe in der Wolkensäule an den Eingang des Zeltes, um mit Mose zu reden."[2] ("According to the description given, Num. chs. 2, 3, the tabernacle is to stand in the middle of the camp (comp. Ex. 25: 8; Ezra 37: 26, 28), and the Levites next; then the twelve tribes to encamp round about it, in symmetrical order, always three toward one of the four regions of heaven; and, according to a like regulation, the sanctuary on the march is to go in the middle of the train, Num. 10: 11 ff. According to the other narrators, however, the tabernacle stands outside of the camp, and the ark of the covenant goes before the people. Yahwe speaks with Moses from the cover of the ark of the covenant standing in the most holy, Ex. 25: 22; 30: 6; 36; Num. 7: 89. . . . According to the other narrators Yahwe entered into the cloud-pillar to speak with Moses.")

[1] Gen. 44: 1.   [2] *Geschichtlichen Bücher des Alten Testaments*, pp. 64, 65.

These claims of contradiction are put forward as proofs that the account of the tabernacle and the ark are not historical, but poetic and imaginative. The critic, however, himself in this case deals wholly in the imaginary and unreal. It is not recorded anywhere that the Lord spake to Moses through the cloudy pillar, and even if there had been such a record it would not be inconsistent with the declaration and the fact that God communed with Moses "from between the two cherubim which are upon the ark of the testimony." The Almighty could communicate his will to Moses in more ways and places than one.

As for the representation of the tabernacle as being both within and without the camp, we remark: (1) That the tabernacle, or *a* tabernacle, is spoken of as being pitched without the camp at the time of the shameful affair of the golden calf.[1] But this was clearly only a temporary arrangement, introduced on the occasion of Israel's great sin. (2) This tent was not the Mosaic tabernacle, for that had not yet been erected. (3) But even if this tent pitched by Moses without the camp had been the true Mosaic tabernacle, its outside position is never again mentioned after Israel's idolatry had been fully put away.

There is, therefore, nothing in this particular passage inconsistent with the uniform representation of the Mosaic tabernacle and ark in the Pentateuch as having their rightful and actual place within the camp of the Israelites.

7. Colenso, like some other critics, maintains that the sacred narrative represents the six hundred thousand footmen of the Israelites as being armed previously to their departure from Egypt. On this assumption several imaginary difficulties are suggested. Among other things it is asked why the Israelites, with arms in their hands, did not fight for their liberty and their children in Egypt. It is, however, a question whether the Israelites were really armed before they crossed the Red Sea. Our Authorized Version reads that "the children of Israel went up *harnessed* out of the land of Egypt."[2] But for the word "harnessed" the words "by five in a rank" are placed in the margin. But the Revised Version has the word "armed," and Colenso is very sure that this is the correct rendering.[3] This view, however, is not sustained by the best scholarship. Gesenius gives a different rendering. Reuss has it "marchant en bon

---

[1] Ex. 33:7.   [2] Ex. 13:18.   [3] *Pentateuch and Book of Joshua*, p. 98.

ordre"[1] ("marching in good order"). Professor W. H. Green recognizes the fact that the original word is one "whose meaning and derivation are exceedingly doubtful."[2]

We do not care to discuss this point farther. When Reuss, the stepfather of analytic criticism, decides against translating the original word by "armed," the dogmatism of Colenso is unavailing.

But it is asked, Where, then, did the Israelites obtain the weapons with which they defeated the Amalekites about a month after crossing the Red Sea?[3] We answer that the Israelites, after coming out of Egypt, may have obtained supplies of arms from several sources: (1) From the drowned Egyptians. The statement that "Israel saw the Egyptians dead upon the seashore"[4] is very suggestive. Josephus may be correct in his statement that the day after the crossing "the Israelites collected the weapons of the Egyptians."[5] This may be only an inference of the Jewish author, but if so it is a very natural and proper one. (2) The Israelites may have *manufactured* weapons. In one month six hundred thousand men might manufacture all the weapons needed by those who went to meet the Amalekites; for those chosen to go on that expedition were perhaps no more than twelve thousand men,—one thousand from each tribe,—and hence arms would be needed only for that number. (3) After the defeat of the Amalekites there was of course an easy supply of weapons. In one, or in all, of these ways there was a possibility of the Israelites' obtaining arms.

8. Even Wellhausen furnishes some pretty good specimens of imaginative criticism. In denying the Mosaic origin of the decalogue, he says that the trustworthiness of the account in Exodus of its being written on two tables of stone and placed in the ark is impaired by the fact that it is recorded that Deuteronomy was written on twelve stones and deposited in the ark. The critic thinks that because this second account cannot be true therefore the first is also probably untrue. His words are, "Indessen auch vom Deuteronomium wird bezeugt, einerseits es sei auf zwölf Steinen eingeschrieben, andererseits es sei in die Lade gelegt worden, Deut. 31 : 26"[6] ("Yet also concerning Deuteronomy this testimony is given, that, on the one hand, it was written on twelve stones, and, on the other, deposited in the ark, Deut.

---

[1] *L'Histoire Sainte*, Vol. II., p. 38.　　[2] *Pentateuch Vindicated*, p. 74.
[3] Ex. 17 : 8-13.　[4] Ex. 14 : 30.　[5] *Antiquities*, 2 : 16 : 6.　[6] *Prolegomena*, p. 410.

31 : 26"). In the passage thus cited there is not a word about Deuteronomy being written on twelve or any other number of *stones*. The declaration there is, that it was "the book of the law"—not a copy in stone, but a *book* copy of the law—that was placed in the ark. Nor is it stated anywhere in the Pentateuch that a stone copy of Deuteronomy was placed in the ark.

Again, Wellhausen affirms that we have two decalogues, quite different from one another, preserved to us in Exodus. His words are, "Indem zwei ganz verschiedene Dekaloge, Exod. 20 und Exod. 34 überliefert werden"[1] ("Two entirely different decalogues are given, Exodus 20 and Exodus 34). There are, indeed, two sets of tables mentioned in connection with these two chapters. But they are declared to be identical in their contents. "And the Lord said unto Moses, Hew thee two tables of stone like unto the first; and I will write upon these tables the words that were in the first tables, which thou brakest."[2] The identity of the contents of the first two and second two tables is also emphatically affirmed in Deuteronomy.[3]

Thus Wellhausen, as well as other analytic critics, is sometimes indebted to his imagination for facts to support his theories. We do not, of course, say that all their reasoning, or their reasoning in general, is such as we have been dealing with in this chapter. There are some difficulties involved in the Mosaic authorship of the Pentateuch, and these the analytic critics employ with much skill. Many of their arguments are characterized by more or less plausibility and strength; but, on the other hand, much of their argumentation is founded on fancy and misrepresentation. We have thought proper to take some notice of arguments of this kind, as well as of those that are stronger and more respectable.

[1] *Prolegomena*, p. 411.   [2] Ex. 34 : 1.   [3] Deut. 10 : 2, 4.

CHAPTER VIII

PLURALITY OF AUTHORS

THE documentary hypothesis is not inconsistent with the Mosaic authorship of the Pentateuch. Moses may have employed several documents in its composition. In this there is nothing inherently incredible or improbable. Astruc, who is regarded by many as the originator of the documentary hypothesis (but was not), was at least a *professed* advocate of the traditional belief. As Kuenen remarks, the very title of his work shows how little he questioned the Mosaic authorship of Genesis.[1] More than half a century before Astruc, Vitringa, an orthodox Protestant, propounded the documentary hypothesis, as follows: There were "documents of the fathers preserved among the Israelites, which Moses collected, digested, embellished, and supplemented."[2] Abraham may have brought family records and other written memorials from Ur of the Chaldees. Moses may have had access, in Egypt, to documents much older than Abraham, and may have taken copies of them, or retained a knowledge of them. Jethro, his father-in-law, who was both priest and statesman, may have had in his possession records that came down from former generations. Moses may have employed some of his own contemporaries to write for him and to furnish him with narratives and statements. These various documents, consisting of registers, narratives, and statements, Moses may have put together, condensing, curtailing, and filling out, and thus making the whole his own. If there were any literary monuments of the past in Moses' time, we think there were none more likely than he to be acquainted with them, and to utilize them in his own writings.

Nor is this hypothesis inconsistent with the most thoroughgoing doctrine of supernatural inspiration. Luke, the writer of the third Gospel, intimates in the outset that much of the

[1] *Hexateuch*, p. 58: "Conjectures sur les Memoirs originaux dont il paroit que Moïse s'est servi pour composer le livre de la Genèse."
[2] *Observationes Sacræ*, Vol. I., p. 36.

knowledge of the events he is about to relate had been derived from natural sources.[1] This is undoubtedly true of Moses and of every other divinely guided and inspired writer. The knowledge which Moses acquired by his residence in Egypt and at the court of Pharaoh was undoubtedly utilized in writing Genesis and Exodus. It is more reasonable to suppose that God gave him knowledge by putting family records and other memorials of the past into his possession than that he communicated with him in every case by direct, supernatural revelation. The hypothesis of Cave that J of the critics is Moses, is not to be rejected on account of any antecedent improbability, but, if at all, on account of the want of positive evidence in its support.

The documentary hypothesis, then, or rather *a* documentary hypothesis, is not incompatible with Mosaic authorship. Though it should be shown that the Pentateuch embraces several documents, consisting of extracts, sketches, statements, family records, taken from various sources, yet may Moses have been the one who, by his own hand, or by amanuenses, collected, arranged, curtailed, condensed, supplemented, corrected, and also added much of his own, and thus constituted himself the real author, and secured that remarkable unity which even analysts are forced to admit is a striking feature of the Pentateuch as a whole.

If, then, the hypothesis of a plurality of writers were proved, the Mosaic authorship of the Pentateuch would not thereby be disproved.

But has the hypothesis of plural authorship been established? or can it be established? Let us examine.

1. One of the arguments employed in its favor, based on claimed inconsistencies, has already been considered. We have but little to add to what has already been said in Chapter V. on this subject.

(1) We have shown that, in many cases, the claimed inconsistencies and contradictions are the results of misinterpretation, or exist only in the imagination of the objectors.

(2) As has often been remarked concerning claimed discrepancies in the Bible in general, it may truly be said of those that are claimed in the Pentateuch that they involve most generally names and numbers, in which copyists are most likely to make mistakes.

---

[1] Luke 1: 1-3.

(3) The analysts, in much of their argumentation on this point, proceed on the theory that Moses was plenarily inspired as a writer, or was in some way rendered infallible. They argue that the Pentateuch was not written by him because it contains inconsistencies and other errors.

(4) Some of the analytic critics are on this point discreditably illogical. We refer to those of them who admit the Bible, including the Pentateuch with all its claimed errors, to be in some sense the word of God, or that at least it contains the word of God, but, because of these claimed errors in the Pentateuch, deny that Moses is, in any sense, its author. If, notwithstanding these supposed errors, it contains God's word, may it not contain the word of Moses as well? Is God less free from error than Moses?

(5) This argument from claimed errors proves in many cases too much. If the Pentateuch contains such contradictions and incredibilities as are claimed, the conclusion must be that neither Moses nor any man of common sense wrote, compiled, or redacted it. Their hypothesis amounts to this, that a crowd of writers worked on the Pentateuch, combining documents, supplementing, curtailing, and amending, doing the work of compilers, editors, and redactors, but that not one of them had sense enough to remove palpable contradictions and absurdities. Yet these same writers, so destitute of common sense, have at last succeeded in working up these five books into such a unity of thought and such literary excellence that they have been the admiration of the civilized world for hundreds of years.

2. Another argument in favor of the hypothesis of a plurality of authors is that in many places two narratives are combined in one. It is claimed that the two narratives in many cases can be separated, and that each narrative, taken by itself, constitutes a complete and consistent whole. We will test this claim by the presentation of some of the so-called *distinct stories*.

Separating the account of the flood into what are called the "P" and "J" stories, we have for the "J" story the following: "And Yahweh said unto Noah, Come thou and all thy house into the ark: for thee have I seen righteous before me in this generation. Of every clean beast thou shalt take to thee seven and seven, the male and his female: and of the beasts that are not clean two, the male and his female; of the fowl also of the air seven and seven; to keep seed alive upon the face of all the earth.

For yet seven days, and I will cause it to rain upon the earth forty days and forty nights; and every living thing that I have made will I destroy from off the face of the ground. And Noah did according unto all that Yahweh commanded him. . . . And Noah went in, and his sons, and his wife, and his sons' wives with him, into the ark, because of the waters of the flood. Of clean beasts, and of beasts that are not clean, and of fowls, . . . there went in unto Noah into the ark, as God commanded Noah. And it came to pass, after the seven days, that the waters were upon the earth. . . . And the rain was upon the earth forty days and forty nights. . . . And Yahweh shut him in. . . . And the waters increased, and bare up the ark, and it was lifted up above the earth. . . . All in whose nostrils was the breath of life, of all that was in the dry land, died. And every living substance was destroyed which was upon the face of the ground: . . . and Noah only was left, and they that were with him in the ark. . . . And the rain from heaven was restrained; and the waters returned from the earth continually; . . . and it came to pass at the end of forty days that Noah opened the window of the ark, which he had made; and sent forth a raven, and it went forth to and fro, until the waters were dried up from off the earth."[1] Such is the account of the flood as attributed by the critics to J. We can scarcely realize how abrupt, broken, and incoherent this account is, because, as we read it, we supply ideas which have been made familiar to us by reading the full account. In this fragmentary account there is no information as to what the ark was, and no information as to who made it, or whether it was made at all, until near the close, where it is incidentally stated that Noah made it. The account begins with the statement that Noah found favor with God, and then comes the command, "Come into the ark," there being no allusion to the ark before. Also the sentence, "And Yahweh shut him in," stands dislocated and alone. So, too, the sentence, "And it came to pass after forty days," has no meaning; but as it stands in Genesis it means forty days after the tops of the mountains had been seen. This is the way the analysts cut up and mangle the Scriptures, while claiming to separate them into their independent and distinct parts.

The so-called "J" story of the selling of Joseph is as follows: "And Israel said unto Joseph, Do not thy brethren feed the flock in Shechem? come, and I will send thee unto them. . . . So

[1] Gen. 7:1–8:7.

he sent him out of the vale of Hebron, and he came to Shechem. . . . And before he came near unto them, they conspired against him to slay him. . . . And Reuben heard it, and delivered him out of their hand; and said, Let us not take his life. . . . And it came to pass, when Joseph was come unto his brethren, . . . the coat of many colors that was on him. . . . And they lifted up their eyes and looked, and, behold, a traveling company of Ishmaelites came from Gilead, with their camels bearing spicery and balm and myrrh, going to carry it down to Egypt. And Judah said unto his brethren, What profit is it if we slay our brother, and conceal his blood? Come, and let us sell him to the Ishmaelites, and let not our hand be upon him; for he is our brother and our flesh. And his brethren were content. . . . And sold Joseph to the Ishmaelites for twenty pieces of silver: . . . And they sent the coat of many colors. . . . Joseph is without doubt torn in pieces. . . . And all his sons and all his daughters rose up to comfort him; but he refused to be comforted: and he said, For I will go down to the grave to my son mourning. And his father wept for him."[1]

Here, again, the narrative called "J," when taken by itself, is broken and disconnected. Some of the sentences are cut in two, mangled in meaning as well as in form.

We give, as follows, the so-called "J" account of the first journey to Egypt to buy corn: "And the famine was over all the face of the earth. And Joseph opened all the storehouses, and sold unto the Egyptians; and the famine was sore in the land of Egypt. . . . And he said, . . . Get you down thither. . . . For he said, Lest peradventure mischief befall him. And the sons of Israel came to buy among those that came: for the famine was in the land of Canaan. . . . He it was that sold to all the people of the land. . . . And Joseph saw his brethren, and he knew them, but made himself strange unto them; . . . and he said unto them, Whence come ye? And they said, From the land of Canaan to buy food. . . . And as one of them opened his sack, to give his ass provender in the lodging-place, he espied his money; and, behold, it was in the mouth of his sack. And he said unto his brethren, My money is restored; and, lo, it is even in my sack: and their heart failed them. . . . And he said, My son shall not go down with you; for his brother is dead, and he only is left: if mischief befall him by the way in the which ye go, then shall ye bring down my gray hairs with sorrow to the grave."[2]

[1] Gen. 37 : 13-35.   [2] Gen. 41 : 56–42 : 38.

The so-called "E" account is as follows: "Now Jacob saw that there was corn in Egypt, and Jacob said unto his sons, Why do ye look one upon another? . . . Behold, I have heard that there is corn in Egypt: . . . and buy for us from thence; that we may live, and not die. And Joseph's ten brethren went down to buy corn from Egypt. But Benjamin, Joseph's brother, Jacob sent not with them. . . . And Joseph was governor over the land, . . . and Joseph's brethren came, and bowed down themselves to him with their faces to the earth. . . . And spake roughly with them. . . . And Joseph knew his brethren, but they knew not him."[1,2]

Comment is unnecessary. The Pentateuchal narratives cannot be decomposed without violence and distortion. Neither the so-called "J" nor "E" document taken by itself constitutes a narrative characterized either by continuity or sense. The attempt to separate the historical portions of the Pentateuch into distinct and coherent stories is a failure. All that has been done in decomposing the Pentateuchal narratives might be done with Macaulay's History of England and Bancroft's History of the United States.

3. Another argument in favor of the hypothesis of a plurality of the authorship of the Pentateuch is drawn from the differences in style. It is claimed that a plurality of authors is necessary to account for these differences. The analytics hold that if Moses wrote the five books of the Pentateuch they would all be written throughout in one style. The weakness and inconclusiveness of this argument are shown by several considerations.

(1) The assumption on which this argument is based is incorrect. It is not true that authors do not vary in style. Many authors have written in different styles at different periods of their lives, and many authors have written in different styles at the same period of life. Most authors become less ornate and florid as they advance in age. At least, there are many examples of this. But there are examples of change in the other direction. Of these Bacon is one. His mind, to use Macaulay's illustration, reversed the order of nature, producing fruit first (which remained to the last), and blossoms much later. The writings of his later years are much superior to those of his youth in variety of expression, in richness of illustration, in sweetness and vigor, in everything that constitutes eloquence. A

[1] Gen. 42: 1-8.
[2] These quotations are taken from *Die Heilige Schrift des Alten Testaments*, by Kautzsch-Socin.

similar change took place in the style of Burke. At the age of twenty it was simple and unadorned; at forty it was rich and copious; at fifty, ornate and florid, and at seventy, gorgeous. Macaulay declares it strange that the essay on the "Sublime and Beautiful" and the "Letter to a Noble Lord" (the former, one of Burke's early, and the latter one of his late, productions) should have been written by the same man.[1] But they were; and this, with other similar facts, shows the unreasonableness of the conclusions drawn by the critics from the differences of style in the Pentateuch.

Not only do authors write in different styles at different periods of their lives, but many of them write in different styles at the same period. Every poet has his prose as well as his poetic style. There is a greater difference between the prose writings and the poetry of most modern authors, so far as style is concerned, than between different parts of the Pentateuch. According to the argumentation of the critics, the prose works of Milton and the "Paradise Lost" must have been written by different authors. According to their way of reasoning, Scott's "Life of Napoleon" and the "Lady of the Lake" cannot be the productions of one man. The same may be said of Cowper's poems and epistles, and the prose and poetic writings of many other authors.

Authors vary much also in poetic style. Judging by style alone, we would conclude that the "Pucelle," the "Henriade," and the dramas of Voltaire, to say nothing about his "Charles XII." of Sweden and other prose works, must have been produced by three different authors. According to the way the analytics reason, Byron's "English Bards and Scotch Reviewers," his "Childe Harold," and his "Don Juan" owe their origin to a triple authorship. Each of these productions has marked peculiarities of style. An argument founded on *archaisms* may be employed to prove that "Childe Harold" was written long before Byron's time, for it abounds in obsoletisms, such as *mote, whilome, idlesse, eld, fytte, fere*, and other words, which are not found even in Byron's other poems. If we follow the linguistic argument, we must conclude that the author of this poem lived centuries before the time of Lord Byron. Coleridge, too, sometimes wrote in a weird and antique style. Our critics, to be consistent, ought to maintain that the author of "Christabel"

---

[1] Macaulay's *Essay on Bacon.*

and the hymn "Before Sunrise in the Vale of Chamouni" could not have written the "Rime of the Ancient Mariner." The views of our critics about style are shown to be absurdly incorrect by the example of the writings of Burns. He was master of two styles of language, the broad Scotch dialect and the pure Anglo-Saxon English. We have the pure English in such poems as "To Mary in Heaven" and "Man was Made to Mourn"; and the broad Scotch in the "Twa Dogs" and the "Twa Brigs." "Tam O'Shanter" is written mainly in the Scotch dialect, but a small portion is characterized by the purest and most elegant English, as follows:

> "But pleasures are like poppies spread,
> You seize the flow'r, its bloom is shed;
> Or like the snow-falls in the river,
> A moment white—then melts forever;
> Or like the borealis race,
> That flit ere you can point their place;
> Or like the rainbow's lovely form
> Evanishing amid the storm."

The two styles appear also in "Bannockburn." The first four stanzas of this poem are in Scotch, and the last two in pure English. Besides, there are two distinct styles of *thought* in Burns's poems. Some of them contain only noble and pure ideas, and some of them are characterized by vulgarity and obscenity. The author of "The Cotter's Saturday Night" was apparently a man of good moral ideas, but some of Burns's pieces would seem to have been written by a drunkard and a debauchee. Thus we have in Burns's works four or five diverse styles of thought and diction—prose style and poetic style, Scotch style and English style, and a pure and elevated style of thought in contrast with a vulgar and obscene style. We must admit that all these different styles were practiced by one man, and sometimes in writing one poem, or else maintain that there were four or five different authors of the productions attributed to Burns. Yet the analytics go on reasoning about the Pentateuch just as if no author ever wrote in more than one style, and just as if Moses, who lived one hundred and twenty years, and whose literary activity may have continued for eighty years or more, could not have changed his style of thought or diction during all that time.

(2) The extreme weakness of the linguistic argument is shown by other facts. One of these is that in the Pentateuch,

as well as in other parts of the Old Testament, poetry and prose are mingled together. How can the critics be sure that what they regard as transitions from one author to another, as from E to J and from J back to E, are not in some cases alternations of poetry and prose, or adaptations of style to subject, by the same author? If men should judge of the alternations of style in Goethe's "Faust" as the analysts do of the Pentateuch, what would be the result?

(3) Besides, the uncertainty of all theories founded on differences of style in the Pentateuch is increased by the fact that if the hypothesis of the critics be correct there is very little to determine what the style of Hebrew writing was in the Mosaic age. According to their showing, there are indeed a few pieces of composition of that age found in the Pentateuch. Is there any difference between these few pieces and the Pentateuch in general, as to style of language and thought? This is a point which the critics ignore, and thereby tacitly admit that the facts are against them. But aside from this, with what is the style of the Pentateuch to be compared? The critics can only reason thus: The style of it is a good deal like that of Jeremiah or Joel, and therefore it is not like the style of Moses. Yet they fail to consider the style of what they admit Moses actually wrote.

(4) The weakness and uncertainty of all this reasoning are admitted by the ablest of the analytics themselves. Kuenen says, "The extant Israelitish literature is too limited in extent to enable us to determine the age of any work with certainty from mere considerations of language and style."[1] Even Cheyne quotes approvingly from Kuenen, as follows: "Linguistic arguments do not furnish a positive or conclusive argument."[2] Wellhausen expresses his contempt for linguistic arguments, as well as for some others, by saying that "the firemen kept at a distance from the spot where the conflagration raged." He takes the ground that the battle must be fought out "in the regions of religious antiquities and dominant religious ideas."[3]

(5) The weakness of the linguistic argument is further shown by the efforts that have been made to point out peculiarities of style in the books of the Pentateuch. Take, for example, Driver's list of phrases which he claims are characteristic of

[1] *Hexateuch*, p. 268.   [2] *Founders of the Old Testament Criticism*, p. 281.
[3] *Prolegomena*, p. 12.

Deuteronomy.[1] The number of such phrases as presented by him is forty-one. But the number of obsoletisms, called by philologists archaisms, in "Childe Harold" is found by actual count to be fifty-five.[2] Here, then, are fourteen more linguistic facts to prove that Byron did not write that poem than Driver produces to prove that Moses did not write Deuteronomy. On examination, however, we find that very many of these phrases said to be characteristic of Deuteronomy are really not such. The author admits that the first ten are found in Exodus.[3] This admission does not go far enough, for, according to his own showing, nearly all of these ten phrases are found not only in Exodus, but elsewhere. Number one is found in Exodus, and also in Joshua and Hosea. Number two is found in Exodus and Joshua, often in Kings and Jeremiah. Number three is found in Exodus, and in Isaiah, Proverbs, and Ecclesiastes. Number five is found in Exodus, Judges, Micah, and Jeremiah. Number nine is found in Exodus and in Genesis and Joshua. Nearly all of the first ten phrases said to be characteristic of Deuteronomy are found not only in Exodus, but also elsewhere. The same is true of most of the other thirty-one examples. The eleventh, said to be very characteristic of Deuteronomy, is admitted also to be "characteristic of II. Isaiah," and is found also in I. Kings and in Jeremiah. The fourteenth is found in Exodus, Jeremiah, and Ezekiel. The seventeenth is found in Genesis, Isaiah, and frequently in Ezekiel. The nineteenth is found in Joshua and I. Chronicles. The twenty-sixth is found in Numbers, often in the Book of Judges, in Kings and Jeremiah occasionally. The thirty-fifth is found in Kings, Ezra, Nehemiah, and Jeremiah. The fortieth is found in Leviticus, Numbers, and Joshua. Very few of these forty-one phrases are found in Deuteronomy alone. The most of them are found in other books, many of them frequently. To call these phrases in general characteristic of Deuteronomy is absurd. But Driver has a way of construing things to his own mind and of representing them to others that covers up the absurdity. He claims that many of these phrases were incorporated into Deuteronomy from JE, and that JE was incorporated afterward into the Book of Exodus. The viciousness of this procedure from a logical point of view is manifest; for the thing in dispute is the existence of these supposed authors,

---

[1] *Introduction to the Literature of the Old Testament*, pp. 91-95.
[2] See above, p. 109. [3] *Introduction*, p. 91.

J, E, D, and P. And now comes Driver, and, in order to prove that certain phrases are characteristic of Deuteronomy, brings in the existence of JE as an established fact. The fact of characteristic phrases being thus proved is then used in turn to prove the existence of such writers as J and E. Another absurd procedure in this undertaking is the claiming that phrases are characteristic of Deuteronomy which yet are found in several other books—some of them frequently thus found. Since these phrases are used by many writers, they are not characteristic of any one in particular. Driver's list and argumentation confirm the admissions of Kuenen and Wellhausen concerning the weakness and inconclusiveness of the linguistic argument as employed against the Mosaic authorship of the Pentateuch.

4. The argument in favor of the documentary hypothesis drawn from the use of the divine names in Genesis, though doubtless the strongest adduced by the analytic critics, is by no means conclusive or satisfactory. It is as follows: In Genesis 1 : 1-31 and 2 : 1-3 the Divine Being is designated exclusively by the name "God" (*Elohim*); in 2 : 4-25 and 3 : 1-24 the name "Lord God" (*Yahweh Elohim*) is generally employed; in 4 : 1-26 "Lord" (*Yahweh*) is generally employed; in 5 : 1-32 "God" is generally employed; in 6 : 1-8, "Lord"; in 6 : 9-22, "God." Now this varied use of the divine names may be accounted for by the hypothesis that in Genesis extracts from several documents written by different authors have been pieced together, and that one of these authors employed the name "God," another, "Lord," and perhaps another, "Lord God." It is further claimed that the phenomenon in question is not satisfactorily accounted for in any other way. It is hence inferred that the hypothesis that Genesis is made up largely of extracts from documents written by different authors must be accepted; and a further inference is that Genesis is not the production of any single author, and hence not the production of Moses.

The argument certainly has plausibility and force. But there are several considerations by which it is very much weakened, if not altogether destroyed.

(1) One of these is the union of the two names "Lord" and "God," as in Genesis 2 : 4-25 and 3 : 1-24. It is, indeed, very easy to say that this is a JE document, an amalgamation of extracts from a Jehovistic and an Elohistic writer; but not a word is claimed from an Elohistic document except the name "God"

(*Elohim*). After all, then, the critics cannot claim this passage as a JE document, but are compelled to take the ground that it is purely Jehovistic, and that the name "God" (*Elohim*) was interpolated in it at least sixteen times by some unknown person for an unknown purpose. For the fact of the interpolation they have, and claim, no other evidence than that there is no other way of reconciling this passage with their hypothesis.

(2) Another weak place in the argument is suggested by the fact that frequently the name "Lord" (*Yahweh*) is found in the so-called Elohistic document[1] and the name "God" (*Elohim*) in the Jehovistic.[2] Hence, again, in more than half a dozen places the analytic critic is under the necessity of supposing, in order to conform the text to his hypothesis, that an interloping redactor inserted sometimes *Jahweh* for *Elohim* and sometimes *Elohim* for *Jahweh*. No reason can be assigned for this arbitrary tampering with the text of the original writer, except a wanton disposition to make changes. We are not aware that any of the critics have gone so far as to maintain that the intention of the interpolator in making these arbitrary substitutions was to remove traces of plural authorship and thus deceive mankind.

(3) Still further, the interchange of divine names is not found in the last ten chapters. In all these chapters the name *Jahweh* appears but once.[3] In every case, with this one exception, *Elohim* is employed to designate the Divine Being. Yet the critics, notwithstanding, go right on with their analysis, dividing up this portion of Genesis between E and J, assigning to the latter even whole chapters in which *Elohim* is exclusively employed.[4]

Such are some of the facts in regard to the use of the divine names in Genesis and the analysis of this book into several documents written by different authors. *Elohim* is found very many times joined to *Jahweh* in a so-called Jehovistic document. The analysts easily reconcile this fact with their hypothesis by supposing that this is the work of an interpolator. *Jahweh* is found in a so-called Elohistic document, and again the aid of an interpolating redactor is invoked. Repeatedly are the names *Jahweh* and *Elohim* found, each just where, according to the hypothesis, it ought not to be. But our critics again show

---

[1] Gen. 15:1; 21:1; 22:11; 28:21. [2] Gen. 7:9, 17; 31:50.
[3] Gen. 49:18. [4] Gen. 43, 44.

themselves equal to the emergency by suggesting that some redactor sometimes substituted *Elohim* for *Jahweh*, and sometimes *Jahweh* for *Elohim*, making these arbitrary changes in mere wantonness; or else that there were two redactors, a Jehovist and an Elohist, and that the former got his work in on the original E document, and the latter his work in on the original J document. If, in chapter after chapter, the interchange of the divine names disappears altogether, the critic still sets up his analysis just as in the chapters where the varied use of the divine names is the most apparent. Thus are the facts and the text conformed to the analytic hypothesis. Thus what seems the best argument for this hypothesis loses in a great degree its plausibility and strength through the very efforts that must be made in its behalf. An argument is scarcely admissible which creates a necessity for supposing interpolations, substitutions, or other alterations in the biblical text. Violence of this kind is generally resorted to in desperate cases, just as the taking of human life is considered justifiable only in self-defense. The frequency with which the analysts resort to the supposition of interpolations, redactions, or other changes in the text of Genesis, in order to carry out their argument derived from the use of the divine names, is certainly suspicious, and suggests the desperateness of the case.

5. The documentary hypothesis, as it is at this time held and advocated by critics, is to be accepted only on positive and strong evidence. The authors designated as E, D, J, P, Q, R, E^2, J^2, P^1, P^2, P^3, etc., are absolutely unknown. Their names and places are not even conjectured. E is supposed to have been an Ephraimite, and J of the tribe of Judah. But this is a mere fancy, without a scintilla of evidence in its favor. The absolute ignorance that prevails in regard to these authors is evinced by the fact that not even a conjecture is offered that any one of them bore a name that is given in the biblical histories or genealogies. In all the writings of all these men and in all the other writings contained in the Bible, there is not a hint nor an allusion in regard to the name, place, position, or character of any of them. History knows nothing of them. Tradition knows nothing of them. The very writings attributed to them know nothing of them. The whole Bible knows nothing of them. The analysts themselves do not name a single man who they even suppose might be one of them. The argument from

silence is, at best, perhaps only presumptive, but in this case the presumption is exceedingly strong that the supposed host of authors, compilers, interpolators, and redactors had no existence. Such a presumption is to be overcome only by conclusive evidence. Such evidence in this case does not seem to be forthcoming.

6. Let it not be forgotten that a documentary hypothesis is not incompatible with the Mosaic authorship of the Pentateuch. Such an hypothesis seems to have been suggested by one who firmly held the traditional belief.[1] Principal Cave, an advocate of that belief, has suggested that Moses is the Jehovist of the critics. Truly he may have acted, as before suggested, as compiler, editor, and redactor, as well as author. The documentary hypothesis, then, even if proved, does not disprove Mosaic authorship.

We have now reviewed a number of the arguments that are urged against the traditional belief. Some of them, such as the arguments founded on the silence of succeeding books, the centralization of worship and divergences of the Mosaic laws, the non-adaptation of these to the Israelites in the wilderness, and the account of the finding of the book of the law in the time of Josiah, have not been considered. These will be attended to as we proceed in the presentation of evidence and arguments on the other side. We will present the internal evidence in the first place, and then the external.

[1] Vitringa, *Observationes Sacræ*, p. 413.

PART III
INTERNAL EVIDENCE

PART III

INTERNAL EVIDENCE

CHAPTER I

THE ADAPTATION OF THE FIVE BOOKS OF THE PENTATEUCH TO THE POSITION WHICH THEY OCCUPY IN THE SACRED VOLUME

THIS argument involves the principle that adaptation indicates design. The Pentateuch is adapted to serve as an introduction to the rest of the Bible, and each one of its five books is adapted to the place in which it is found. No change in the order of these books can be made without derangement and confusion. The displacement of the Pentateuch from its position as the introductory part of the Scriptures would produce a similar result.

Organic unity characterizes the Bible in all its parts, not excepting the Pentateuch. The Old and New Testaments are complements of one another. The New cannot be understood without the Old; the Old would be incomplete and comparatively meaningless without the New. The opening verse of Matthew involves the Old Testament history, ritual, and prophecy: "The book of the generation of Jesus Christ, the son of David, the son of Abraham."[1] Who was Christ, the Anointed, the Messiah? who was David? and who was Abraham? These questions can be answered only in the light of Old Testament history, prophecy, ritual, and types. The Epistles presuppose the Acts of the Apostles; the Acts presuppose the Gospels; the Gospels presuppose the prophecies and Psalms, the history, sacrifices, and types of the Old Testament.

Also, among the Old Testament books there is an orderly succession. This fact was recognized and is formally suggested by

[1] Matt. 1: 1.

the authors themselves. Every book after Genesis to Nehemiah begins with the copulative "And" (Hebrew, *Waw*), with but two exceptions, Deuteronomy and the First Book of Chronicles, which are in the main repetitions, and to some extent overlap preceding books. The Book of Nehemiah is no exception; for, after the title, which consists only of three words, we have the *Waw* connecting what follows with the Book of Ezra. Thus it is with all the preceding books. There is no gap left in the history, in the transition from one book to another, and with the two exceptions above mentioned (where the initial *Waw* is omitted), there is no overlapping, each book taking up the history precisely where the preceding book left it. Though Deuteronomy and Chronicles in part repeat and overlap what precedes, yet are they necessary as connecting links. They each carry the history beyond the point reached in the preceding book. The Book of Ezra takes up the historical thread just where it is dropped by Chronicles, and the Book of Joshua just where it was dropped by Deuteronomy. The initial sentence of Joshua, *And it came to pass after the death of Moses*, presupposes Deuteronomy, which closes with an account of the death and burial of Moses. In like manner Deuteronomy presupposes Numbers. Without this book there would be a gap of nearly forty years between Leviticus and Deuteronomy. Besides, Deuteronomy presupposes in another way the preceding books. In the judgment of Christendom, as the name indicates, Deuteronomy is a repetition of preceding laws, laws that are found only in the preceding books. Numbers presupposes Leviticus. It begins with "And" (*Waw*), indicative of continuation, and it takes up the history precisely where Leviticus leaves it, at the close of the account of the laws enacted at Sinai. Leviticus in turn presupposes Exodus. It has the connecting *Waw*, and at the very outset refers to the tabernacle as described in the preceding book. Leviticus is a continuation of the ritualistic legislation which is begun in Exodus. Without the latter, the former is like a bough lopped off, or a severed limb. Then again, Exodus, true to the suggestion of its copulative initial, is the continuation of the history begun in Genesis. That history relates to the chosen people, and it runs through all the books from Genesis to Nehemiah. But it was important to know who the chosen people were. They were the descendants of Abraham, and hence the life of Abraham is given. But who was Abraham? This involves the origin of mankind and their division into races and nations, and, as a preface to the whole, a brief account of the origin of the world is given. Thus Genesis stands properly as the first book of the Pentateuch and of the whole Bible.[1] It brings the history of the peculiar people down to their happy settlement in Egypt and the death of Jacob. Then Exodus takes up the story and gives a history of the oppression, the deliverance, and the earliest legislation. Leviticus continues the record of the legislation. Numbers relates the thirty-eight years' wandering in the wilderness and accounts for the failure of the Israelites to march on to the promised land. Then Deuteronomy gives a review of the history and the legislation, and closes with an account of Moses' viewing the promised land from the top of Pisgah and of his death and burial.

Thus every book of the Pentateuch is in its proper place. Each would be out of place anywhere else than where it is. Now adaptation and orderly arrangement suggest preparation and design. Reverent and thoughtful minds are not disposed to think that things exist or happen by chance. The hat is adapted to the head. The hat, then, was made for the head, and the head is before the hat in the order of existence. Paul teaches that the woman was created for the man.[2] Then the man was before the woman. Now each book of the Pentateuch is precisely adapted to the place it occupies. Exodus is adapted to follow Genesis; hence the natural conclusion is that it was intended to follow Genesis, and that Genesis was first in the order of existence. It is not natural, it is almost unreasonable, to suppose that some author first wrote Exodus, and then that the same or another author wrote another book adapted to go before the other. So of all the books of the Pentateuch. Deuteronomy is adapted to the place it occupies. It is not suited to precede Numbers, nor immediately to follow Leviticus. It is natural and reasonable to conclude that it was intended to be the fifth book of the Pentateuch.

But the hypothesis of the analysts is, that Deuteronomy was written first, and that the other books were not written till several hundred years afterward. It is, perhaps, conceivable that the orderly arrangement of the Pentateuchal books and the adaptation of each to its place were the work of editors, com-

[1] Kuenen says, speaking of the Hexateuch, "The Book of Genesis figures as an indispensable introduction" (*Hexateuch*, p. 4). [2] I. Cor. 11 : 8, 9.

pilers, and redactors, who, by combining, curtailing, condensing, and expanding original documents, and by substitutions, additions, transpositions, and other emendations, worked up books nicely adjusted to each other and characterized by an admirable organic unity. It is, perhaps, conceivable that these shrewd, skillful, and far-seeing manipulators, whose wonderful handiwork, according to the hypothesis, deceived even the Lord Jesus Christ and his apostles and led the church and the world astray until the advent of Voltaire and his criticism, had not sense enough, according to the showing of the analytic critics, to remove the most palpable absurdities and most glaring contradictions from the documents which they altered and amended with so much freedom and skill. This hypothesis, we must admit, is conceivable; for critics have conceived it, though it took many minds, striving many years, to work it out. But, conceivable though it be, it is extremely improbable, and ought to be received only on the best of evidence.

But, to resume, the Pentateuchal books are nicely adjusted to one another. Each book would be incomplete without the others. Each one is adapted to the place it occupies. There is reason to believe, therefore, that each book was prepared and intended to succeed the one that precedes it, in the order in which we have them. If this be so, Deuteronomy was the last written, and the hypothesis of the analysts that the other four books were not written till the exile or after it must be abandoned.

CHAPTER II

DEUTERONOMY PRESUPPOSES OTHER PENTATEUCHAL BOOKS

THAT Deuteronomy presupposes other Pentateuchal books has already been suggested, but is worthy of further consideration.

That Deuteronomy is, in the judgment of Christendom, a repetition of previously existing laws, the name itself indicates. This is also the judgment of the analytics themselves. Reuss, speaking of Deuteronomy in the time of Josiah, says, "Il n'y avait donc là de nouveau que la form"[1] ("There was nothing new in it except the form"). Graf presents the same view, as follows: "Das Buch lehrte ja nichts an und für sich Neues, ... und der Verfasser, indem er Mose seine Ermahnungen in den Mund legte, hatte nur den Zweck, dass Jeder aufs Neue daran gemahnt würde dem alten Gesetze treu zu bleiben. ... Wie hätte auch Josia so darüber erschrecken können, dass das in diesem Buche Vorgeschriebene von den Vätern nicht beobachtet worden und darum das Volk den Zorn Jahwe's auf sich geladen, wenn er sich nicht bewusst gewesen wäre, dass ihnen diese Gebote bekannt waren?"[2] ("The book teaches nothing that is really new, ... and the composer, while he put his exhortations in the mouth of Moses, had in mind only to admonish anew every one to be faithful to the old law. ... How could Josiah have been so alarmed at non-observance, by the fathers, of the things written in this book and at the wrath of Jehovah brought upon the people by themselves, if he himself had not been aware that these commands were known to them?") Wellhausen makes similar declarations: "Die literarische Abhängigkeit des Deuteronomiums von den jehovistischen Gesetzen und Erzählungen ohnehin erwiesen und anerkannt ist"[3] ("The literary dependence of Deuteronomy on the Jehovistic laws and narratives is independently shown and is acknowledged"). Wellhausen, unwilling to admit that any of the first four books of the Pentateuch had an existence before Deuteronomy, supposes that the

---
[1] *L'Histoire Sainte*, Vol. I., Int., p. 160.
[2] *Die Geschichtlichen Bücher des Alten Testaments*, p. 25.   [3] *Prolegomena*, p. 34.

prophets had written down some of their speeches, and the priests some of their precepts, and that Deuteronomy presupposes still earlier documents and borrows materials largely from them.

Though Kuenen dogmatically asserts that "a written regulation of the cultus did not exist in the pre-Deuteronomic times,"[1] he admits that Deuteronomy is largely a repetition of what is contained in the preceding books. Some of his declarations are as follows: "Deuteronomy 2:2-23 is a free recension of Numbers 20:14-23; 21:1 sqq.; and Deuteronomy 2:24-3:11, of Numbers 21:21-25. Beneath Deuteronomy 3:12-20 lies the same conception of the settlement in the transjordanic district which we find in Numbers 32. With regard to the events at Sinai, Deuteronomy 5, 9, 10 reproduce the representations of Exodus 19, 24, 32, 34."[2]

Many other such statements are made by this author. He, of course, does not *mean* that Deuteronomy refers to and quotes Exodus and Numbers, yet such are his declarations. According to the rigid law of criticism laid down by the analytic critics, Kuenen's book on the Pentateuch must have been written by two authors, or at least been worked over by a redactor. Though he, of course, stoutly maintains that Exodus and Numbers came into existence centuries after Deuteronomy, he makes various declarations which literally affirm the fact that the latter refers to and quotes from the former.

The fact thus admitted by the leaders of the analytic school of critics, that the laws contained in the middle books of the Pentateuch are recognized in Deuteronomy by repetition, quotation, reproduction, and reference, demonstrates the prior existence of these laws, and also suggests, and at least renders probable, the prior existence of the books containing them.

To escape the latter conclusion, the analytic critics maintain that the Deuteronomist did not refer to, quote, and reproduce laws as they are contained in the middle books, but as contained in older documents that have perished. But the existence of such documents is a mere hypothesis, and is one of the points in dispute. Thus we have here one hypothesis brought in and employed to help prove another. To this procedure, so vicious from a logical point of view, there are serious objections. In the first place, the laws as reproduced in Deuteronomy are found in

---

[1] *Hexateuch*, p. 273. [2] *Hexateuch*, p. 169.

the middle books, as is admitted; and they are found nowhere else. They are not found in the prophetic books, nor in any known document other than the middle books of the Pentateuch. Of the many books referred to and quoted in Chronicles, it is not claimed that any of them contained the laws reproduced in Deuteronomy. If the Deuteronomist did not reproduce these laws from Exodus and Numbers, he copied them from an utterly unknown book, by an utterly unknown author.

Besides, there are clear indications that the laws as contained in Deuteronomy are of a later form than as contained in Exodus and Numbers. Take, as an example, the legislation in regard to the avenger of blood and the cities of refuge. In Exodus it is simply provided that there should be a place of refuge for the unintentional homicide, and that the altar should be no protection to the willful murderer.[1] In Numbers it is enacted that there shall be six cities of refuge, three on each side of the Jordan, and regulations are established for the treatment both of intentional and unintentional manslayers.[2] In the fourth chapter of Deuteronomy there is an account of the actual appointment of three cities of refuge east of the Jordan, and their names are given.[3] This was done at the time when the Israelites were in possession only of the transjordanic portion of Canaan. Further on in Deuteronomy the appointment of three cities of refuge in western Canaan is enjoined, together with the construction of roads to facilitate the flight of the manslayer. There is also this additional regulation, that in case of the future enlargement of territory three additional cities of refuge should be appointed. Another supplementary regulation set forth in this passage is the intervention of the elders in the trial of cases as the representatives of the congregation.[4] Then, in Joshua the record is completed by the account of the appointment of three refuge cities in west Palestine. Thus the progressive history of the institution of refuge cities and of the legislation pertaining thereto proves that what is contained in Deuteronomy on this subject presupposes and continues what is contained in Numbers.

The institution of the Passover furnishes a similar illustration. We have the first account of it in Exodus, where many laws are enacted with regard to it.[5] In Leviticus it is referred to as already a well-known institution,[6] and is mentioned in order to

---

[1] Ex. 21 : 13, 14.   [2] Num. 35 : 11-29.   [3] Deut. 4 : 41-43.
[4] Deut. 19 : 1-13.   [5] Ex. 12 : 1-28.   [6] Lev. 23 : 4-8.

be placed on a legal footing along with the other feasts. Again, in Numbers the Passover is referred to as being well-known, and as being kept according to laws previously enacted;[1] yet there is supplementary legislation in Numbers on this subject. It is enacted that those who, by reason of uncleanness, or by reason of being on a journey, could not keep the Passover on the fourteenth day of the first month should keep it on the fourteenth day of the second. Deuteronomy also contains supplementary legislation on this subject. In Exodus, while as yet the tabernacle had no existence, the Israelites were allowed to kill and eat the passover at their own homes. In Leviticus, after the erection of the tabernacle, it was enacted that the Israelite should kill neither ox, nor lamb, nor goat, either in the camp or out of it, but should bring all animals for slaughter to the door of the tabernacle.[2] But the tabernacle in the wilderness was constantly moving from one place to another, hence the place of sacrifice and of killing the paschal lamb was constantly changing. What, then, was to be done when the Israelites should be settled in Canaan, and the tabernacle cease to wander and be fixed in one place, and many Israelitish families be living at great distances from it? This emergency is provided for by supplementary legislation in Deuteronomy. It mentions the Passover as established and known, enjoins its observance (without mentioning on what day of the month), and prescribes that in Canaan the place of observance should be that chosen for sacrifice and worship.[3] This supplementary regulation implies and presupposes the legislation contained in the preceding books on the same subject.

Again, Exodus forbids the loaning of money on interest to Hebrews, but says nothing about foreigners.[4] Leviticus forbids the loaning of money or of *food* on interest to a poor Israelite or a poor sojourning stranger, but is silent in regard to foreigners in general.[5] Deuteronomy forbids the lending of money, food, or anything to a Hebrew on interest, but allows the lending on interest to foreigners in general.[6] We have here repetition, but also supplementary additions. Exodus forbids the charging of interest on money. Leviticus forbids it on money *and food*. Deuteronomy forbids it on money, food, *and everything else*. Here is progress in legislation, suggesting the order of enact-

[1] Num. 9 : 1-5.   [2] Lev. 17 : 3, 4.   [3] Deut. 16 : 1-8.
[4] Ex. 22 : 25.   [5] Lev. 25 : 35-37.   [6] Deut. 23 : 19, 20.

ment as being the same as that of the books of Exodus, Leviticus, and Deuteronomy.

Once more, two entire chapters (one hundred and sixteen verses) of Leviticus are taken up with the subject of leprosy, giving minute directions as to how it is to be detected and treated.[1] Deuteronomy contains but one verse in regard to this subject, as follows: "Take heed in the plague of leprosy, that thou observe diligently, and do according to all that the priests the Levites shall teach you: as I commanded them, so ye shall observe to do."[2] This is an exact reference to the laws in Leviticus, which were extensive and minute, and were committed to Aaron and his successors.[3] Take another example of progressive legislation: In Numbers it is enacted that the death penalty shall not be inflicted on the testimony of *one* witness; there must be witnesses, but how many is not specified.[4] This law is supplemented in Deuteronomy with two additions, one of which fixes the minimum number of witnesses at not less than two, and the other requires the witnesses to be foremost in the execution.[5]

Thus it is shown that the laws are reproduced in Deuteronomy in their complete and latest form, and that the laws as set forth in Numbers and Exodus are clearly in their earlier and less complete form. This fact clearly proves that the middle books preceded Deuteronomy in time, unless it can be shown that the laws and history reproduced in Deuteronomy were copied from another source. Of our argument, then, this is the sum:

1. Deuteronomy is largely a reproduction of preëxisting laws.
2. These are found in Exodus and Numbers, and are found nowhere else.
3. The literary dependence of Deuteronomy on these middle books, or on what is contained in them, is thus demonstrated, and is also admitted by some of the analytic school.
4. Deuteronomy reproduces the laws in supplemented and extended, and hence *later*, forms. Exodus and Numbers set forth these laws evidently in their earlier forms.
5. It is natural and logical to conclude that the books which contain the laws in their older form are the older books, and the book which reproduces these laws in their later form is the later book.
6. The opposite opinion, namely, that Deuteronomy pre-

[1] Chs. 13, 14. [2] Deut. 24: 8. [3] Lev. 13: 2. [4] Num. 35: 30. [5] Deut. 17: 6, 7.

ceded Exodus and Numbers, involves the conclusion that the writer of these two books recorded the laws in their more ancient form for the purpose of deceiving mankind in regard to the time of his writing. How very shrewd, skillful, and far-seeing he must have been, though not entirely honest!

As an offset to these undeniable facts the analytic critics bring in an hypothesis, or rather a series of hypotheses equal in number to the plagues of Egypt. That Deuteronomy was unknown until the time of King Josiah, is an hypothesis; that the preceding books were not written until several centuries afterward, is an hypothesis; that before Josiah's time there were documents in circulation, but which afterward perished, that embodied much of the history and legislation contained in Exodus and Numbers, is an hypothesis; that these documents were amalgamated in time into one, is an hypothesis; and there are many points that come in as hypotheses subsidiary to the above. The authors and amalgamators, editors and redactors, of these documents are utterly unknown; their names are not even conjectured. The existence of these writers and their writings is, at best, a mere matter of inference, and is a subject of dispute.

Now, this bringing in of mere hypotheses in order to set aside the fact that Deuteronomy does in reality reproduce much of the history and legislation recorded in Exodus and Numbers, is not a procedure that will commend itself to the sober judgment of thinking men. Such argumentation may be interesting and convincing to critics, who have an overweening confidence in their own methods, but will assuredly be repudiated in the end by the common sense and logical thinking of mankind. Since every subsidiary hypothesis is a weak point, it is seen that the analytic theory and argumentation are largely made up of weak points.

CHAPTER III
STYLE

WE have already dealt with the objection that the Pentateuch is written in different styles, and therefore could not have been written by Moses or any other single author. In reply, we showed that many authors have employed different styles at the same period of life, and that many an author has varied in style at different periods of life. The literary activity of Moses may have continued eighty years, or longer. Owing to his varied and wonderful experiences, the varied subjects of which he treated, and his surpassing and versatile talents, there need be no difficulty in believing that his style, both in thought and in diction, varied with his age and circumstances, mood and subject. Certainly, so far as style of language is concerned, he may have written the Pentateuch. He undoubtedly spoke and wrote the Hebrew language in its purity. The parting address,[1] the Ninetieth Psalm, the song at the Red Sea, and other compositions that are expressly ascribed to him,[2] are not failures in point of diction. We do not, however, forget that our critics deny that Moses is the author of any of these compositions. They indeed call attention to the fact that the Pentateuch nowhere calls itself by his name, and is not ascribed to him as its author; yet, in the case of compositions that are directly and expressly ascribed to him, they do not hesitate to declare the record false. But, after all, they admit that in the Pentateuch we have some genuine Mosaic productions—the book of the covenant, perhaps,[3] or other groups of laws, though they claim that it cannot be certainly known what Moses did actually write; but, most assuredly, whatever he wrote was in pure Hebrew, like the rest of the Pentateuch. The fact that the critics have difficulty in deciding in their own minds what Moses wrote, indicates that the Hebrew of Moses and of the Mosaic age is the Hebrew of the Pentateuch. Possibly it is fear of being confronted with this

[1] Deut. 32.   [2] Ex. 17:14; 24:4.   [3] Ex. 20:1–23:33.

troublesome fact that makes some of the critics so cautious about admitting that there is anything in the Pentateuch that Moses wrote. Driver does indeed venture to say that the song at the Red Sea is probably Mosaic; but Professor Cheyne, who is a faithful follower of the analysts, calls this declaration "a startling phenomenon," and "hesitates to contemplate the consequences which might possibly follow from the acceptance of this view."[1] What this critic so much dreaded is the damage that might be done to the post-Mosaic theory of the analysts. They guard that theory more carefully than watch-dogs, and they recognize the fact that the admission of the decalogue, or of anything else contained in the Pentateuch, to be of Mosaic origin or of the Mosaic age involves conclusions in regard to the state of the Hebrew language of that period that conflict with their views. Arguing as they do about style, they must maintain that there was a marked change in the language during the time between Moses and Josiah, a period of more than eight hundred years. As their hypothesis is that Deuteronomy first appeared in Josiah's time, and the four preceding books during the exile or after it, for the sake of their theory they feel constrained to maintain that Moses wrote nothing contained in the Pentateuch. They may admit that Moses originated some of the Pentateuchal laws, but they must insist that they were recodified and recast in post-Mosaic Hebrew.

But after all the care and caution exercised by these critics, the argument from style may be turned against them. The first four books, according to their hypothesis, originated at a time when the Hebrew language had begun to take on Aramaic corruptions. Jeremiah's style is not purely Hebraic, though he was contemporary with King Josiah. One entire verse is in Aramaic.[2] In Ezra and Daniel there are long Aramaic passages. There are Aramaic words and idioms in many other of the later books. They are found, or at least claimed, in Chronicles, Ecclesiastes, Canticles, Ruth, Proverbs, and later Psalms. Professor W. R. Smith says that such writers as the authors of Chronicles and Ecclesiastes use "Aramaic words and idioms which would have puzzled Moses and David."[3]

Now the question for these critics to answer is this: How is the fact to be accounted for that the Pentateuch is free from

---

[1] *Founders of Old Testament Criticism*, p. 265. [2] Jer. 10:11.
[3] *Old Testament in the Jewish Church*, p. 48.

Aramaisms if Deuteronomy was written in the time of Josiah and Jeremiah and the other books were gotten up in the time of Ezra and Nehemiah? We have not very much confidence in these linguistic arguments, but it seems to us that these books must all have originated a good while before exilic times in order to escape Aramaisms which, to use Professor Smith's phrase, would have proved a puzzle to Moses as well as David. To be sure, according to the documentary hypothesis, E, J, and P may have lived and written early enough to retain the purity of the earlier Hebrew style, but how about the editors, revisers, and redactors who worked up the supposed ancient documents into the first four Pentateuchal books as we now have them? Why were no Aramaic peculiarities thrust into the text by these officious manipulators, who are supposed to have been the contemporaries of Ezra?

CHAPTER IV

JOURNALISTIC FORM

A CONSIDERATION of more importance than that of mere style, as bearing on the question of the age of the Pentateuch, is the journalistic form of certain portions of it. The book as a whole is certainly not a journal, but some portions of it give evidence of having been written from time to time, just as the events recorded in them occurred. Portions of the Pentateuch—the Book of Genesis, for instance—could not have been thus written, and have neither the form nor appearance of a journal. A journal records only what the writer himself sees and hears, or experiences in some other way. Of course, then, much of the Pentateuch was not thus written. But from the exodus to the close of the wandering many events might be recorded in this way. And, as a matter of fact, the removal of the camp from place to place, the speaking of God to Moses, the enactment of laws, and many other events appear just as if set down in the order and at the time of their occurrence in a journal kept by Moses, or one of his contemporaries. Take, as an example, the account of the marching of the Israelites in the desert: "These are the journeys of the children of Israel, which went forth out of the land of Egypt with their armies under the hand of Moses and Aaron. And Moses wrote their goings out according to their journeys by the commandment of the Lord: and these are their journeys according to their goings out."[1] In the declaration that "Moses wrote their goings out according to their journeys" it is clearly implied that Moses kept a journal. Then follows the journal, or extracts from it. The date of the exodus is first given—the fifteenth day of the first month. Then follows a list of marches and stations: Rameses, the starting-point; first encampment, Succoth; second encampment, Etham; third, Migdol; fourth, Marah,—forty-one encampments in all. The journalistic form is maintained throughout: From Rameses to Succoth; from Succoth to Etham; from Etham to Midgol; from

[1] Num. 33: 1-49.

Migdol to Marah; thus on and on until the arrival at Jordan, near Jericho, in the plains of Moab.

There are traces of journalistic composition elsewhere in the Pentateuch. After the defeat of the Amalekites, the record is, "And the Lord said unto Moses, Write this for a memorial in a book."[1] A correct rendering requires the definite article — "*the* book." Not long after the affair of the Amalekites, we read of Moses delivering the words of the Lord orally, but also of his committing these words to writing. "And Moses came and told the people all the words of the Lord, and all the judgments: . . . And Moses wrote all the words of the Lord."[2] "And Moses wrote this law."[3] "Now therefore write ye this song for you, and teach it the children of Israel"[4] (God's command to Moses). "And it came to pass, when Moses had made an end of writing the words of this law in a book, until they were finished, that Moses commanded the Levites, which bare the ark of the covenant of the Lord, saying, Take this book of the law, and put it in the side of the ark of the covenant of the Lord your God."[5]

The analytics admit that many passages in the Pentateuch purport to have been written as a journal. Reuss, speaking of the Pentateuch, says, "It is composed in such a manner that one may regard it in great part as the journal of Moses, in which he intermingles the recital of events and the texts of laws, with scarcely any rational order."[6] And again: "If the history of the emigration had been written by Moses himself, and if the code which is framed into this history had been composed by him, it would be very necessary to admit that we have the journal of the prophet. That alone would explain the incoherence of the matters treated of in it and the absence of all systematic order in the innumerable articles of laws, everywhere connected with certain localities or to certain epochs of the sojourn in the desert. The idea of a journal is everywhere recommended by two facts which will not fail to be used in its support. If the narrative part is detached from what pertains to the legislation properly so-called, an almost continuous narrative will be obtained of the life of Moses from his birth till his death, in an order which may be called chronological, and often determined by precise dates. On the other hand, the numerous repetitions and contradictions in the legislative part lose in their actual form

---

[1] Ex. 17 : 14.   [2] Ex. 24 : 3, 4.   [3] Deut. 31 : 9.
[4] Deut. 31 : 19.   [5] Deut. 31 : 24-26.   [6] *L'Histoire Sainte*, Int., p. 159.

whatever is embarrassing to us; because it may be admitted that in a considerable space of time many a prescription might be repeatedly inculcated, or even changed, according to the necessities of the moment, or in consequence of a more exact appreciation of the means of execution."[1]

In regard to these declarations, for the present we only remark that they pretty clearly indicate that the real reason why Reuss did not fully accept the journal theory, as applied to considerable portions of the Pentateuch, was his opposition to its Mosaic origin.

The journalistic feature of the Pentateuch is recognized also by Wellhausen, though not in express terms. In speaking of what he calls "the breaking of the joints of the narrative by the enormous growth of the legal contents," he says, "Und in dieser Weise gehört die Thora hinein in die Geschichtsdarstellung, nicht nach ihrem Stoff als Inhalt irgend eines Kodex, sondern nach ihrer Form als das berufsmässige Thun Mose's"[2] ("In this way the Tora enters into the historical representation, not according to its matter as contents of a code, but according to its form as the professional doings of Moses").

Here we have the essential features of a journal—the laws presented, not in a body, as finally completed, but as they were issued from time to time by Moses. We do not quote Wellhausen as saying that any part of the Pentateuch consists of matter taken from a journal kept by Moses. As a matter of course, such an admission by him is not to be expected. He means only that some unknown person, designated by the symbol PC, shrewdly put his writing, long after the time of Moses, into the form of a journal, in order to deceive his readers. Hence he speaks of "the appearance of historical reality which the priestly code creates by its learned art."[3] Kuenen suggests the same view. He admits that many texts concur with Deuteronomy 30: 9 in testifying that Moses committed to writing chapters 5 to 26 of that book, but he immediately suggests that this may be "a literary artifice."[4]

This much may be stated, that these critics all admit that a good deal of the Pentateuch has the form and appearance of a journal, and were not the question of Mosaic authorship involved it is pretty clear that they would admit that the Penta-

---

[1] *L'Histoire Sainte*, Int., p. 126. [2] *Prolegomena*, p. 358.
[3] "Gelehrter Kunst," *Prolegomena*, p. 363. [4] *Hexateuch*, p. 15.

teuch is in this respect what it purports to be. As quoted above, Reuss says, "If the history of the emigration had been written by Moses himself, and if the code which is framed into this history had been composed by him, it would be necessary to admit that we have the journal of the prophet."[1] But may we not in turn say, that if any one kept a journal and recorded in it much that is contained in the Pentateuch it must have been Moses? The conclusion of this whole matter may be stated as follows:

1. Much of the Pentateuch is in the form of a journal. This the critics admit.

2. Much of it not only appears, but *purports*, to be a journal. The writer desired and intended that it should be so regarded. This also is admitted by the critics.

3. If the passages which purport to be from somebody's journal are not really such, the writer *practiced artifice for the purpose of deceiving*. This is also admitted by the critics.

4. It is expressly stated that some portions of the Pentateuch, among these the larger part of Deuteronomy, were committed to writing by Moses at the very time when the events related took place. If this is not true, the author of Deuteronomy is chargeable with falsehood. This, if not admitted, at least ought to be.

In view of all these facts, is it not probable that a portion of the Pentateuch is in reality a journal? This conclusion is favored by form and purport, the style of the writing, and express declarations of the Pentateuch itself. We do not claim that the book throughout is a journal, nor is this necessary to our argument. If the Book of Numbers, more than half of Deuteronomy, and portions of other books are journalistic, as they seem to be, the author must have been on the ground, recording events as they occurred; and in that case the theory which ascribes the origin of the Pentateuchal books to an author, or to authors, who lived long after the time of Moses will have to be abandoned.

[1] *L'Histoire Sainte*, Int., p. 126.

CHAPTER V

ACQUAINTANCE WITH EGYPT

Our proposition is, that the Pentateuch was written by a man who had a minute and familiar acquaintance with Egyptian affairs, and for people who had a minute and familiar acquaintance with Egyptian affairs. The establishment of this proposition will be a virtual refutation of the hypothesis of the critics concerning the origin of the Pentateuch. For a minute and familiar acquaintance with Egyptian affairs presupposes a long residence in Egypt. Moses and the Israelites had a long residence in Egypt, and before they left it had acquired a thorough knowledge of its affairs. Even the analysts have not had the hardihood as yet to deny the story of the exodus altogether. Moses and the Israelites then meet the requirements of our proposition. But if that proposition be true,—and we intend to demonstrate its truth,—the Pentateuch could have originated only in the Mosaic age. There is no evidence that E, D, J, P, and R, the supposed authors of the Pentateuch, ever lived in Egypt. Indeed, there is no evidence but an hypothesis that they ever lived at all, and there is not even an hypothesis that they ever lived in Egypt; nor is there any reason to believe that the Israelites, after the Mosaic age, were at any time minutely acquainted with Egyptian affairs.

Even on the theory of supernatural and plenary inspiration, it is not probable that any one not well acquainted with Egypt would be selected by divine wisdom to write the Pentateuch. God utilizes human knowledge and talents as far as possible. Christ's disciples, those conversant with his acts and sayings, were employed to write the Gospels. Luke, the companion of Paul, was employed to write the Acts of the Apostles. The most thoroughgoing doctrine of divine inspiration, then, would incline us to expect that the Pentateuch would prove to be written by a man who spent some time in Egypt and had an extensive and accurate knowledge of it, and not by a man, or (if the reader insists on a plurality of authors) by men, who lived at a distance from it and never saw it.

The point to be proved is, that the author of the Pentateuch possessed a minute and familiar acquaintance with Egyptian affairs, and that he assumes the same minute and familiar acquaintance on the part of those for whom it was more immediately written. We proceed to state, in proof and illustration of this proposition, a few of the many facts that might be presented for this purpose. A volume would not exhaust this subject.

1. The allusion to the Egyptian custom of shaving. "Then Pharaoh sent and called Joseph, and they brought him hastily out of the dungeon: and he shaved himself, and changed his raiment, and came in unto Pharaoh."[1]

Nearly all the races and tribes with whom the ancient Hebrews came in contact let their hair and beard grow;[2] but the Egyptians were an exception in this respect. Herodotus states that they were accustomed to let their hair grow only in time of mourning.[3] Wilkinson says that "foreigners who were taken to Egypt as slaves, having beards on their arrival, were compelled, on entering the service of Egyptian masters, to have their beards and heads shaved," and that "to be unshaven was regarded as the mark of a low condition, or of a slovenly person."[4]

Now it is to be observed that Joseph, though he was called hastily to appear before the Egyptian king, was allowed time to shave himself. No explanation is made, just as if none were needed; and there was none needed if the account was written by Moses, or in the Mosaic age, for he and the contemporary Israelites were well acquainted with the Egyptian customs and ideas, which made it necessary that Joseph should appear shaven before Pharaoh.

2. The account of the storm of hail and thunder.[5]

It was the hail, not the thunder, that constituted the plague. "And the hail smote throughout all the land of Egypt all that was in the field, both man and beast; and the hail smote every herb of the field, and brake every tree of the field."[6] From this declaration, and from the whole passage,[7] it is evident that the hail did all the damage. But though this fact is emphasized, yet Pharaoh evidently was much more alarmed by the thunder than by the hail. He exclaimed, "Entreat the Lord (for it is enough) that there be no more mighty thunderings and hail." The reply

---
[1] Gen. 41 : 14.   [2] Sayce's *Races of the Old Testament*.   [3] 2 : 36.
[4] *Ancient Egyptians*, Vol. II., pp. 326, 327.   [5] Ex. 9 : 18-26.   [6] Ex. 9 : 25.
[7] Ex. 9 : 19, 22.

of Moses was, "As soon as I am gone out of the city, I will spread abroad my hands unto the Lord; and the thunder shall cease, neither shall there be any more hail."[1] It is quite evident that it was the thunder, though harmless, that Pharaoh especially feared. He mentions in his entreaty the mighty thunderings first. Why was this? Why was Pharaoh more concerned about the harmless thunder than about the destructive hail? To those well acquainted with Egypt no explanation is needed. The fact that rain and thunder are almost unknown in Egypt makes the whole matter plain. Pharaoh had never heard thunder, at least very loud thunder, before, and it was very natural, therefore, that he should be frightened more by it than by the flashing lightning and crushing hail. But the historian says nothing about the absence of thunder and hail from Egypt, or their infrequency, taking it for granted that his readers will understand all these matters. He assumes that his readers, like himself, were familiar with the climatic peculiarities of the country of the Nile.

3. Deuteronomy 11: 10, 11: "For the land, whither thou goest in to possess it, is not as the land of Egypt, from whence ye came out, where thou sowedst thy seed, and wateredst it with thy foot, as a garden of herbs: but the land, whither ye go to possess it, is a land of hills and valleys, and drinketh water of the rain of heaven."

Here the Israelites are addressed as being familiar with the facts referred to; namely, that Egypt was a level plain, not watered by showers from heaven, but irrigated by artificial means. These facts are mentioned, not as being strange or new, but as well known, and as illustrations to show what kind of a country Canaan was. To the Israelites Egypt is the well-known, familiar country, while Canaan is *terra incognita*. This is applicable to the Israelites in the time of Moses, but at no subsequent time. It may be objected that the above passage purports to be part of an oral address of Moses to the people, and therefore forms no part of the Pentateuchal history. To this it may be replied, first, that one thing in dispute is whether Moses and the historian are the same person; and, second, that the point which we have quoted this passage to prove is clearly presented in many passages which purport to have been written by the author as historian, of which we proceed to give further illustrations.

[1] Ex. 9: 28, 29.

4. Embalming.

This process of embalming is referred to without explanation, as a custom well known both to the author and also his readers. "And Joseph commanded his servants the physicians to embalm his father: and the physicians embalmed Israel."[1] The accuracy of the author in his account of the embalming and funeral of Jacob is very remarkable, and will be mentioned hereafter. At present we only call attention to the fact that the embalming of Jacob and afterward that of Joseph[2] are mentioned as things well known. No description or explanation is given. It was to the Hebrews in general a foreign custom. Jacob and Joseph appear to have been the only Hebrews that ever were embalmed in the Egyptian manner, yet it is referred to as if it were just as well understood as burial itself. In striking contrast with this is the account of the funeral of King Asa: "And they buried him in his own sepulchers, which he had made for himself in the city of David, and laid him in the bed which was filled with sweet odors and divers kinds of spices prepared by the apothecaries' art; and they made a very great burning for him."[3] The burial of Asa was in some respects unusual, and hence there is a description of it. The author tells what the embalming in his case was. But it is not so in the account of the embalming of Jacob and Joseph. All that the author deems necessary to say in their case is that they *were embalmed*. Undoubtedly, the reason for his not giving either explanation or description is that he thought none was needed. These facts point to the time of the exodus. To the Israelites who had lived in Egypt the process of embalming was entirely familiar; but this cannot be said of the Israelites at any subsequent period.

5. The diseases prevalent in Egypt are alluded to in the Pentateuch as being well known to the Israelites. "And the Lord will take away from thee all sickness, and will put none of the evil diseases of Egypt, which thou knowest, upon thee; but will lay them upon all them that hate thee."[4] "The Lord will smite thee with the botch of Egypt, and with the emerods, and with the scab, and with the itch, whereof thou canst not be healed."[5] "Moreover he will bring upon thee all the diseases of Egypt, which thou wast afraid of; and they shall cleave unto thee."[6] "If thou wilt diligently hearken to the voice of the Lord thy

---

[1] Gen. 50 : 2. [2] Gen. 50 : 26. [3] II. Chr. 16 : 14.
[4] Deut. 7 : 15. [5] Deut. 28 : 27. [6] Deut. 28 : 60.

God, and wilt do that which is right in his sight, and wilt give ear to his commandments, and keep all his statutes, I will put none of these diseases upon thee, which I have brought upon the Egyptians: for I am the Lord that healeth thee."[1]

In all these passages the Israelites are addressed as being well acquainted with the nature and virulence of the diseases which prevailed in Egypt. They are not informed as for the first time of these diseases, but are simply reminded of what they knew well already.

6. The process of brick-making is referred to in the same way.

The use of straw in making brick, unusual in other countries, is mentioned, but not explained. The writer presumes on the knowledge of his readers.[2]

7. Cities and places in Egypt are referred to as well known.

As a general thing, cities and places are mentioned without any indication of their geographical position, and without any mark of identification, the author evidently assuming that none was needed. Where the land of Goshen was we are not informed, except that it seems to be identified with the land of Rameses. It is a matter of inference that it was in the eastern part of Egypt, as indicated in the account of the journey of Jacob and his family.[3] The writer evidently took it for granted that his readers needed no information in regard to Goshen. The residence of the Egyptian king is never once mentioned. What the capital city of Egypt was is nowhere stated. The city of On is mentioned, but no information is given concerning it. The river is mentioned repeatedly, but no name given. Pithom and Rameses are mentioned, but no further information given concerning them than that they were treasure cities, built by the Hebrews. Everywhere the writer assumes that his readers knew all about the geography of Egypt. But as soon as he begins to speak of towns and places but a little distance from Egypt and Goshen, he particularizes, describes, and identifies. The first record of the march out of Egypt is as follows: "And the children of Israel journeyed from Rameses to Succoth."[4] Succoth is another name for Pithom,[5] a fact for the knowledge of which we are indebted to antiquarians and excavators. But the writer assumes that those for whom he especially wrote needed no in-

---

[1] Ex. 15: 26. [2] Ex. 5: 6-19. [3] Gen. 46: 28, 29; 47: 11.
[4] Ex. 12: 37. [5] Sayce, *Fresh Light from the Monuments*, p. 60.

formation concerning the identity and the geographical position of these cities. The second record of the march is as follows: "And they took their journey from Succoth, and encamped in Etham, in the edge of the wilderness."[1] Here the author gives information about the position of the last-named place. In the third record of the march the geography of the places mentioned is indicated with much particularity: "Speak unto the children of Israel, that they turn and encamp before Pi-hahiroth, between Migdol and the sea, over against Baal-zephon: before it shall ye encamp by the sea."[2] This particularization begins just as soon as the Israelites are out of the land of Egypt. It is very noticeable in the references to places in Palestine as well before as after the exodus. "And Abram passed through the land unto the place of Sichem, unto the plain of Moreh."[3] "And he removed from thence unto a mountain on the east of Bethel, and pitched his tent, having Bethel on the west, and Hai on the east."[4] "And he went on his journeys from the south even to Bethel, unto the place where his tent had been at the beginning, between Bethel and Hai."[5] "Then Abram removed his tent, and came and dwelt in the plain of Mamre, which is in Hebron."[6] "Kirjath-arba; the same is Hebron in the land of Canaan."[7] "And the field of Ephron, which was in Machpelah, which was before Mamre."[8] "And Jacob came unto Isaac his father unto Mamre, unto the city of Arba, which is Hebron, where Abraham and Isaac sojourned."[9] "And they [the spies] ascended by the south, and came unto Hebron; where Ahiman, Sheshai, and Talmai, the children of Anak, were. (Now Hebron was built seven years before Zoan in Egypt.)"[10]

A comparison of the way in which places in Egypt are referred to in the Pentateuch with the way in which places in Palestine are described and identified, certainly indicates that the former were well known, the latter unknown—at least not so well known. In regard to the latter the author assumes that his readers need information, and he embraces every opportunity to give it to them. These facts are explained by the supposition that the Pentateuch was written in the Mosaic age for people who had lived in Egypt, were interested in Palestine, and yet were ignorant of its geography. These facts are accounted for in no other way. But how could a writer who had never been

[1] Ex. 13: 20. [2] Ex. 14: 2. [3] Gen. 12: 6. [4] Gen. 12: 8. [5] Gen. 13: 3.
[6] Gen. 13: 18. [7] Gen. 23: 2. [8] Gen. 23: 17. [9] Gen. 35: 27. [10] Num. 13: 22.

in Palestine be so well acquainted with its geography? To say nothing about supernatural inspiration, Moses had abundant opportunity of acquiring such information at the court of Pharaoh. There was a long war between Egypt and Canaan immediately preceding the exodus and during the reign of Rameses II., the Pharaoh of the oppression.[1] Reports of military men and travelers brought information to the Egyptian court concerning cities and places in Palestine.[2] From the Karnak inscriptions, the Tel-el-Amarna tablets, and other sources of information, it is in evidence that in the age preceding the exodus the cities and towns of Palestine were well known to the ruling class in Egypt. Jerusalem, Hebron, Salem, Gibeon, and nearly all the geographical names with which we are so familiar are mentioned in the lately exhumed Egyptian monuments.[3] Palestine was indeed an Egyptian province, governed by the deputies of Pharaoh.[4] Now, Moses, brought up in the court of Pharaoh and associating with the ruling class, would of course acquire the current information concerning the topography of Palestine. All these facts point to the author of the Pentateuch as one familiar with the topography of Egypt, knowing, indeed, the topography of Palestine, but not so familiar with it, and writing for people who knew all about Egypt, but who needed instruction concerning places in Palestine. But for preconceived views and theories these considerations would doubtless lead to the conclusion that the Pentateuch was written in the Mosaic age and by Moses himself.

[1] Sayce's *The Hittites*, pp. 24-39.
[2] Sayce's *Fresh Light from the Monuments*, pp. 57, 58.
[3] Brugsch-Bey, *Egypt Under the Pharaohs*, ch. 13; Sayce, *Fresh Light from the Monuments*, ch. 3.
[4] Sayce, *Races of the Old Testament*, pp. 101, 102.

CHAPTER VI

SCIENTIFIC ACCURACY

THE opponents of the Mosaic authorship of the Pentateuch maintain that it is characterized by inaccuracies and errors, and that, therefore, it cannot be the production of Moses. In using this argument they seem to be almost ready to assert his infallibility. At least, much of their reasoning on this point is irrelevant, except on the hypothesis that he was divinely and plenarily inspired. We now, however, take up the argument drawn from the accuracy of the Pentateuch in favor of its Mosaic authorship. We do not insist that the books which compose it, as we *now have them*, are free from error; but we maintain that these books are characterized by an accuracy far above all other ancient books,—an accuracy, indeed, that indicates that the author was guided by superhuman wisdom. This proposition, if established, will carry conviction to most minds that God and Moses were the authors of these books, as mankind have so long believed.

The account of creation in Genesis is eminently sober, truth-like, and accurate. We are not going to attempt to demonstrate that it is *perfectly* accurate. This cannot be done in the present state of human knowledge, though we confidently expect science to do this hereafter. But even now it is shown that the Mosaic account of the creation in respect to accuracy is far above every other cosmogony. The Mosaic cosmogony is, indeed, the only one that any intelligent man believes, or can believe. It is admired even by skeptical scientists for its remarkable accuracy and its deep insight into nature. In proof that it is thus admired, we quote the German scientist Haeckel, as follows:

"The Mosaic history of creation, since in the first chapter of Genesis it forms the introduction to the Old Testament, has enjoyed, down to the present day, general recognition in the whole Jewish and Christian world of civilization. Its extraordinary success is explained, not only by its close connection with

Jewish and Christian doctrines, but also by the simple and natural chain of ideas which runs through it, and which contrasts favorably with the confused mythology of creation current among most of the other ancient nations. First, the Lord God creates the earth as an inorganic body; then he separates light from darkness, then water from the dry land. Now the earth has become inhabitable for organisms, and plants are first created, animals later, and among the latter the inhabitants of the water and the air first, afterwards the inhabitants of the dry land. Finally, God creates man, the last of all organisms, in his own image and as the ruler of the earth.

"Two great and fundamental ideas, common also to the non-miraculous theory of development, meet us in this Mosaic hypothesis of creation with surprising clearness and simplicity—the idea of separation or *differentiation*, and the idea of progressive development or *perfecting*. Although Moses looks upon the results of the great laws of organic development (which we shall later point out as the necessary conclusions of the doctrine of descent) as the direct actions of a constructing Creator, yet in his theory there lies hidden the ruling idea of a progressive development and a differentiation of the originally simple matter. We can, therefore, bestow our just and sincere admiration on the Jewish law-giver's grand insight into nature and his simple and natural hypothesis of creation without discovering in it a so-called 'divine revelation.' That it cannot be such, is clear from the fact that two great fundamental errors are asserted in it, namely: first, the *geocentric* error that the earth is the fixed central point of the whole universe, round which the sun, moon, and stars move; and, secondly, the anthropocentric error that man is the premeditated aim of the creation of the earth, for whose service alone all the rest of nature is said to have been created."[1]

In regard to the two errors thus charged on Moses, we remark: (1) That the *geocentric* theory is not contained in his account of creation. There is not a word in it about the sun, moon, and stars moving round the earth. (2) He does, however, set forth the anthropocentric idea, and is justified by the facts. Man is master of all the lower animals and the subduer of the earth. He is pressing the elements and forces of nature more and more

[1] Professor Haeckel's *History of Creation* (Lankester's translation), Vol. I., pp. 37, 38.

into his service. If the earth and nature were not made for man, he is an egregious usurper. The anthropocentric theory is true, and Moses is right, notwithstanding Haeckel's assumption to the contrary. It is not strange that this skeptical scientist should endeavor to counteract his own commendation of the Mosaic cosmogony as a testimony to its divine inspiration; for it is highly improbable, scarcely credible indeed, that any merely human author in ancient times should conceive and indite so admirable an account of creation as our skeptical professor admits the first chapter of Genesis to be—"simple and natural chain of ideas"; "surprising clearness and simplicity"; "grand insight into nature"; "simple and natural hypothesis of creation"; "contrasts favorably with the confused mythology of creation current among most of the other ancient nations"; commanding the "just and sincere admiration" of the skeptical scientist, and, above all, so remarkably harmonious, as is admitted, with the teachings of modern science.

The Mosaic account of creation embraces the following points, accepted by modern scientists:

1. That the heavens and the earth—all things, nature, the universe, had a beginning.
2. That nature, the creation, is a consistent whole.
3. The existence of things at first in a state of chaos, in which there was neither light nor life.
4. That the bringing of the chaotic materials into a state of order and beauty was a progressive work.
5. The existence of light independent of the sun.
6. The formation of continents by the emergence of land from the water.
7. The existence of vegetable before animal life.
8. That the seas swarmed with life before land animals appeared.
9. That fishes, birds, beasts, and reptiles all appeared on the earth before the creation of man.
10. That man appeared as the head and master of all the lower animals.

These and other scientific truths are crowded into one short chapter. That first chapter of Genesis, like the decalogue and the Sermon on the Mount, for brevity and comprehensiveness, is unparalleled by anything outside of the Bible. Though its aim, like that of the rest of the Pentateuch and of the whole

Bible, is not to teach science, but religion and morality, yet here we have more scientific truth presented, in an unscientific way, than can be found within the same space anywhere else; and so accurate is the whole presentation, so conformed to all that modern science has discovered and demonstrated, that the only way the skeptical German professor has of meeting the argument derived from it in favor of supernatural inspiration is to charge upon it the geocentric and anthropocentric doctrines, the latter of which, however, it teaches correctly, and the former of which it does not teach at all.

Now, how did the Hebrew cosmogonist learn all these scientific truths? How was he enabled to describe so accurately the progressive series of gradations in the world's formation as to strike the modern scientist with surprise and admiration? Whence all this scientific knowledge in the author of Genesis, when there was no scientific knowledge anywhere else?

It is noticeable, further, that the first chapter of Genesis reveals profound knowledge and insight at *the very points about which science knows nothing and has nothing to say.* One of these is the origin of matter—the elements of which things are composed. Science maintains that no particle of matter ever ceases to exist, but knows nothing and says nothing as to how particles of matter came into existence. But here Genesis comes in and declares that God *created* them—created all things in the beginning. Science cannot tell how life began on the earth. It teaches that the earth was at one time red-hot, and afterward cooled so as to render life on it possible. But how did living things begin? Spontaneous generation has been demonstrated to be an unscientific dogma. Life on our earth comes only from life. Then, when there was no living thing on earth, not even a seed, how could life originate? Science is again struck dumb; but Genesis answers by declaring that plants grew out of the earth at the creative fiat of the living God. But how did the animals originate? Did some of the plants develop into animals, and thus furnish a starting-point for the animal species? To this question science gives no answer. Scientists, many of them, probably most of them, do indeed accept the hypothesis that species have been derived from species—the higher from the lower, and the lower from the lowest. But whence the lowest species? The Darwinian theory is, that all existing species have been derived from a few primordial forms; probably from one.[1] But no account is given of the origin of those few primordial forms, or that one primordial form from which all existing species are supposed to have descended. If a primordial form were mere dead matter, no living thing could be derived from it. If it were a *living* form, whence came it? To account for the origin of animal life science and scientists have nothing to propose, unless it be the exploded and discredited dogma of spontaneous generation; but the author of Genesis bridges the chasm between dead matter and animal life by declaring that living creatures were produced from the waters and the earth by the creative word and power of God.

As to the origin of man, many of the scientists, as Darwin and Haeckel, go the whole figure and suppose that mankind, as well as all other species of animals, have been derived from other species—that among the ancestors of man are to be included the monkey and the oyster. But this hypothesis has its difficulties, and even Darwin declared, "I can never reflect on them without being staggered."[2] Other scientists have been repelled by difficulties other than those which made Darwin stagger. Professor Max Müller has said that "it is inconceivable that any known animal could ever develop language,"[3] and that "language is our Rubicon, and no brute will dare to cross it."[4] Professor Mivart, whom Huxley declared to be a man of "acknowledged scientific competence,"[5] has declared the Darwinian conception of man's origin to be "utterly irrational" and "a puerile hypothesis," and has declared that "no arguments have been adduced to make probable man's origin from speechless, irrational, non-moral brutes."[6] Professor Virchow, of Germany, has said that, according to the evidence, "an ape can never become a man," and that "facts seem to teach the invariability of the human species."[7] Alfred R. Wallace, the simultaneous originator, with Darwin, of the Darwinian theory, maintains that "natural selection" is not sufficient to account for man's origin, and that his large brain, his voice, and his mental and moral powers must have been developed through the guidance of a higher power and intelligence.[8] Many similar declarations of

---

[1] Darwin's *Origin of Species*, p. 419. [2] *Origin of Species*, p. 154.
[3] Lecture, *Eclectic Magazine*, July, 1873, p. 154.
[4] *Science of Language*, First Series, p. 354. [5] *Critiques and Addresses*, p. 219.
[6] *Genesis of Species*, p. 300; *Lessons from Nature*, pp. 180, 185, 186.
[7] *Cranium of the Man and Ape*, in *Popular Science*.
[8] *Action of Natural Selection on Man*.

distinguished scientists might be quoted. Then, there is the difficulty about "the missing link." It is admitted that there is a wide gap between man and the catarrhine (perpendicular-nosed) monkeys, that are claimed by Darwin[1] and Haeckel[2] to be the nearest known human progenitors. A single link seems insufficient to bridge so wide a chasm. But not a trace of the ape-like man has been found, and the chasm is without even the semblance of a bridge. Besides, the distinguished scientist Sir John Lubbock maintains, and has succeeded in proving, that the ant, of which there are about a thousand species, ranks next to man in the scale of intelligence, and that the anthropoid apes approach nearer to him only in bodily structure.[3] It is clear, then, that the tiny race must be admitted somewhere between the monkey and the man. But, then, how shall the gap between the crawling ant and the God-like man be filled? Science, or rather the scientists, have been struggling with this problem in vain. The author of Genesis, however, solved it long ago by representing the origin of man to be different from that of other species—his body, indeed, to have been produced by derivative creation from the earth, but his soul coming directly, like a breath, from the Almighty.[4]

Thus, at the very points where science has nothing to say, and where scientists are dumb or weary themselves to no purpose, staggering under difficulties and perhaps calling each other's views irrational and puerile, or at best insufficient, the Mosaic cosmogony declares that God's creative power intervened and operated. Thus the silence of science on these points is justified, since it is not its business, but that of theology, to trace effects to the great First Cause. But how did the ancient author know the points beyond which science could not go, and in the presence of which scientists would be silent, or only differ and wrangle? Whence the knowledge and foresight that led him to locate the intervention of creative power at the origin of things, in the beginning, at the origin of life, and the origin of man's soul, and at the same time to set forth an orderly and progressive gradation in cosmic arrangements, so exactly conformed to all that science teaches on the subject? Haeckel, as we have shown, speaks of "the Jewish lawgiver's grand insight into nature," and expresses his profound admiration for it. But this

---

[1] Darwin's *Descent of Man*, pp. 153-157.
[2] Haeckel's *History of Creation*, Vol. II., pp. 270-274.
[3] *Ants, Bees, and Wasps*, p. 1. [4] Gen. 2:7.

grand insight is a fact that must be accounted for in some way. May it not be that Moses was divinely inspired and that his "grand insight into nature" came as a special gift from God? The possibility, probability, or certainty that there is a supernatural element in Genesis and the other books of the Pentateuch may be legitimately employed as an argument in favor of the Mosaic authorship. For if divine inspiration, or, in other words, if God Almighty had anything to do in the production of these books, the views of the anti-Mosaic critics must certainly be abandoned; for assuredly inspired communications from heaven would not be embodied in frauds, fictions, and historical misrepresentations and perversions.

We have called attention to the profound insight into nature brought to view in the first chapter of Genesis, and to the remarkable and admitted conformity of its declarations to the teachings of modern science. It may be said that the author of Genesis merely recorded in the first chapter some old tradition current among the people in the region of the Euphrates. It is indeed very probable, even certain, that Abram took traditions with him from Ur of the Chaldees, and possibly traditions in written form; for, according to the chronology, he was contemporary with Noah for more than fifty years, Noah was contemporary with Methuselah, who died the year of the flood, about six hundred years, and Methuselah was contemporary with Adam two hundred and forty-three years. Thus Adam could instruct Methuselah and his generation two hundred and forty-three years; Methuselah had six hundred years to transmit all that he had learned from Adam, and what he had found out for himself, to Noah and his generation, and about one hundred years to instruct Shem and his generation; Noah had about fifty years and Shem more than two hundred years to impart all their stores of knowledge to Abram and his generation.

It is thus suggested that all that Adam knew about the creation of the world and of himself and also about the garden of Eden and the fall, and all that Noah knew about the flood, may have been transmitted to Abraham and his descendants. Adam could have had no traditions concerning the creation, and whatever knowledge he and the ancient races possessed on this subject must have come originally as a special gift from God. For in primitive times, when science was unknown, the knowledge of the origin of the world and of plants and animals must have been imparted by the Almighty in some special way, or have been the result of mere conjecture. Will the ground be taken that the Mosaic cosmogony, so sober, so truth-like, and so conformed to all that science has yet been able to discover, is mere guesswork, the creation of fancy in an unscientific and unenlightened age?

We again remind the reader that we are not now maintaining that the Mosaic account of creation is perfectly accurate in a scientific sense. This cannot now be conclusively established, though its scientific accuracy is becoming more and more a matter of demonstration. The skeptical scientist from whom we have above quoted declares that "the authority of the Mosaic history as an absolutely perfect, divine revelation was destroyed" by the demonstration of the Copernican theory. As we have already said, the Mosaic books do not approve the geocentric error, though they do indeed speak of the rising and the setting of the sun, and of the apparent motion of the heavenly bodies in general, just as do all mankind, including astronomers and all other scientists.

But the conformity of the cosmogony in Genesis to truth and fact, as evinced more and more by advancing science, to the surprise and admiration even of skeptics, instead of being accounted for, is rendered more striking, by comparison with cosmogonies preserved in Babylonian and other traditions. The cosmogonies of the ancient nations in general are confused and absurd. Not one of them has been, or can be, accepted by enlightened people.

The Babylonian account of creation is perhaps the most worthy of being compared with that of Genesis. It is supposed to have been current among the dwellers along the Euphrates 2000 B.C., though copied on the tablets of Asurbanipal about 700 B.C. This cosmogony is fragmentary, confused, and obscure, yet in some points is similar to that of Genesis. It appears to speak of six days in creation, a time of chaos, the original commingling of earth and water, the production of animal life by supernatural power, and the placing of the heavenly bodies in relation to the earth.[1] This Chaldaic account of the creation and that of Genesis very likely had the same origin. The similarity between them suggests that in one sense they are the same story, the latter being the original in contents and

---

[1] George Smith, *Chaldean Account of Genesis*, pp. 61-100.

character, and the former being the mutilated and corrupt form which the story assumed when disfigured and obscured by polytheistic and pantheistic perversions and additions. But all this leaves the origin of the original story untouched, and even makes the simplicity, accuracy, and truth to nature retained in the Mosaic account all the more wonderful. If this account contains the information which God imparted originally to mankind concerning the origin of the world and of man, why was it not disfigured and obscured, shorn of its simplicity, truth, and grandeur, and thus assimilated to all the other cosmogonies current among the ancient nations? Whence the difference? And if the hypothesis of the analytic critics in regard to a plurality of Pentateuchal authors is correct, why did not some of these numerous writers, combiners, editors, compilers, revisers, interpolators, and correctors, who touched up almost everything they got their hands on, not alter and mar this grand old story of the creation?

But there are other illustrations of the scientific accuracy of the Pentateuch. The unity of the human race is now an admitted fact. The teaching of Genesis on the oneness of the human race was formerly called in question. But by the aid of chemistry, physiology, philology, ethnology, and history this truth has been triumphantly established, and is accepted by scientists and enlightened people in general. On this subject Genesis was for a long time in advance of the scientists. The original sameness of human speech is another subject in regard to which the accuracy of Genesis has been fully vindicated. We say nothing just now in regard to the story of Babel. But we call attention to the fact that what that story teaches as to the original sameness of human speech, the common origin of languages, and the relationship between them has been in very modern times established as scientific truth. The presumption seemed for a long time to be against these truths as well as against the unity and universal brotherhood of men. But after much investigation and conflict, these truths have been fully established and are generally accepted. This fact is an illustration of the scientific accuracy of the author of Genesis, and furnishes evidence that he was guided by more than human wisdom.

CHAPTER VII

HISTORICAL INTEGRITY

OPPONENTS of the Mosaic authorship of the Pentateuch have called its historical character in question. One of their arguments is that the Pentateuch is not true, and, therefore, Moses did not write it. If the argument is valid, it disproves divine inspiration; for if an untrustworthy book is not to be ascribed to Moses, much less is such a book to be ascribed to God.

We maintain, however, that the Pentateuchal history is true, and, therefore, the books containing it are divinely inspired, and that they were written by Moses. Of course, the mere truthfulness of a book does not prove that it was divinely inspired, nor that it was written by the author to whom it is ascribed. But if the Pentateuchal history is trustworthy, there is reason to believe that God had something to do in the production of the books which contain it, and that they were written by Moses, or at least that they were not gotten up by a host of nameless writers, as claimed by the analysts. We do not claim that every historical statement contained in the Pentateuch can be proved to be true by external testimony. We claim, however, that its principal statements—even those that have been objected to the most—can be thus substantiated. Much has been done to vindicate the historical accuracy and truthfulness of the Pentateuch by the discoveries of antiquarian research, and the work is still going on. New discoveries are being made almost continually. The result of every fresh discovery that bears on the question is to demonstrate, or to render probable, some statement in the Pentateuchal history. Every difficulty and all possible doubts have not as yet been removed; but, judging by what has already been accomplished, we have reason to believe that, ere long, the discoveries of the Egyptologists and other archæologists, together with what is known from history and tradition, will have convinced all, except stubborn doubters, that the Pentateuch is entirely trustworthy as a book of history.

1. Genesis does not very definitely fix the place of man's

origin, but by implication it was near the garden of Eden, the place of his earliest residence. This is placed by the record "eastward in Eden," somewhere in the region of the Euphrates.[1] This account of the place of man's origin has not, indeed, been universally accepted. Darwin was disposed to place "the cradle of the human race" in Africa, for the reason that the catarrhine monkeys, from which he supposed men to be descended, had their early home in that continent.[2] Haeckel, though agreeing with Darwin in holding that "man has developed out of the *Catarrhini*," suggests that the primeval home of the human race was in Lemuria, an imaginary continent connecting Asia and Africa, supposed to be now lying under the Indian Ocean, but formerly inhabited by Lemurian apes.[3] But history, tradition, and current opinion point to Asia as the original home of mankind. The region of the Euphrates evidently was the home of the earliest civilization and presumably of primitive men. As investigation goes on, this opinion receives additional confirmation, and is now generally accepted by mythologists, philologists, historians, antiquarians, and ethnographers. Thus the evidence is shown to preponderate in favor of the Mosaic account of the place of man's origin, early home, and geographical distribution.

2. The Mosaic account of man's primitive condition also receives confirmation from current tradition. Lenormant declares that "the idea of the Edenic happiness of the first human beings constitutes one of the universal traditions,"[4] and that belief in a primeval age of human innocence and happiness prevailed not only among the Semitic races, but among the Aryans, as well, Chaldeans, Assyrians, Egyptians, Persians, Indians, Greeks, and ancient nations in general. Little need be said on this point, inasmuch as the primeval state of innocence and happiness is presupposed by the subject to which we shall immediately advert.

3. The fall of man into a state of sin and suffering is another point in regard to which the statements of Genesis are corroborated by traditions almost universally current among mankind. Some of the ancient nations, as the Hindus and Greeks, represented the primeval state of innocence as a golden age, and these, of course, conceived of the fall as an age of declension,

---

[1] Gen. 2: 8, 14. [2] *Descent of Man*, p. 155.
[3] *History of Creation*, Vol. II., pp. 326, 400. [4] *Beginnings of History*, p. 67.

and as a gradual lapse from virtue and happiness. But more generally the fall is represented as a single event, similar to the eating of the fruit of the tree of knowledge, as related in Genesis. Of this there are many examples. Speaking of the trees that are represented in the Assyrian sculptures, Layard says, "The sacred tree, or tree of life, so universally recognized in Eastern systems of theology, is called to mind, and we are naturally led to refer the traditions connected with it to a common origin." In a foot-note he adds, "We have the tree of life of Genesis, and the sacred tree of the Hindus, with its accompanying figures — a group almost identical with the illustrations of the fall in our old Bibles."[1] Lenormant remarks that this emblem is presented on the Babylonian cylinders as frequently as in bas-reliefs in the Assyrian palaces, and says, "It is difficult not to connect this mysterious plant with the famed trees of life and knowledge which play so important a part in the story of the first sin."[2] The ancient Persian tradition is suggested in the Zend-Avesta by the declaration that "Agra-mainyus, who is full of death, in opposition to the works of the good God, created a great serpent and winter, through the agency of the demons."[3] In some of the later parts of the Zend-Avesta, the story of the fall is given with variations. Apples, a woman, and the author of all evil figure in the fall as related in the Scandinavian Edda.[4] The Greek traditions of Pandora and of the garden of the Hesperides, with its golden apples guarded by a dragon, may with propriety be regarded as an altered and variant story of the garden of Eden and of the fall.

4. The deluge.

The traditions of this event are nearly universal. They are found among all mankind, with the exception of the black races.[5] Though perhaps no reason can be assigned why such traditions are not found among the African races, the evidence is none the less strong for the reality of the deluge than if their prevalence were absolutely universal. Without detailing the traditions as prevalent among the Babylonians, Assyrians, Hindus, Persians, Phrygians, Greeks, Scandinavians, Cherokees, Mexicans, Aztecs, Toltecs, and other races and tribes in the Old and the New World, we will call attention only to that of Babylonia. Of this there are two versions, one given by Berosus, a

---

[1] *Nineveh and Its Remains*, p. 356. [2] *Beginnings of History*, p. 83.
[3] *Vendidad*, 1 : 5-8. (Spiegel's German translation, pp. 61, 62.)
[4] *Beginnings of History*, p. 81. [5] *Beginnings of History*, p. 382.

Babylonian, who wrote probably about 300 B.C. He was the priest of Bel, and in that capacity had access (it is supposed) to the public archives. The similarity between his account of the flood and that contained in Genesis is very striking. Berosus relates that Xisuthrus was divinely warned beforehand of the impending deluge and was commanded to build a huge vessel and to take with him into it his family and friends, and also every species of land animals, together with a sufficient supply of food. He further relates that Xisuthrus obeyed the divine command, built the vessel, and placed in it his wife, children, and friends, who with himself were alone of all mankind saved from drowning. He states that after the waters had begun to abate Xisuthrus sent out birds from the ship, to ascertain whether the ground was yet dry, and that the ship finally landed on a mountain in Armenia, and that the people in that region scraped off the bitumen for charms and antidotes to poison.[1]

The other Babylonian account of the deluge, deciphered from the cuneiform tablets by the celebrated George Smith, is more ancient than that of Berosus. These tablets were copies made by Asurbanipal, the Assyrian king, about 700 B.C. The original tablets are believed to date back at least to the seventeenth century B.C. They existed, therefore, almost as far back as the time of Abraham. The traditions were, of course, older than the tablets on which they were printed. This tablet account harmonizes still more closely with Genesis than does that of Berosus. The divine premonition of the deluge and the command to build the ark, or ship; the caulking of it with bitumen or pitch; the collection of the animals and of the food; the advent of the waters; the floating of the vessel; the sending out of the birds; the landing on the mountain — in all these and in some other points there is entire agreement.[2] There are some discrepancies. Genesis makes the dimensions of the ark to be three hundred cubits in length, fifty in breadth, and thirty in height. The tablets make it six hundred cubits long, sixty cubits broad, and sixty high; according to Berosus, it was five stadia long (five-eighths of a mile) and two stadia (or a quarter of a mile) wide, height not given. The tablet account states that the deluge culminated in seven days; Genesis, in one hundred and fifty. Berosus states that three birds were sent out of

[1] Cory's *Ancient Fragments*, pp. 56-63.
[2] Smith's *Chaldean Account of Genesis*, pp. 263-294; Lenormant's *Beginnings of History*, pp. 575-588.

the ark, without naming them; the tablet names them—dove, swallow, and raven; and Genesis mentions only the raven and the dove, but states that the dove was sent out twice. Berosus mentions the landing of the ship on a mountain in Armenia; the tablets mention the mountain Nizir as the landing-place; and Genesis mentions the mountains of Ararat. The two Babylonian accounts call the builder of the vessel Xisuthrus; Genesis calls him Noah. The Babylonian accounts are disfigured with polytheistic notions, while of course Genesis recognizes but one God.

These differences, however, suggest that all these accounts have a common origin, and that the one contained in Genesis is the original and true account. It must have originated before polytheism became prevalent, if it is to be regarded as traditional at all, while the polytheistic corruptions manifest in the Babylonian accounts mark them as later variations of an older account. So, too, of the dimensions of the vessel as given in these three accounts, Genesis making the length three hundred cubits, the tablets making it twice as great (six hundred cubits, nearly a quarter of a mile), and Berosus making it eleven times greater—five furlongs (five-eighths of a mile), and two furlongs in breadth (a quarter of a mile). These facts are just such as we should expect on the hypothesis that the tablet account is later than that of Genesis, and that the account given by Berosus is still later.

Thus the Mosaic account of the deluge is corroborated in all its points by the almost universally prevalent traditions of mankind, and by traditions that are shown to have been in existence not very long after the time given as that of the deluge itself.

5. The confusion of tongues.

The story of the tower of Babel is also corroborated by tradition, but not so fully as that of the deluge. Josephus quotes a sibylline tradition, as follows: "When all men were of one language and one speech, some of them built a high tower, as if they would thereby ascend up to heaven; but the gods sent storms of wind and overthrew the tower and gave every one his peculiar language; and for this reason it was that the city was called Babylon."[1] Precisely the same tradition is given by Abydenus, as quoted by Eusebius: "They say that the first inhabitants of the earth, glorying in their own strength and size,

---

[1] *Antiquities*, 1 : 4 : 3.

and despising the gods, undertook to build a tower, whose top should reach the sky, upon that spot where Babylon now stands. But when it approached the heaven, the winds assisted the gods and overturned the work upon its contrivers (its ruins are said to be at Babylon), and the gods introduced a diversity of tongues among men, who till that time had all spoken the same language. And a war arose between Kronos (that is, Saturn) and Titan; and the place in which they built the tower is now called Babylon on account of the confusion of the languages; for confusion is by the Hebrews called Babel."[1]

Besides these traditions, the account of the building of Babel is confirmed by a number of facts and coincidences. Centralization was the aim of the Babel-builders, and even before their time Sargon, the king of Accad, aimed at universal empire. After his conquest of Syria, "he appointed that all places should form a single kingdom." Long afterward, in the century before the exodus, there was a partial realization of this dream of consolidation in the prevalence of one literary language throughout western Asia. This language was the Babylonian, which, it may be added, was at that time almost identical with that of Canaan, called Hebrew. The country where the tower was built is one of brick and bitumen, not of stone. Correspondingly Genesis states, "They had brick for stone, and slime [bitumen] had they for mortar."[2] The fragment of a tablet found by George Smith tells "how small and great mingled the holy mound in Babylon and how the god in anger destroyed the secret design of the builders and made strange their counsel."[3]

6. The expedition of Chedorlaomer into Palestine, as related in the fourteenth chapter of Genesis.

Sayce claims that this account has been proved to be historical. He says, "Oriental archæology has vindicated its authenticity in a remarkable way and disproved the ingenious skepticism of a hasty criticism." We refer the reader to his discussion of this subject.[4]

7. Besides the confirmation of particular narratives as presented above, the archæologists have furnished, and are still furnishing, evidence of the truth of the Pentateuchal history in

[1] Cory's *Ancient Fragments*, p. 55.   [2] Gen. 11:3.
[3] Smith's *Chaldaic Account of Genesis*, p. 160; Sayce, *Fresh Light from the Monuments*, pp. 35, 36.
[4] *Fresh Light from the Monuments*, pp. 44-47; *Higher Criticism and the Monuments*, pp. 161-169.

general. They report nothing that contradicts it, or is in any way inconsistent with it. Their discoveries, so far as they bear on the Pentateuchal history, demonstrate either its certainty, or probability, or possibility. The monuments do not, indeed, furnish a biography of Abraham, but the site of Ur, his native city, has been discovered, and it is claimed that the contract-tablets found there contain the names of Abram, Sarah, and Milcah. It is in evidence, too, that polytheism prevailed in that ancient city, as suggested in Joshua 24: 2. The archæologists do not report that they find the name of Melchizedek on any of the tablets, but they testify that they find that in the century before the exodus there reigned in Uru-salem (*city of the god of peace*) a priestly king, who, though subject to Pharaoh, king of Egypt, was not appointed nor confirmed by his authority, but claimed to rule by the authority of the God-king on Mount Moriah.[1] This royal priest, styled Ebedtob, might well be the successor of Melchizedek, king of Salem, and priest of the most high God.[2] The name *Bethel* (*house of God*) is not given in the monuments as a place where Abraham or Jacob worshiped, but they give the significant names *Jacob-el* and *Joseph-el* as designating places in Palestine.[3] It is in evidence that the Hyksos kings were expelled from Egypt, and were succeeded by a new dynasty about the time in which, according to Exodus, "there arose up a new king over Egypt, which knew not Joseph."[4] It is ascertained that a famine, lasting many years, occurred during the time of the Hyksos.[5] It is agreed among Egyptologists that Rameses II. was the Pharaoh of the oppression, and his son, Menephtah II., the Pharaoh of the exodus.[6] The mummy of the former has been discovered, and is on exhibition in Egypt; the mummy of the latter, whose army was overwhelmed in the Red Sea, has not as yet been heard of. Pithom, one of the store-cities[7] built by the Israelites for the king of Egypt, has been discovered—enormous brick walls enclosing a space of about fifty-five thousand square yards. These walls furnish evidence of the truth of the historical statement that the Egyptian oppressors refused straw to the Israelites for the making of brick.[8] Naville, using the words of another, says: "I carefully examined the chamber walls, and I noticed that some of the

---

[1] Sayce, *Higher Criticism and the Monuments*, pp. 174-178. [2] Gen. 14: 18.
[3] *Higher Criticism and the Monuments*, p. 337. [4] Ex. 1: 8.
[5] Brugsch-Bey, *Egypt Under the Pharaohs*, pp. 121, 122.
[6] *Idem*, p. 318. [7] Ex. 1: 11. [8] Ex. 5: 7-19.

corners of the brickwork throughout were built of bricks *without straw*. I do not remember to have met anywhere in Egypt bricks so made. In a dry climate like Egypt it is not necessary to burn the bricks; they are made of Nile mud and dried in the sun. Straw is mixed with them to give them coherence."[1] Succoth, the first stage in the exodus of the Israelites,[2] has been identified as the civil name for Pithom and the country lying around it.[3] The other store-city, built for Pharaoh by the Israelites (Rameses), is mentioned in the papyri, and has been identified with Phacus.[4] At the time of the oppression and of the exodus there was in Egypt a numerous and heterogeneous race of tributaries and captives, who were much in the same condition of bondage and degradation with the Hebrews.[5] Thus is explained and verified the declaration that "a mixed multitude" (literally, "a very great mixture") went up with them.[6] The route of the exodus has been determined,[7] notwithstanding the singular opinion of Brugsch-Bey.

Voltaire objected to the statement that the Israelites in the time of Moses conquered sixty fortified cities, besides many unwalled towns, in the region of Argob in Bashan, on the ground that it is improbable that so many cities and towns existed in one small canton, and he suggests, in the style that has become very prevalent, that some reviser has exaggerated the number.[8] Modern research, however, has demonstrated that ancient Bashan was exceedingly populous. The density of its ancient population is attested by the number of ruined towns and cities found to-day in the country. Burckhardt found the ruins of two hundred villages within a short distance of one another. Dr. Robinson gives the names of more than two hundred places in the Hauran and more than eighty in Batanea or Bashan.[9] Tristram says, "The ruined villages lie thick in every direction, seldom more than half a mile apart."[10] The ancient fertility of the soil is also abundantly attested. Voltaire's objection is groundless.

Furthermore, the names of Kadesh, Megiddo, and of nearly all the cities and towns are found in the inscriptions, tablets,

---

[1] *Store-city of Pithom and the Route of the Exodus*, pp. 10-12. [2] Ex. 12: 37.
[3] Brugsch-Bey, *Egypt Under the Pharaohs*, pp. 96, 317. [4] *Idem*, p. 96.
[5] *Idem*, pp. 301, 317, 318. [6] Ex. 12: 38.
[7] Naville, *Store-city of Pithom and Route of the Exodus*, pp. 27-31.
[8] *Dictionnaire Philosophique*, Article "Moses."
[9] *Biblical Researches*, Vol. III., App., pp. 150-159. [10] *Land of Moab*, p. 330.

or other monuments. In the same way the existence of the Hittites, Amorites, and other Canaanitish races and tribes referred to in the Pentateuchal history has been demonstrated. It is shown that in the century before the exodus the Hittite kingdom in Palestine was strong enough to withstand the Egyptian empire, then the most powerful in existence, and to compel its head, the great Rameses II., to enter into a league with it on equal terms.[1] It is further shown that the races and tribes in Palestine had been so weakened by long-continued wars immediately before the advent of the Israelites as to be incapable of making effectual resistance.

But for the want of space many other illustrations might be given of the way in which archæology is vindicating the historical character of the Pentateuch and other portions of the Bible. We close this chapter with a quotation from Professor Sayce: "What has been achieved already is an earnest of what will be achieved when the buried cities and tombs of the East have all been made to deliver their dead. We cannot expect to find everything verified, but the historian will be content if it is permitted him to turn with the same confidence to the books of Moses as he does to Thucydides or Tacitus." And again, "In glancing over the preceding pages, we cannot fail to be struck by the fact that the evidence of Oriental archæology is, on the whole, distinctly unfavorable to the pretensions of 'the higher criticism.'"[2]

[1] Brugsch-Bey, *Egypt Under the Pharaohs*, pp. 258-286.
[2] *Higher Criticism and the Monuments*, pp. 233, 561.

CHAPTER VIII

EXACTNESS.

IN addition to the historical trustworthiness of the Pentateuch, its accuracy in minute details is to be considered. We regard this minute accuracy as one of its most remarkable characteristics, and it constitutes unmistakable evidence that the book was written by one who witnessed the scenes described. God might, indeed, have employed and inspired, for the purpose of writing an account of the exodus and succeeding events, some one who was ignorant of them, and have imparted to him the necessary knowledge. But this is not God's way of doing. He is disposed to utilize human talent as far as practicable and to work miracles only so far as may be necessary. The minute accuracy of the Pentateuch presents these two alternatives for our adoption: either its author lived in Egypt and was an eye-witness of the exodus, or divine knowledge was communicated to him by the inspiration of the Almighty. It makes little difference which alternative the analytic critic accepts. Either is fatal to his views.

The kind of accuracy to which we refer is virtually conceded to the Pentateuch. We are far from saying that the analytic critics admit it to be accurate in every respect. On the other hand, they charge upon it contradictions, inconsistencies, exaggerations, and almost all sorts of errors. Some of them regard all accounts of miracles as myths, fictions, or incredible stories. But we speak now of geographical, historical, and chronological references and statements — references and statements concerning the history, geography, climate, and soil of Egypt, Palestine, and other countries; the mountains, lakes, seas, and rivers; the inhabitants, their manners and customs; the governments and laws. Inaccuracy in matters of this kind has often been charged upon the Pentateuch, but has never been proved. The charge, however, has been abandoned, or virtually withdrawn. All efforts of this kind have failed. To-day the Pentateuch is virtually admitted to be free from the errors that characterize even trustworthy historians. Not an Egyptologist nor any archæologist finds a single error in all the Pentateuchal books. The result of the archæological discoveries of modern times, so far as the Pentateuchal books are concerned, has only been to demonstrate their accuracy and vindicate their historical character. Hence "the higher criticism" regards modern archæology with disfavor, if not with downright hostility.

In the case of other ancient books the result has been very different. Archæological investigation has been making their inaccuracy more and more evident.

The inaccuracies of Herodotus are notorious. Though truthful himself, and though he gives us more information about Egypt than any other ancient writer, yet he accepted in many cases the incorrect statements of others, and added some mistakes of his own. He is frequently inaccurate in matters that seemingly came under his own observation. He declares that the Egyptians had no vines in their country.[1] This has been conclusively shown to be incorrect by Kenrick, Wilkinson, Brugsch-Bey, and others.[2] Even Herodotus virtually contradicts himself by referring, as he repeatedly does, to wine and raisins in Egypt.[3] In regard to vines and wine in Egypt the Pentateuch[4] is accurate, the Father of History inaccurate. Herodotus further declares that the use of wheat and barley bread as food was considered disgraceful.[5] Both Wilkinson[6] and Kenrick[7] declare this statement to be incorrect. The inaccuracy of Herodotus in saying that the Egyptians drank only out of brazen cups[8] is also noticed by Wilkinson,[9] and is demonstrated by the monuments. The Egyptologist further claims that "but little reliance can be placed on his measurements of the pyramids."[10] Kenrick declares that the history given by Herodotus of all that precedes 800 B.C. "cannot be accepted as true, either in its facts or its dates," and he suggests that the priests, with whom he conversed, were of a very subordinate rank, and ignorant of the history of their country, and that they had invented such a history as would satisfy the curiosity and excite the imagination of visitors.[11]

[1] 2 : 77.
[2] *Egypt Under the Pharaohs*, Vol. I., p. 161 ; *Ancient Egyptians*, Vol. I., pp. 39-53 ; *Ancient Egypt Under the Pharaohs*, p. 300.   [3] 2 : 37 ; 2 : 39.   [4] Gen. 40 : 9-13.
[5] 2 : 36.   [6] *Ancient Egyptians*, Vol. I., p. 179.
[7] *Ancient Egypt Under the Pharaohs*, Vol. I., pp. 158, 159.   [8] 2 : 37.
[9] *Ancient Egyptians*, Vol. I., p. 280.   [10] *Ancient Egyptians*, Vol. II., p. 256.
[11] *Ancient Egypt Under the Pharaohs*, Vol. II., pp. 60, 62.

Other ancient writers are still more inaccurate. The editor of Brugsch-Bey claims that, "notwithstanding the many attacks which have been made on the veracity of the ancient historian, modern excavations and the deciphering of texts prove that his statements from his own personal knowledge are, on the whole, to be trusted," and then adds, "Next to him in rank, but greatly his inferiors, are Diodorus Siculus, Strabo, Josephus, and Plutarch."[1]

The testimony of Professor Sayce to the inaccuracy of Herodotus and other ancient writers is as follows: "Let us now turn to the classical writers who have left accounts of the ancient history of the East. Among these Herodotus, and Ktesias of Knidos, naturally claim our first attention. Herodotus has been termed 'the Father of History,' since the later classical conceptions of Oriental history were in great measure based upon his work. Ktesias was the physician of the Persian king Artaxerxes, and thus had access to the state archives of Persia; on the strength of these he maintained that Herodotus had 'lied,' and he wrote a work with the object of contradicting most of the older historian's statements. But when confronted with contemporaneous monuments, Herodotus and Ktesias alike turn out to be false guides. In Egypt, Herodotus placed the pyramid-builders after the time of Rameses or Sesostris, and but shortly before the age of the Ethiopians Sabaco and Tirhakah, although in reality they preceded them by centuries. Among the Egyptian kings a Greek demigod and Lake Mœris in the Fayûm are made to figure, and the work of Herodotus abounds with small inaccuracies in the explanation of Egyptian words and customs, and in the description of the products of the country. His account of Assyria and Babylonia is still more misleading. The Assyrian and Babylonian empires are confounded together, just as they are in the Book of Judith; Sennacherib is called king of the Arabians, and Nebuchadnezzar is transformed into Labynêtos I. (or Nabonidos), and made the father of the real Nabonidos. The fortifications of Babylonia are ascribed to a queen Nitôkris, who bears an Egyptian name, and is placed five generations after Semiramis, a title of the Babylonian goddess Istar or Ashtoreth; while Ninos, that is, Nineveh, is supposed to be an Assyrian monarch, and termed the son of Belos or Baal. In the fragments of Ktesias Assyrian history fares no better."[2]

[1] *Egypt Under the Pharaohs*, p. 443.
[2] *Witness of Ancient Monuments to the Old Testament Scriptures, Living Papers*, Vol. VI., Essay 32, pp. 42, 43.

Thus is set forth the inaccuracy of the classical writers. In complete contrast with all this is the view presented by the archæologists in regard to the Pentateuch. They allude to the Pentateuchal history again and again as confirmed by the monuments. The most distinguished of the archæologists and Egyptologists, Kenrick, Wilkinson, Lepsius, Brugsch-Bey, Naville, Maspero, Palmer, and all the rest, though pointing out the inaccuracies of the classical writers in treating of ancient Oriental affairs, have not indicated a single error in all the five books of the Pentateuch—not a single error in history, chronology, or geography, not a single erroneous statement as to fact or date. Whatever light comes from the ancient monuments, from papyri and inscriptions, from tablets of clay and tablets of stone, from tombs and mummies of the dead, from mounds in Babylonia and ruined palaces in Assyria, whatever light comes from these sources and falls on the Pentateuchal history, serves but to explain, to prove, or to confirm. Not every difficulty has yet been removed, and perhaps never will be, but enough has been done to give assurance that as archæological investigation advances the accuracy of the Pentateuch, even in minute affairs, will continue to be vindicated.

Among the internal proofs of the minute accuracy of the Pentateuch we may refer to its chronology. Without maintaining at this time its absolute correctness, we propose to point out its remarkable definiteness and self-consistency.

According to Genesis, ten generations preceded the flood. Each generation is represented by a patriarch. These patriarchs are all mentioned by name; the order of their succession is indicated; the time elapsing between the birth of each predecessor and that of his successor is stated, and the age at which each died is given. It is stated that the deluge took place in the six hundredth year of Noah. These dates and facts are all clearly and definitely stated. They indicate unmistakably that the deluge occurred 1656 A.M., that Methuselah died that very year, and that Lamech died 1651 A.M., five years previous.

According to the sacred history, the deluge was designed to destroy mankind for their wickedness, and only righteous Noah and his family were to be preserved. The history states that, as a matter of fact, these alone were preserved. Now, if the date of the deluge had been fixed at any other year than precisely 1656 A.M., the result would have been confusion and contradiction in the record. Had it occurred one year earlier, it would have destroyed Methuselah, who lived to the year 1656. Lamech lived only seven hundred and seventy-seven years, whereas the average length of life among the antediluvian patriarchs, including Noah, was eight hundred and fifty-seven and one-half years. Had he attained to this average age, he would have lived seventy-five and one-half years after the deluge. Had that event occurred five years before the six hundredth year of Noah's life, both Lamech and Methuselah must have entered the ark or been drowned with the wicked. As the latter died 1656 A.M., and as the flood began on the seventeenth day of the second month of that year,[1] it is evident that Noah attended the funeral of his grandfather only a short time before the flood came. These conclusions are inevitable, if we accept the facts and dates as given. Adam lived nine hundred and thirty years, and, of course, died 930 A.M. Adding together the times elapsing between the birth of father and of son on down to Noah, we find that Noah's six hundredth year was 1656 A.M.; that Methuselah was born 687 A.M., was contemporary with Adam two hundred and forty-three years, and died the year of the deluge, 1656 A.M.; and that Lamech, being born 874 A.M., died 1651 A.M., five years before the flood.

We thus have an example of remarkable accuracy. If the date of the deluge had been fixed at any year preceding 1656 A.M., it would have involved the Pentateuchal history and chronology in contradiction. On the hypothesis of fiction, or any hypothesis other than that of veritable history, how very shrewd and how carefully exact the author, or authors, of Genesis must have been! Or will the analytic critic assume that in this case there was merely an accidental and fortunate escape from the committal of a damaging blunder?

An example of inaccuracy is furnished by the Septuagint text in this very matter of antediluvian chronology. It adds in most cases one hundred years to the time intervening between the births of father and son, thus placing the flood in the year 2242 A.M., and the birth of Methuselah 1287 A.M. It assigns nine hundred and sixty-nine years as the duration of Methuselah's life, and thus places his death fourteen years after the flood, though it represents, of course, only Noah and his family as having been saved in the ark. The Samaritan text decreases the

[1] Gen. 7: 11.

time intervening between the births of father and son, in one case by one hundred years and in two cases by more than one hundred, and thus places the deluge at 1307 A.M. It succeeds in allowing Methuselah and Lamech to die before the flood (which it thus places in the year 1307 A.M.) by shortening the life of the former from nine hundred and sixty-nine to seven hundred and twenty years, and of the latter from seven hundred and seventy-seven to six hundred and fifty-three, thus representing them as dying younger than any of the other antediluvian patriarchs, and representing Methuselah's life as being one hundred and thirty-seven and one-half years, and Lamech's as two hundred and thirty-four and one-half, shorter than the average of human life before the flood.

Moreover, the Hebrew chronology of men and generations after the flood is characterized by definiteness and accurate self-consistency. Noah lived nine hundred and fifty years, dying three hundred and fifty years after the flood—2006 A.M.[1] Arphaxad was born two years after the flood, in the one hundredth year of Shem, and died at the age of four hundred and thirty-eight.[2] Thus the account goes on, indicating the time of the birth and death, and the length of life, of the postdiluvian patriarchs on down to Abraham.[3]

Possibly some one may claim that there is a discrepancy in the account of Shem's age and Arphaxad's birth. Shem, at the age of one hundred years, begat Arphaxad, two years after the flood. But Noah, being six hundred years old at the time of the flood,[4] was, of course, six hundred and two years old two years after the flood. But it may be claimed that Noah was five hundred years older than Shem; for it is expressly declared that "Noah was five hundred years old: and Noah begat Shem, Ham, and Japheth."[5] This doubtless means that Noah was five hundred years old when his oldest son was born. Now, if Shem was the oldest son, there was a difference of five hundred years between his age and that of his father. At the time of the flood, Noah being six hundred years old,[4] Shem must have been one hundred; and at the birth of Arphaxad, two years after the flood, Shem must have been one hundred and two years old. But according to the record he was only one hundred. Thus inaccuracy may be inferred. Shem, however, was not the oldest son, though he had the preëminence

[1] Gen. 9: 28, 29. [2] Gen. 11: 10-13. [3] Gen. 11: 10-32. [4] Gen. 7: 11. [5] Gen. 5: 32.

and was accounted the first-born, as being the progenitor of Abraham, of the chosen race, and of Christ. Ham was the youngest son,[1] and Japheth was older than Shem.[2] It was Japheth, then, that was born when Noah was five hundred years old; and Shem, according to the record, next in age to Japheth, was ninety-eight years old at the time of the flood.

Inconsistency is claimed also in the record of the ages of Terah and Abraham. "And Terah lived seventy years, and begat Abram, Nahor, and Haran."[3] The difference, then, between the ages of Terah and Abram was seventy years, if Abram *was the oldest son*. Terah died at the age of two hundred and five,[4] and the next event mentioned after Terah's death is the departure of Abram from Haran, at the age of seventy-five.[5] If these events are mentioned in the order of their occurrence, either Abram must have been one hundred and thirty-five years old at the time of his departure from Haran, or there must have been a difference of one hundred and thirty years between his age and Terah's. In either case there is a discrepancy in the record. But it is possible that events are not mentioned in the order of their occurrence in this case. The death of Ishmael is recorded more than half a century out of its chronological order.[6] Isaac's death is mentioned many years in advance of its actual place in the chronology. So, too, the death of Terah may have occurred many years after the departure of Abram, though mentioned in the history before. Stephen indeed refers to the death of Terah as preceding the departure of Abram from Haran. But the author of the Acts merely quotes the statement of Stephen without approving it. But while the death of Terah may be mentioned out of its chronological order, and in this way the accuracy of the record be vindicated, we think that this hypothesis is unnecessary. The record does not say that the age of Terah was seventy at the time of Abram's birth, but that he "lived seventy years and begat Abram, Nahor, and Haran." Certainly all the three sons were not born just when their father was seventy years old. There is no reason to believe that they were triplets. We understand that the record gives the age of Terah at the time of the birth of his oldest son, just as in the case of Noah; and that Abram, like Shem, was not actually the first-born, but was accounted as such. There is

[1] Gen. 9:24. [2] Gen. 10:21. [3] Gen. 11:26. [4] Gen. 11:32.
[5] Gen. 12:4. [6] Gen. 25:17.

reason to believe that Haran was the oldest son. Nahor married his daughter, and probably Abram's wife, Sarai, was also his daughter.[1] This suggests that Haran was older than his brothers. Hence the charge of inconsistency is in this case without proof. Abram may have been born when Terah was one hundred and thirty years old, Abram may have been of the age of seventy-five at the time of his departure from Haran, and Terah may have died immediately before, at the age of two hundred and five.

It may be said that we have here an instance at least of indefiniteness in the fact that we are not at once informed which son was born to Terah in his seventieth year. Be it so. This is the only instance of the kind in the whole record. All the other facts and dates are clear.

Abram left Haran (at or before his father's death) at the age of seventy-five.[2] After a residence of ten years in Canaan, Abram, at the age of eighty-five (seventy-five plus ten), took Hagar as his wife.[3] Ishmael was born when Abram was eighty-six years old.[4] At the time of the circumcision Abram was ninety-nine and Ishmael thirteen.[5] The difference between their ages was eighty-six (ninety-nine minus thirteen). At the time of Isaac's birth Abraham was one hundred years old.[6] The difference between the ages of Ishmael and Isaac was fourteen years. Ishmael died at the age of one hundred and thirty-seven.[7] Isaac was married at forty,[8] and twenty years afterward Jacob and Esau were born, when Isaac was sixty years old.[9] There was, then, an interval of one hundred and sixty years between the birth of Abraham and that of Jacob. Abraham died at the age of one hundred and seventy-five.[10] Jacob and Esau were therefore born fifteen years before the death of their grandfather.

Jacob was married at the age of eighty-four, and seven years afterward Joseph was born; for there was a difference of ninety-one years between the ages of Jacob and Joseph, which is shown as follows: When Jacob was one hundred and thirty years old, Joseph was thirty-nine; for Joseph was made prime minister to Pharaoh at the age of thirty;[11] and nine years (seven of plenty and two of famine) elapsed after this before the second visit of Jacob's sons to Egypt and the migration.[12] Joseph's age at the time of the migration was thirty-nine, and Jacob's age was one

[1] Gen. 11 : 29. [2] Gen. 12 : 4. [3] Gen. 16 : 3. [4] Gen. 16 : 16.
[5] Gen. 17 : 24, 25. [6] Gen. 21 : 5. [7] Gen. 25 : 17. [8] Gen. 25 : 20.
[9] Gen. 25 : 26. [10] Gen. 25 : 7. [11] Gen. 41 : 46. [12] Gen. 45 : 6.

hundred and thirty.[1] The difference, then, in their ages was ninety-one (one hundred and thirty less thirty-nine). Joseph was born the seventh year after Jacob's double marriage, at the close of the fourteenth year of his residence in Padan-aram.[2] Jacob served seven years for Leah, seven for Rachel, and was for six years a partner in business with Laban.[3] He remained therefore, all together, in Padan-aram twenty years (seven plus seven plus six). Joseph, being born at the close of the fourteenth year, was six years old at the time of the departure of the family from Padan-aram. Jacob, therefore, was ninety-seven (ninety-one plus six). At the time of his flight from Esau he was seventy-seven (ninety-seven minus twenty). At the time of his double marriage he was eighty-four (seventy-seven plus seven). Joseph, at the time of his arrival as a slave in Egypt, was seventeen,[4] and Jacob was one hundred and eight (seventeen plus ninety-one). The difference in age between Joseph and his grandfather Isaac was one hundred and fifty-one (sixty plus ninety-one). At the time of Joseph's sale to the Ishmaelites Isaac's age was one hundred and sixty-eight (seventeen plus one hundred and fifty-one). Isaac died at the age of one hundred and eighty,[5] twelve years after the sale of Joseph.

The time between the return to Canaan and the sale of Joseph was eleven years (seventeen minus six, or one hundred and eight minus ninety-seven). The time between the return to Canaan and the emigration to Egypt was thirty-three years (thirty-nine minus six, or one hundred and thirty minus ninety-seven).

The time of the sojourn of the patriarchs Abraham, Isaac, and Jacob in Canaan, that is, the time from the entrance into Canaan to the migration to Egypt, is represented as follows: From the entrance into Canaan to the birth of Isaac, twenty-five years; then to the birth of Jacob, sixty years; and, next, to the migration to Egypt, two hundred and fifteen years (twenty-five plus sixty plus one hundred and thirty). All these facts and dates are either stated with unmistakable exactness, or are made out with mathematical precision.

The same precision characterizes the subsequent chronological and genealogical statements of the Pentateuch. In Exodus 12: 40, 41 we have a statement as explicit historically and chronologically as could be made in regard to the duration of the sojourn in Egypt. It is declared to have been four hundred and

[1] Gen. 47:9. [2] Gen. 30:25. [3] Gen. 31:38-41. [4] Gen. 37:2. [5] Gen. 35:28.

thirty years — no more and no less. The very year, month,[1] and day of the month in which the exodus began and the four hundred and thirty years terminated, are indicated. This date, with all its exactness, is again given in Numbers 33:3, which claims to be written by Moses. We do not enter into defense of the absolute correctness of the passage. It is not our business now to notice what the critics say about its authorship. We simply call attention to the fact that this clear and explicit statement is a part of the Pentateuch, and is not inconsistent with anything else contained in it. The initial statement of the Book of Numbers is similar in character: "The first day of the second month, in the second year after they were come out of the land of Egypt."[2] Here again the year, month, and day are indicated. Again, in Numbers 10:11 is the statement that the Israelites set out from the wilderness of Sinai "on the twentieth day of the second month, in the second year." In both these cases the event referred to is dated from the exodus. In like manner the second celebration of the Passover is dated from the exodus, and hence declared to be in the second year.[3] This was in accordance with the record of this event itself, the month to be "the beginning of months," and the "night to be much observed."[4]

Chronological precision characterizes the record concerning the forty years' wandering in the desert. The forty years were emphasized. "After the number of the days in which ye searched the land, even forty days, each day for a year, shall ye bear your iniquities, even forty years; and ye shall know my breach of promise"[5] (rather, "my recall of promise"). But as all events were dated from the exodus, the forty years of wandering were to be counted from that epoch. This was all the more proper for the reason that the Israelites, since their departure from Egypt, had been all the time in the wilderness. In harmony with these chronological views, and marked by the usual exactness, is the record in Deuteronomy concerning Moses, very near the close of the forty years' wandering: "And it came to pass in the fortieth year, in the eleventh month, on the first day of the month, that Moses spake unto the children of Israel."[6]

The same characteristics mark the chronological record concerning Moses and Aaron. Aaron was the elder of the brothers,

---

[1] Ex. 12:2, 18.   [2] Num. 1:1.   [3] Num. 9:1.   [4] Ex. 12:2, 42.
[5] Num. 14:34.   [6] Deut. 1:3.

and he is named first in the genealogy.[1] At the time of their first interview with Pharaoh, Aaron was eighty-three years old, and Moses eighty.[2] Moses lived one hundred and twenty years, and Aaron one hundred and twenty-three. Aaron died on Mount Hor, in the fortieth year after the exodus, on the first day of the fifth month, one hundred and twenty-three years old.[3] But of the death of Moses scarcely any particulars are given. Neither the day, nor the month, nor even the year is mentioned. We infer that he died at the close of the fortieth year after the exodus, or early in the forty-first; for Aaron, who was three years older, died in the fifth month of the fortieth year, aged one hundred and twenty-three. Moses, then, must have died not long after his brother. In the record of his death not even the place is mentioned, except to say that it was somewhere in the land of Moab.[4] The only information we have as to the particular place of his death is, that God had directed him to ascend Mount Nebo, in order to look across the Jordan, and to die. But this meagerness of information and this absence of particulars that characterize the record of Moses' death are very significant, inasmuch as they set in a stronger light the definiteness, particularity, and precision of preceding statements. It would seem that the account of the great lawgiver's death was not from the hand that wrote the passages to which we have called attention as examples of particularity and precision. This accords with what we conceive to be the truth in the case, namely, that Moses wrote the Pentateuch substantially as we have it, but that, of course, he did not write the account of his own death and burial.

Not only the same definiteness and precision and self-consistency, but also the same chronological ideas and system, pervade the Pentateuch throughout. In the time of Moses, and afterward, events were dated from the exodus. The exodus was preceded by the sojourn of four hundred and thirty years in Egypt. This sojourn and the exodus were associated in the mind of the author of the Pentateuch. The sojourn in Egypt was preceded by the sojourn of the patriarchs Abraham, Isaac, and Jacob two hundred and fifteen years in Canaan. These patriarchs were preceded by the ten postdiluvian patriarchs, who filled the period of three hundred and sixty-five years between the flood and the call of Abraham; and these were preceded by

[1] Ex. 6: 20; Num. 26: 59. [2] Ex. 7: 7. [3] Num. 33: 37-39. [4] Deut. 34: 5.

the antediluvian patriarchs, who filled the period of one thousand six hundred and fifty six years between the creation and the flood. This is the chronological system of the Pentateuch: forty years between the entrance into Canaan and the exodus; four hundred and thirty years between the exodus and the migration to Egypt; two hundred and fifteen years between the migration to Egypt and the migration to Canaan; three hundred and sixty-five years between the migration to Canaan and the flood; and one thousand six hundred and fifty-six years between the flood and the creation,—all together, two thousand six hundred and sixty-six years from the creation to the exodus.

1. This system is clear, well defined, and self-consistent.

2. So self-consistent, precise, and accurate is this chronological system in its general features and in its details, that there is no internal evidence against its absolute correctness. Assailants are compelled to employ exclusively external proofs.

3. The only doubtful point in all the details of this system is the birth-time of Abraham; that is, whether he was born in the seventieth or one hundred and thirtieth year of Terah. Aside from this, all the dates, facts, figures, and statements are clear and distinct, and are absolutely consistent with one another.

4. The only place in the Pentateuch where definiteness, precision, and particularity in chronological details are not found, is the last chapter of Deuteronomy, which Moses, of course, did not write. Had Moses given an account of his own death and funeral, it would doubtless have been as exact and minute as the account of the death and burial of Aaron at Mount Hor, near to Mosera.[1]

5. The precision and self-consistency of this chronology are in striking contrast with the alterations, inaccuracies, and inconsistencies of Josephus and of the Samaritan and Septuagint text.

6. The Pentateuchal chronology, if self-contradictory or erroneous in any respect, affords, by its definiteness and particularization, a fine opportunity for attack and refutation. Why do not the critics attack it? Wellhausen merely shakes his lance at it. He remarks that the chronology is carried forward without a break ("lückenlos") from the creation to the exodus.[2] But instead of attacking it as incorrect or false, he ventures only to sneer at the exactness of details and the bold-

---

[1] Num. 33:38, 39; Deut. 10:6.   [2] *Prolegomena*, pp. 7, 363.

ness with which numbers and names are stated. The manly thing for him to have done was either to point out errors in it, or frankly to admit its seeming correctness.

But further, outside of chronological matters, the statements of the Pentateuch are exact and self-consistent.

Let us take the genealogy of Jacob's family as an example.[1] Though this genealogical account has often been assailed as false, or at least incorrect, it is at least entirely and precisely self-consistent. Two totals are given in Genesis,[2] and another in the Acts by Stephen.[3] These totals are sixty-six, seventy, and seventy-five. Now if we count the children of Leah as named in the register, we shall find the number to be thirty-three, as given;[4] so of the number of Zilpah's children, sixteen; also of the number of Rachel's children, fourteen; and so, too, of Bilhah's children, seven. If we add these numbers together, we have seventy (thirty-three plus sixteen plus fourteen plus seven). This is the total referred to in the declaration, "All the souls of the house of Jacob, which came into Egypt, were threescore and ten."[5] But this total of seventy includes Joseph and his two sons, who did not go with Jacob to Egypt, but were there before his arrival. It includes, also, Jacob himself, who is expressly named as one of the seventy.[6] Deducting these four from seventy, we have sixty-six (seventy minus four). This accords with the declaration, "All the souls that came with Jacob into Egypt, which came out of his loins, besides Jacob's son's wives, all the souls were threescore and six."[7] The phrase "came with Jacob into Egypt" excludes Joseph and his sons, and also Jacob himself, from the total sixty-six. The total seventy-five is not mentioned in the Pentateuch,[8] and therefore does not specially concern us. But if any one should refer to it as evidence of Pentateuchal inaccuracy, we would remind him that Stephen includes in that total of seventy-five *all the kindred* whom Joseph invited to Egypt: "Then sent Joseph, and called his father Jacob to him, and all his kindred, threescore and fifteen souls."[3] The phrase "all his kindred" includes Jacob's sons' wives. If there were eight of his sons' wives in addition to Joseph's still living, we would have, including Jacob, the total seventy-five (sixty-seven plus eight). Stephen doubtless quoted the Septuagint, which we shall soon see was inexact in its

[1] Gen. 46 : 8-27. [2] Gen. 46 : 26, 27. [3] Acts 7 : 14. [4] Gen. 46 : 15.
[5] Gen. 46 : 27. [6] Gen. 46 : 8. [7] Gen. 46 : 26.

statements; but he corrected them by including all of Jacob's kindred in the seventy-five.

If it seems strange that Jacob should be counted as a member of his own family, that does not detract from the accuracy of the account. The fact that he is so counted is expressly mentioned, thus: "Jacob and his sons." Accordingly, he must be reckoned with Leah's family, in order to make the totals thirty-three and seventy. Thus this account of Jacob's family is precisely self-consistent, and in this regard is perfectly accurate. In these matters the Septuagint text differs from the Hebrew, and runs into self-contradiction and inaccuracy. It gives the number of the families of Leah, Zilpah, Rachel, and Bilhah respectively as thirty-three, sixteen, eighteen, and seven, which make a total of seventy-four. The Septuagint, however, gives the totals sixty-six and seventy-five. It reads that nine sons were born to Joseph in Egypt.[1] If we count Joseph and these nine sons as added to the sixty-six, we will have seventy-six; and if we deduct them from the second total (seventy-five), we will have but sixty-five. The Septuagint is inaccurate also in saying that the seventy-five as well as the sixty-six came "*with Jacob* into Egypt."[2] In Exodus 1: 1-5 the Septuagint reads that "all the souls of Jacob were seventy-five," and yet in Deuteronomy 10: 22 it reads that the fathers of the Israelites "went down into Egypt with seventy souls." Thus at every point the Septuagint is inconsistent and inexact. The contrast between it and the Hebrew text in this respect is marked.

The accuracy of the Pentateuch in its references to Egyptian affairs has already been in part illustrated. Many of the facts mentioned to show the acquaintance of the author with Egyptian affairs serve equally well to prove his minute accuracy. In this case, too, we claim, not, as in some of the foregoing points, simply precision and self-consistency of statement, but real and absolute accuracy. Thus the allusions to Joseph's shaving before his presentation to Pharaoh, to brick-making, to embalming, and other Egyptian affairs, are precisely correct, as is evinced by the statements of ancient authors and the investigations of modern Egyptologists.

In addition to the illustrations of this sort above presented, we will call attention to some others.

The allusion in the chief baker's dream to his carrying three

---

[1] Gen. 46: 27.   [2] Gen. 46: 26, 27.

baskets on his *head*[1] is in exact accordance with ancient Egyptian custom. Herodotus mentions, as one of the things by which the Egyptians were distinguished from all the rest of mankind, the fact that they carried burdens on their heads.[2] In Pharaoh's dream, the dependence of the fertility of Egypt on the Nile is correctly assumed, and is accurately represented by the circumstance that both the fat and the lean cows, the rank and good stalk with seven full ears and the stalk with the seven thin and blasted ears, all came up out of the river.[3] When Joseph's brethren dined with him, they *sat*[4] while eating, which was in accordance with Egyptian custom.[5] The Jews, and also the Grecians and Romans of the later time at least, reclined at meals.

The account of the embalming of Jacob bears marks of correctness. "And forty days were fulfilled for him; for so are fulfilled the days of those which are embalmed: and the Egyptians mourned for him threescore and ten days."[6] Herodotus speaks of the embalming process lasting seventy days.[7] Diodorus Siculus speaks of the body being prepared "with cedar oil and other substances for more than thirty days," and he further says that the friends of the deceased mourn for him until the body is buried.[8] The author of Genesis, more accurate than either of these classical writers, mentions both periods, forty days ("more than thirty days," says Diodorus Siculus), and seventy days, the whole time of the embalming, and also the time of the mourning.

The closing words of Genesis contain an allusion to an Egyptian custom: "So Joseph died, being an hundred and ten years old: and they embalmed him, and he was put in a coffin in Egypt."[9] The mummy-cases so frequently found in Egypt corroborate the truth and accuracy of this statement.

We have not space, nor is it necessary, to speak of all, or of a majority, of the many accurate allusions in the Pentateuch to the customs and affairs of Egypt. In discussing such points we could only reproduce what has been said by others. This subject has been well discussed by Hengstenberg.[10]

The geographical statements and allusions of the Pentateuch have of late years received many confirmations. Their accuracy has in most cases been demonstrated. In no instance have they been falsified. Goshen, On, Rameses, Pithom, Succoth, Etham, Migdol, and Pi-hahiroth have been identified. The remains of

[1] Gen. 40: 16. [2] 2: 32. [3] Gen. 41: 2-6. [4] Gen. 43: 33.
[5] Wilkinson, *Ancient Egyptians*, Vol. I., p. 167. [6] Gen. 50: 3. [7] 2: 86.
[8] 1: 91. [9] Gen. 50: 26. [10] *Egypt and the Books of Moses.*

Pithom, one of the store-cities built by the Israelites for Pharaoh, have been discovered, consisting of huge walls built of bricks made, some with straw, and some without.[1] The route of the Israelites from Rameses to the Red Sea has been determined.[1] The Israelites reached the sea by a three-days' march, and it is ascertained that the distance from Memphis to Pi-hahiroth is just three days' journey.[2] It is in evidence that the allusions to places in the account of the march from the Red Sea to Sinai — the wilderness of Shur, in which they went three days without water; Marah, with its bitter waters; Elim, with its twelve wells and seventy palm trees; the wilderness of Sin; Rephidim, "where there was no water for the people to drink"; and, finally, Sinai, the mount of God—the statements and allusions in regard to these places have led scientific observers and experienced travelers to declare, after careful investigation, that "the physical facts accord with the inspired account" and also prove "the accuracy of Scripture details."[3] Humboldt declared that the historical narratives of the Old Testament (among which are, of course, embraced those of the Pentateuch) "are most true to nature, a point on which the unanimous testimony of modern travelers may be received as conclusive, owing to the inconsiderable changes effected in the course of ages in the manners and habits of a nomadic people."[4]

This "unanimous testimony of modern travelers" to the truth of the historical narratives of the Pentateuch and of the entire Old Testament, as well as the testimony of the archæologists and the monuments, "the higher critics" almost entirely ignore. This policy of prudence or of contemptuous silence Professor W. R. Smith broke through so far as to venture to say that "the Pentateuch displays an exact topographical knowledge of Palestine, but by no means so exact a knowledge of the wilderness of the wandering." He further declares that "geographers are unable to assign with certainty the site of Mount Sinai, because the narrative has none of that topographical color which the story of an eye-witness is sure to possess."[5] But Professor Smith here deals only in assertion. He cites no authorities and gives no proofs. He makes no specifications, except to say that geographers cannot agree as to the site of Mount Sinai. It is, however, *almost* universally agreed that the mount called by the

---

[1] Naville, *Store-city of Pithom and the Route of the Exodus*, pp. 11, 24-31.
[2] Professor E. H. Palmer, *Desert of the Exodus*, p. 224.
[3] *Idem*, p. 230. [4] *Cosmos*, Vol. II., pp. 412, 413.
[5] *Old Testament in the Jewish Church*, p. 324.

natives "Jebel Musa" is the ancient Sinai. Lepsius, indeed, opposed this view, but says, "I am not aware that there are any modern travelers and savants who have thrown doubts on the correctness of this assumption."[1] Thus Lepsius stood alone. Professor Sayce has lately opposed the prevalent view, but he admits that "it may seem a pity to disturb a traditional faith which has supported so many tourists among the desolate wadies and monotonous scenery of the Sinaitic Peninsula."[2] He has not, however, succeeded in producing any "disturbance," for he speaks not from personal observation, and the testimony of nearly all the travelers and explorers, except that of Lepsius, is against him.

Now as to the opinion of Professor Smith that the Pentateuch does not indicate an exact knowledge of the wilderness of the wandering on the part of its author, we deem it a full refutation to cite the testimony of a trustworthy and competent eye-witness. Professor Palmer, of England, professor of Arabic at Cambridge, had so familiar an acquaintance with that language that he could converse freely with the native Bedouin of the desert. He made two visits to and through the Sinaitic Peninsula. He accompanied the Ordnance Survey Expedition to the peninsula in 1868-69. He also visited Et Tih, Idumea, and Moab in 1869-70, on behalf of the Exploration Fund. He declares that he had the company of scientific men and experienced explorers, and that he wandered over a greater portion of the desert than had been previously explored. This man of learning and science, who could speak the Arabic like a native, and who traveled through the desert in various directions, seeing with his own eyes the sands and the rocks, the streams and wadies, hills, and mountains, and plains, had no difficulty in following the track of the Israelites and in identifying the mount of the law. His testimony is that the desert is a proof and a monument, not only of the truth of the general statements of the Pentateuch, but also of the accuracy of the details. One of his closing declarations is as follows: "We cannot ever hope to identify all the stations and localities mentioned in the Bible account of the Exodus, but enough has been recovered to enable us to trace the more important lines of march, and to follow the Israelites in their several journeys from Egypt to Sinai, from Sinai to Kadesh, and from thence to the promised land."[3]

[1] *Egypt, Ethiopia, and the Peninsula of Sinai*, p. 532.
[2] *Higher Criticism and the Monuments*, p. 271.
[3] *Desert of the Exodus*, p. 434.

CHAPTER IX

THE LEGISLATION

THE analysts maintain that the Pentateuchal laws give evidence of a post-Mosaic origin. Kuenen declares that these laws differ so much that they "must, in all probability, be separated from each other by a space, not of years, but of centuries."[1]

1. Among the laws claimed to be contradictory are those which relate to the place of worship. Kuenen claims that Exodus 20: 24 authorizes the offering of sacrifices at different places, and that therefore it conflicts with many passages in Deuteronomy and also with Leviticus 17: 1-9 and Exodus 25 *sqq*.

In regard to this passage,[2] it is to be observed:

(1) That if it does authorize a plurality of sanctuaries, it contradicts all the succeeding parts of the Pentateuch. Kuenen sets against it not only Deuteronomy,[3] but also Leviticus 17: 1-9 and Exodus 25 *sqq*. He might have added that the Book of Numbers knows but one altar and one place of worship. If the claim of Kuenen and other analysts is well founded, what a blunder was committed by the writer of Exodus in placing contradictory laws in the same book! Even the supposed redactor, who so often comes to the help of these critics, is to be blamed for not removing the contradiction, as he might have done by the alteration of a word.

(2) The hypothesis of the analysts is that the middle books of the Pentateuch were gotten up during the exile or after it, with a special view to the establishment of the priestly code. It is admitted that Leviticus and Numbers harmonize with Deuteronomy in regard to the unity of worship. Is it not strange that these exilic writers should have allowed Exodus to contradict the other books and also itself on this vital point?

(3) But the conclusive answer to the arguments and assumptions of the analytics on this subject is this, that Exodus 20: 24 does not authorize a plurality of sanctuaries. Though the pas-

---
[1] *Hexateuch*, p. 25.   [2] Ex. 20: 24.   [3] *Hexateuch*, pp. 24, 25.

sage does, indeed, speak (in the English version) of a plurality of *places* in which God would "record his name," and at which sacrifice was to be offered, yet it does not say that God would record his name in different places *at the same time*, nor that there should be an altar in more places than one *at the same time*. As the Israelites went from place to place during the forty years' wandering, God indicated, by the manifestation of his presence, the spot where he was to be worshiped. A more literal rendering of the passage would be, "in every place [בְּכָל־הַמָּקוֹם] where I record my name." God recorded his name in many places during the wandering in the desert, but never in two places at the same time.

(4) The regulations concerning unity of worship are more definite and emphatic in Deuteronomy than in Exodus and the other middle books, and this fact harmonizes with the traditional theory; for when the Israelites were encamped together, within a short distance of the altar and the tabernacle, and within sight of the pillar of cloud by day and the pillar of fire by night, it was sufficient to tell them to offer sacrifices only in the places where God manifested his presence. But when they were about to enter Canaan, where they would no longer behold either the cloud or the fire, and where they would live, many of them, at a distance from the altar, the ark, and the sanctuary, the great law-giver recognized the propriety of expressing more clearly and urgently the duty of worshiping God at the one place which he himself should choose.

2. Kuenen (also Wellhausen and others) claims that Exodus and Deuteronomy conflict with Leviticus and Numbers, inasmuch as the former two books mention but three yearly feasts,[1] while the latter two mention seven.[2]

But is this a contradiction? The negative view is favored by the following considerations:

(1) It is very improbable that the men who are supposed to have made the Pentateuch what it is, and who are anxious about the establishment of ritual services, would either insert contradictions, or allow contradictions to remain, in regulations which they claimed Moses had enacted concerning religious festivals. These authors, revisers, and redactors must have regarded the Pentateuchal books and laws as harmonious.

[1] Ex. 23: 14-17; 34: 18-24; 13: 3-10; Deut. 16: 1-16.
[2] Lev. 23: 1-44; Num. 28: 18, 25, 26; 29: 1, 7, 9.

(2) Exodus and Deuteronomy are merely *silent* in regard to four of the feasts. Silence is not contradiction. The silence in this case is satisfactorily accounted for by the fact that Exodus [1] and Deuteronomy [2] mention only the feasts at which all the males were required to be present.

3. Kuenen further maintains that Deuteronomy contradicts Exodus, Leviticus, and Numbers in regard to the Levites.[3] His contention is, that according to Deuteronomy all the Levites were priests, while according to the middle books only Aaron and his sons were priests.

But, as has frequently been pointed out, in Exodus, Leviticus, and Numbers the Levites are appointed and set apart to the service of the sanctuary,[4] and thus are really made priests. In this way is conferred on the Levites as extensive a grant of priestly rights and prerogatives as is found in Deuteronomy. There is, however, this difference, that in the middle books the preëminence of Aaron and his sons among the priests is distinctly brought to view, while Deuteronomy on this point is silent. Here again the analysts construe silence as contradiction.

4. Another divergence is claimed in the tithe laws as contained in Leviticus 27:32, Numbers 18:21-32, and those contained in Deuteronomy 14:22; 26:12-15.

In order to make out this divergence, the critic is under the necessity of putting an interpretation on these laws which was rejected by the Jews, as is shown by Tobit[5] and Josephus.[6] But it is an easy thing for Kuenen to say that Tobit, Josephus, and all the Jews, including Solomon and Daniel, misunderstood their tithe law.

5. It is claimed that the laws in regard to firstlings of cattle conflict with one another.[3] This claim, however, is only another example of silence treated as contradiction.

(*a*) Exodus 13:12, 13 and 34:19, 20 set apart the male firstlings of beasts to the Lord, the firstling of an ass to be redeemed, or to have its neck broken.

(*b*) Exodus 22:30 requires the firstlings of oxen and of sheep to be given to the Lord on the eighth day.

(*c*) Deuteronomy 15:19-23 demands that all the firstling males of the herd and flock (except the defective and the deformed) be sanctified unto the Lord, and be eaten at the sanctuary.

---

[1] Ex. 23:17. [2] Deut. 16:16. [3] *Hexateuch*, p. 25.
[4] Num. 1:49, 50; 3:5, 6; 8:10-16. [5] 1:6-8. [6] *Antiquities*, 4:8:8.

(*d*) Numbers 18: 15-18 provides that all firstlings, both of men and beasts, brought unto the Lord shall belong to Aaron; the unclean firstlings to be redeemed; the firstlings of cows, sheep, and goats not to be redeemed, but their blood to be sprinkled on the altar, their fat to be burned, the wave breast and right shoulder to be given to the priests.

On the above passages we remark:

(1) That what is prescribed in one is not forbidden or repealed in any of the others. The only way to prove inconsistency between them is to construe silence as contradiction, the kind of reasoning to which the analysts so frequently resort.

(2) Why the firstlings, though mainly eaten as food by the people, were regarded as belonging to the Lord and also to the priests, is of easy explanation. These firstlings belonged to the Lord as sacrificial victims, their blood and their fat being offered on the altar. They belonged also as sacrificial victims to the priests, who offered them, and to whom were given the wave breast and right shoulder. The remaining portions were devoted to the Lord's feast, of which all classes partook. There is no contradiction here, except to those who are anxious to find it.

6. It is further claimed that there is divergence among the regulations in regard to the maintenance of the Levites. Numbers 35: 1-8 provides that forty-eight cities should be assigned them, and Joshua 21: 1-42 relates how this was done. Kuenen does not find any contradictory regulation, but he refers to passages which speak of the Levites as sojourning in other cities, and which commend them, along with widows and orphans, as objects of charity; and then he challenges any one to explain "how the law-giver, after having made, in the fortieth year, such ample provision for the support of the priests and Levites, could assume a few days later that his injunctions would not be carried out, and that the Levites would wander about in destitution."[1]

We reply: (1) That not all the forty-eight Levitical cities were situated in one tribe or region, but thirteen cities were assigned out of Judah, Simeon, and Benjamin; ten out of Ephraim, Dan, and Manasseh; thirteen out of Issachar, Asher, and Naphtali, and the half tribe of Manasseh; and twelve out of Reuben, Gad,

[1] *Hexateuch*, p. 31.

and Zebulon.[1] The Levites—twenty-three thousand males a month old and upward,[2] forty-six thousand all told—were not confined to these forty-eight cities, but were scattered everywhere as priests, scribes, teachers, and in other capacities.

(2) Only cities, not farms, were assigned to the Levites. A family that owned only a town-lot and a house, or only a town-lot without a house, might be very destitute. "Ample provision," says Kuenen. One wonders where he got his ideas on this subject. He seems to forget that men, women, and children need food and clothing.

7. Contradiction is claimed in regard to the age at which the Levites entered on their priestly duties. Numbers 4:3 fixes the age at thirty years; Numbers 8:24, at twenty-five. Between these passages, as we have them, there is a discrepancy. This discrepancy is cited by Kuenen to disprove Mosaic authorship.[3]

But, (1) it is possible that the discrepancy arose from an error in transcription. The Septuagint has the number twenty-five in both passages. In such a case many of the analysts, if they thought it would advance their case, would assume that the authors of that version followed a better text than that contained in our Hebrew Bibles of the present day. And perhaps they did.

(2) After all, the difference in the numbers is probably not the result of a various reading, or of any kind of error, but of the thoughtful precaution of the law-giver. The fourth chapter has reference to the duties of the Levites in taking care of the tabernacle *on the march;* the eighth, to the *ordinary* service of the tabernacle. The minimum age for the former might be thirty years, and for the latter twenty-five. After the tabernacle was fixed permanently at Jerusalem, the minimum age was reduced to twenty.[4]

(3) But the alleged discrepancy is not between different authors and different books. According to the showing of the analytic critics, the discrepancy, whether real or only apparent, is between the statements of the author whom they call P.[5] They virtually say that since the statements conflict, therefore not Moses, but P, wrote them. The argument is worthless, except on the ground that Moses was plenarily inspired and infallible. The analyst, of course, says that though both passages were written by P, the number in the one or the other has been

---
[1] Josh. 21: 1-42. [2] Num. 26: 62. [3] *Hexateuch*, pp. 25, 31, 308.
[4] I. Chr. 23: 27. [5] *Die Heilige Schrift des Alten Testaments*, Kautzsch-Socin.

altered by a later hand. But here is involved the groundless assumption that if Moses were the original author that later hand could not have done its work.

8. Kuenen claims that the laws in Exodus 21 : 1-6 and Deuteronomy 15: 12-18 in regard to the manumission of Hebrew servants are opposed to Leviticus 25: 39-43.[1] He declares that the former passages limit the term of service of the Hebrew servant to six years, and that the latter extends it to the year of jubilee.

But the former passages do not limit the term of service to six years. They expressly provide that the service *might* continue after the six years indefinitely, or, as our English version has it, forever. Leviticus 25: 39-43 fixes the utmost limit at the year of jubilee. Should a man emphasize the English auxiliary *shall* in the clause, "Shall serve thee unto the year of jubilee" (fortieth verse), he will get a meaning that is not in the original Hebrew. In this case, as in many others, the contradiction is found only by those who *desire* to find it.

Having thus disposed of the main arguments drawn from the Pentateuchal laws to disprove their Mosaic origin, we proceed to take up the arguments drawn from the same source in favor of the other side of the question.

1. One important consideration is, that all these laws purport to come, in the phraseology of Kuenen, "from Moses and the desert." In the legislative portions of the Pentateuch we have the ever-recurring formula, "And the Lord spake unto Moses, saying." A very large portion of the Pentateuch, especially of Deuteronomy, claims to have been actually delivered by Moses in oral discourse to the Israelites. This is true especially of the legal enactments.

These facts force upon us one of two conclusions: either Moses is the author of the legislation attributed to him and the analytic hypothesis must be abandoned, or the Pentateuch contains a vast amount of falsehood. It is of little avail to attempt to disguise the latter alternative under the euphemism of *legal fiction* or *pious fraud*. These phrases exclude the idea of mere mistake. They mean, not that somebody *blundered*, but that somebody *lied*. Besides the charge of falsehood in putting words into the mouth of Moses which he never uttered, and in attributing to him laws which he never enacted, there is the fur-

[1] *Hexateuch*, pp. 25, 31.

ther charge of falsehood in the ascription of these words and laws to the Almighty. The formula so often employed, "The Lord spake unto Moses, saying," means that God in some supernatural, or at least special, way, communicated his will to Moses, and that the laws which Moses enacted came from God. The denial of the Mosaic authorship of these laws is a denial of their divine authorship as well. In every case, then, in which the analytic critic charges falsehood on the record in ascribing a law to Moses, he must charge further falsehood on the record in its representing the law as coming from God. In other words, the charge involved in the analytic hypothesis against the legislative portions of the Pentateuch is that of wholesale lying. Over and over again—times, indeed, too numerous to be counted, the declaration is made that God, through Moses, gave to the chosen people laws which the critics claim had no existence till many centuries after Mosaic times. According, then, to the analytic view, every such declaration is false. Such views, of course, prepare the way for and involve far-reaching skepticism. Accordingly we find the leaders of the analytic school—Wellhausen, Kuenen, Reuss, Graf—maintaining that the whole account of the tabernacle is untrue, the exodus largely a sham, and the decalogue a purely human invention of post-Mosaic origin. The only way logically to avoid these destructive conclusions is to accept the record that the Pentateuchal laws came from Moses and from God.

2. The literary presentment of these laws indicates that they originated in the wilderness, and therefore in the time of Moses.

It is indeed claimed by the analysts that these laws, including the decalogue, presuppose the settlement in Canaan and a population engaged in agricultural pursuits. The expression, "within thy *gates*," in the fourth commandment,[1] and the regulations in regard to leprous *houses*,[2] are claimed as showing that the Israelites at the time of enactment were dwelling in houses and towns. It is freely admitted that the ten commandments and the Pentateuchal laws in general were intended for people living on farms, in houses, and in towns and cities. The Israelites had been living in houses up to within a short time before the decalogue and the most of the laws were given them. They had houses in Egypt, and dwelt in towns and villages, and on farms and pasture lands. Their law-giver in the wilderness did not

---

[1] Ex. 20: 10.   [2] Lev. 14: 33-53.

forget, nor allow them to forget, that they were to be permanently settled in Canaan; and that their sojourning in the wilderness was to be comparatively brief. This is brought to view in the regulations concerning leprous houses. The preamble is as follows: "When ye be come into the land of Canaan, which I give to you for a possession, and I put the plague of leprosy in a house of the land of your possession."[1] Here it appears on the face of the law that the Israelites at the time of its enactment were not yet settled in Canaan, and were living in tents—at least were not living in houses. Yet this very law has been adduced to show that the Israelites were already settled in Canaan.[2] There are also some other laws that could not be applied in the wilderness, and were not intended to come into operation until after the settlement in Canaan, such as the laws in regard to lands, landmarks, first-fruits, newly-built houses, houses in walled cities and houses in villages, newly-planted vineyards, and the seventh-year rest for the land. All such laws and regulations were intended to be operative among the Israelites, not in the wilderness, but when settled in the land of promise. The prospective aim of such laws is often expressly pointed out, as, for example, the law in regard to landmarks: "Thou shalt not remove thy neighbor's landmark, which they of old time have set in thine inheritance, which thou shalt inherit in the land that the Lord thy God giveth thee to possess it."[3] After all that the critics have said about this passage, the fact remains that the phraseology employed in it implies that the Israelites were not living on separated lands, but expected soon to be.[4] Thus the laws scattered through the Pentateuch, though in many cases plainly intended to be operative only in the future and among an agricultural people, unmistakably point to the nomadic condition of the Israelites in the wilderness as existent at the time of enactment.

The style and terms of the laws indicate the Israelites, at the time of enactment, to be on the way from Egypt to Canaan.

(1) Israel is in the wilderness: Leviticus 16: 10, 21, 22.

(2) Israel is in camp: Leviticus 4: 12, 21; 6: 11; 8: 17; 9: 11; 10: 4, 5; 13: 46; 14: 3, 8; 16: 26, 27, 28; 17: 3; 24: 10, 14, 23. The burnt-offering was to be carried *without the camp;* the sin-offering also was to be carried and burned *without the camp;* the ashes from the altar were to be carried *without the camp;* the

---

[1] Lev. 14: 34.   [2] Kuenen, *Hexateuch*, p. 20.   [3] Deut. 19: 14.   [4] See p. 56.

leper was to stay *without the camp;* the priest was to visit him *without the camp;* and thus throughout the Levitical legislation the Israelites are contemplated as occupying a camp.

(3) The Pentateuchal laws contemplate the settlement in Canaan as being, at the time of their enactment, a future event. "When ye be come into the land of Canaan, which I give to you for a possession."[1] "And when ye shall come into the land, and shall have planted all manner of trees for food."[2] "When ye come into the land which I give you, then shall the land keep a sabbath unto the Lord."[3] "When thou art come unto the land which the Lord thy God giveth thee, and shalt possess it."[4] See also Deuteronomy 15: 4, 7; 12: 9; Leviticus 18: 3; Deuteronomy 19: 1.

(4) At the time of the enactment of these laws, the tabernacle and God's presence and worship had no fixed abiding-place. "In all places [in every place] where I record my name I will come unto thee, and I will bless thee."[5] The Levitical law required sacrifices to be brought to the tabernacle, wherever it might be, and this requisition was declared to be a statute forever unto the Israelites throughout their generations.[6] Again and again is it indicated in Deuteronomy that God had not yet chosen the one place of central worship. "But unto the place which the Lord your God shall choose out of all your tribes to put his name there, even unto his habitation shall ye seek, and thither thou shalt come."[7] See also Deuteronomy 12: 11, 14, 18, 26; 14: 23; 15: 20; 16: 2; 17: 8; 18: 6; 23: 16; 26: 2; 31: 11.

(5) The regulations in Exodus concerning the consecration of priests mention by name Aaron, which shows that these regulations were established before Aaron's death.[8] Also in Numbers, in connection with the regulations concerning the lighting of the lamps in the tabernacle, the consecration of the Levites, and other matters, the name of Aaron is expressly mentioned.

Thus the style and terms of the laws and regulations contained in these last four books of the Pentateuch indicate that they were enacted and published when the Israelites were in the wilderness, unless the suggestive marks above pointed out were placed upon them with the intention of deceiving.

3. Many of the Pentateuchal laws were suited only to Mosaic times.

---

[1] Lev. 14: 34. [2] Lev. 19: 23. [3] Lev. 25: 2. [4] Deut. 17: 14.
[5] Ex. 20: 24. [6] Lev. 17: 3-9. [7] Deut. 12: 5. [8] Ex. 40: 13.

We have shown above that these laws were just such as might be expected from Moses in the wilderness. Laws are made for the present and the future, and the laws of the Pentateuch were adapted to the circumstances of the Israelites in the desert, and also to their future condition in Canaan. The point we now make is, that if these laws originated in the times, or near the times, claimed by the analysts, then whoever got them up must have framed laws neither for the present nor for the future, but for the past,—an absurdity which no statesman, nor perhaps anybody else, ever committed.

(1) The law of the king is, according to the analytic theories, precisely of this character, and carries a lie on its face besides.

(*a*) It claims to have been enacted by Moses before the entrance into Canaan. "When thou art come unto the land which the Lord thy God giveth thee, and shalt possess it."[1] This preamble is a lie, if the law which follows is not of Mosaic origin.

(*b*) The provision that the Israelites should appoint as king only the one whom God should choose, and one of their own nation,[2] is out of place and absurd if enacted in the time of Josiah, or near that time. For long before that time David had been made king by divine appointment and popular choice, and his descendants, by the same right, had long reigned in Jerusalem.

(*c*) That the king should not lead the people back into Egypt[3] is another useless and absurd law, if not enacted till near the close of the monarchy; for all danger of a return to Egypt had ceased many centuries before.

(*d*) The provision against the multiplication of horses and wives by the prospective king[4] was entirely in place, if enacted by Moses; for he had seen the abuses and evils of monarchy in the land of Egypt.

(*e*) The fact that Samuel did not refer to this law of the king in resisting the demands of the people does not prove that he was ignorant of it. The law did not suit his purpose. His effort was to prevent the appointment of a king altogether. The people, however, in urging this measure on Samuel, quoted this law as in their favor—"Nay; but we will have a king over us; that we also may be like all the nations."[5]

(2) The laws of war, as contained in Deuteronomy,[6] are

---

[1] Deut. 17: 14.   [2] Deut. 17: 15.   [3] Deut. 17: 16.   [4] Deut. 17: 16, 17.
[5] I. Sam. 8: 19, 20; Deut. 17: 14.   [6] Deut. 20: 1-20.

suited to the time of the conquest, but not to the later years of the monarchy.

(*a*) These laws speak of the conquest as future — the nations of Canaan as yet to be conquered and destroyed.[1] If this war code did not originate, as it purports, in Mosaic times, the law demanding the extermination of these nations must have been inserted for the purpose of deception.

(*b*) The distinction between cities distant and near, the regulations in regard to captives and tributaries, and the directions for the preservation of fruit-trees during sieges, are all unaccountable anachronisms, if either enacted or published after the time of Solomon.

(*c*) This code, however, furnishes evidence that it was enacted before the establishment of the monarchy. In it the idea of a king as commander of the army is utterly excluded. The priest is to address the soldiers on the eve of battle. The officers are to proclaim liberty to certain classes to withdraw from the army. *Then leaders in battle are to be appointed.* There is no chance here for the exercise of kingly power in the army. But the Hebrew idea of a king was that of a man to lead the army and fight the battles of Israel. Clearly this code was out of place after the appointment of Saul as king.

(3) The command to destroy the Amalekites would have been absurdly out of place after the time of David.[2]

(*a*) This is declared to be one of Moses' commands to Israel shortly before his death.

(*b*) The Israelites were to execute this command after their settlement in Canaan, which is thus represented as not yet accomplished.

(*c*) This command was partially executed by Samuel and Saul,[3] and more fully by David.[4]

(*d*) In commissioning Saul to exterminate the Amalekites, Samuel evidently referred to what is recorded in this passage.[5]

(4) The laws in regard to magistrates and the trial of cases plainly point to the times before the monarchy. These laws provide for government and trials by priests, elders, and judges. Kingly power is excluded by them. Thus provision is made for carrying cases by appeal from the court of the elders in the gate to the court in the place which God should choose — "unto the

---

[1] Deut. 20: 16, 17.   [2] Deut. 25: 17-19.   [3] I. Sam. 15: 1-33.
[4] I. Sam. 30: 11-20.   [5] I. Sam. 15: 2, 3.

priests the Levites, and unto the judge that shall be in those days, and enquire; and they shall show thee the sentence of judgment."[1] It is indeed true, as adverted to above, that the possibility or probability of the appointment of a king, at the demand of the people, is mentioned; but it is mentioned only as a *future* contingency. The laws provide for a commonwealth, are adapted to it, and are so framed that a king and kingly power could come in only as intruders. This is true of all the laws contained in the Pentateuch. Not one of them recognizes the monarchy as having been established, or gives the remotest hint of its existence, except as future.

(5) This consideration is strengthened by the fact that the books which contain these laws, and the whole history in which they are imbedded, observe the same absolute silence in regard to the monarchy, and in regard to the whole history of the nation after the time of Moses. There is not a word in all these laws and in all these law books that betrays knowledge of any event after his death and burial. We reserve this point for further treatment in the next chapter.

[1] Deut. 17: 1-13.

CHAPTER X
ARGUMENT FROM SILENCE

THE analytics claim that Judges, Samuel, the Psalms, Proverbs, and other succeeding books are silent in regard to the Pentateuch, and they argue that therefore these books came into existence before the Pentateuch. We will endeavor to show farther on that the historical, poetic, and prophetic books are not silent in regard to the Pentateuch, but do recognize its existence in various ways. The argument from silence may, however, be employed more effectively on the other side. The Pentateuch does not mention, quote, or allude to, nor in any way indicate, suggest, or recognize any other book of the Bible. The Pentateuch, therefore, must have preceded all the other books of the Bible. It is silent in regard to Hosea, Jeremiah, and Isaiah, and it must, therefore, have been written before their time. It makes no allusion to any of the Psalms, and, therefore, it preceded even the Davidic Psalms. Neither does the Pentateuch in any way allude to or recognize the books of Samuel, Judges, or Joshua. It is, therefore, of earlier date than any of these books. This reasoning would be entirely conclusive, provided silence of one book concerning another were proof of prior existence, which it is not; for many an author has no occasion to mention contemporary or preceding authors.

But if the Pentateuchal books were produced in the exilic age or post-exilic age, their silence in regard to many preceding persons and events is unaccountable. These books are absolutely silent in regard to the whole Jewish history from the exile back to the death and burial of Moses. In all these five books there is not a word about the establishment of the monarchy, the division of the nation into two kingdoms, the destruction of the ten tribes, the exile, or any other event in that long period of more than nine hundred years; not one word about Saul, David, Solomon, or any other king; not one word about Samuel, Elijah, Isaiah, or any other prophet; not one word even about the temple, with its beauty and its priestly service.

Silence in regard to all these persons and all these events so dear to the pride and patriotism and piety of the Jewish heart! It is questionable whether such a silence was psychologically possible on the part of Jewish authors living at or after the time of the exile. It is certain that this silence is very improbable and altogether unaccountable.

This silence becomes still more enigmatical and improbable when viewed in connection with the hypotheses of the analysts concerning the origin of the Pentateuchal books. They suppose that Deuteronomy was written near the close of the monarchy, in the time of Manasseh, probably about 650 B.C. They suppose, further, that the other four books were written, or in some way gotten up, during the exile in Babylonia. And still further, they suppose that in these Pentateuchal books are embraced the writings, or extracts from the writings, of an unknown author, E, who lived 800 B.C., and of another unknown author, J, who lived 900 B.C. They suppose, too, that a host of writers, compilers, redactors, and interpolators, living in exilic times, worked on the Pentateuch. Yet, according to these hypotheses, not one of these many authors, compilers, redactors, and interpolators made any allusion to his own times or country, or in any way indicated when or where he lived, or, indeed, whether he lived at all, or in any way betrayed his knowledge of any event in Jewish history after the crossing of the Jordan to conquer Canaan; or, if the Pentateuch did originally contain any such allusions or suggestions, they were all carefully weeded out by designing redactors. The intention of this silence must have been to deceive, and, according to the views of the analytics, the effort to deceive has been wonderfully successful, leading astray the very elect, even the disciples of Christ, and Christ himself, the great Teacher. What extraordinary men those Pentateuchal authors must have been! How careful, cautious, and self-restrained they were, not saying a word to betray their knowledge of their times and places, avoiding all allusion to the history of the preceding nine hundred years, and projecting themselves, with complete and self-consistent abandon, back into the ideas, laws, and affairs of the Mosaic age! Wonderful men they must have been!

Yet the analysts go right on employing *argumentum e silentio* against the traditional belief, apparently unaware that this argument cuts both ways, and that it cuts with even a keener edge against the analytic theories. Their argument is, that the Psalms and prophecies are silent in regard to the Pentateuch, and therefore came into existence before it. We say that the Pentateuch is silent in regard to the Psalms and prophecies, and therefore came into existence before them.

CHAPTER XI

EGYPTIAN WORDS AND NAMES

The author's ignorance of the Egyptian language and hieroglyphics disqualifies him for a proper handling of this subject. All that shall be attempted is the statement of a few facts.

1. The name *Pharaoh* is the Hebrew title of the Egyptian king. It is Hebrew in this sense, that it is employed by the Hebrew writers and by them alone. It occurs first in the history of Abraham. But *Pharaoh* is an Egyptian word (*Perao*), and means *the great house*, or *palace*. The *Sublime Porte* of the Turks is an analogous phrase.

2. The word *abrech* (translated "bow the knee"[1]) is declared to be of Semitic origin, but is retained in the hieroglyphic dictionary.[2]

3. *Zaphnath-paaneah*,[3] the title given to Joseph, means *governor of the place of life;* i. e., of the capital of the country.

4. *Asenath*, the name of Joseph's wife, is declared to be pure Egyptian, and to be but seldom met with, except in the Old and Middle Empire.

5. *Poti-pherah*, the name of Joseph's father-in-law, means *gift of the sun*.

6. *Ahu*, translated "meadow" in Genesis 41:2, is an Egyptian word, which means *marsh-grass* or *sedge*. It is translated "reed-grass" in the Revised Version.

7. The name *Moses* appears to be of Egyptian origin. It appears in *Rameses*, *Amosis*, and other names. It contains the Egyptian word for *son — mes* or *mesu*. Pharaoh's daughter called the child found in the ark of bulrushes "Moses," claiming him as her son, because she had drawn him from the water and *thus given him birth*.

8. *Rameses* or *Ramesu* means the *son of the sun*.[4]

This list is sufficient to remind the reader that Genesis and

---

[1] Gen. 41:43.   [2] Brugsch-Bey, *Egypt Under the Pharaohs*, p. 122.
[3] Gen. 41:45.
[4] These facts are taken from Brugsch-Bey, Kenrick, Sayce, and Naville.

Exodus contain Egyptian words and names. Their use suggests the residence of the author in Egypt, just as the Aramaic words in the books of Daniel and Ezra suggest the residence of their authors in Babylonia. As the Aramaic words in these books point to the time of the exile, so the Egyptian words in the Pentateuch point to the time of the exodus. The occurrence of such words in Genesis and Exodus is accounted for only in this way.

PART IV

EXTERNAL EVIDENCE

PART IV
EXTERNAL EVIDENCE

CHAPTER I
THE BOOK OF JOSHUA

In regard to the Book of Joshua, its date, and its relations to the other books of the so-called Hexateuch, our critics are all at sea. Reuss at one time declares that it is uncertain whether priority should be assigned to Deuteronomy or to Joshua. At another, he affirms "the necessity of concluding that the Book of Joshua, in its actual form, is posterior to the Deuteronomic code, but contemporary with, or rather an integral part of, the Deuteronomic book."[1] Graf makes the following statement: "Reuss hat darauf aufmerksam gemacht, dass die Beziehung des B. Josua auf den Pentateuch in gesetzlicher Rücksicht sowohl als in historischer sich auf das Deuteronomium und den letzen Theil des B. Numeri beschränkt, ein neuer Beweis, wenn es dessen noch bedürfte, dass die Theile des jetzigen Pentateuchs, die sich uns als nachexilische erwiesen haben, bei der Abfassung des B. Josua noch nicht vorhanden waren"[2] ("Reuss has called attention to the fact that the connection of the Book of Joshua with the Pentateuch, in a legal as well as historical view, is limited to Deuteronomy and the last part of the Book of Numbers—a new proof, if any were needed, that the parts of the present Pentateuch which exhibit themselves to us as post-exilic were not on hand at the composition of the Book of Joshua"). Kuenen is quite sure that there is in Joshua a Deuteronomic recasting of an older story, either by the author of Deuteronomy or by some of its redactors, but in regard to the date of the book he has little to say.[3] Wellhausen pronounces it to be historically untrue, and thus imperiously waves aside whatever in it comes in con-

---
[1] *L'Histoire Sainte*, Vol. I., p. 216.
[2] *Geschichtlichen Bücher des Alten Testaments*, p. 95. [3] *Hexateuch*, pp. 130, 131.

flict with his views.[1] This treatment of the Book of Joshua by the critics, and their conflicting views concerning it, are in consequence of two facts, one of which is that the Book of Joshua presupposes the books of the Pentateuch, and the other is that it was written near the time of the conquest of Canaan. It is these two facts, we think, that produce the paralysis of the critics referred to above.

Let us first attend to the date of the book.

1. Our first proposition is, that it was written before the exile. The proof is as follows: At the time Joshua was written, the city of Ai was lying in ruins, and a place uninhabited. This is expressly stated. "And Joshua burnt Ai, and made it an heap forever, even a desolation unto this day."[2] But Ai was rebuilt and inhabited before the time of Ezra and Nehemiah. It is mentioned once in Ezra[3] and twice in Nehemiah[4] as having been inhabited before the exile. Since the author of Joshua describes Ai as still lying in ruins in his day, it is evident that he lived and wrote before the exile.

2. By parity of reasoning it is shown that he lived and wrote before the time of Isaiah; for Ai is spoken of by this prophet as an inhabited city. "He is come to Aiath."[5] It is generally admitted that this is another name for Ai. Even Professor Cheyne unhesitatingly accepts this opinion.[6] Hence Joshua was written before the time of Isaiah.

3. It is further in evidence that Joshua was written before the time of Solomon, for the author expressly states that in his time, at the very time he wrote, the Canaanites were dwelling in Gezer among the Ephraimites. "And they drave not out the Canaanites that dwelt in Gezer; but the Canaanites dwell among the Ephraimites unto this day, and serve under tribute."[7] But it is further in evidence that the Canaanites ceased to inhabit Gezer in the time of Solomon. This is stated in the Book of Kings, as follows: "For Pharaoh king of Egypt had gone up and taken Gezer, and burnt it with fire, and slain the Canaanites that dwelt in the city, and given it for a present unto his daughter, Solomon's wife. And Solomon built Gezer, and Beth-horon the nether."[8] It is clear that Joshua was written before the destruction of Gezer and its inhabitants by the king of Egypt.

Up to this point our critics make but little resistance. But to

---

[1] *Israel*, p. 442.   [2] Josh. 8:28.   [3] Ezra 2:28.   [4] Neh. 7:32; 11:31.
[5] Isa. 10:28.   [6] Cheyne on *Isaiah*, p. 74.   [7] Josh. 16:10.   [8] I. Kings 9:16, 17.

admit that Joshua was written before the time of Solomon would endanger their theories, and here they begin to contend. Kuenen admits that if the passage in I. Kings 9:16 is taken literally "we should have to place Joshua 16:10 before Solomon,"[1] but he endeavors to get out of the difficulty by the supposition that Gezer did "not become tributary to the Israelites until after its conquest by Solomon's father-in-law."[1] But, in the first place, this is merely a supposition, made without evidence, to avoid an undesirable conclusion. Second, though Kuenen affirms this supposition to be probable, we think it very improbable that Solomon would compel a city which he himself had built "to serve under tribute." Third, the supposition, even if admitted, would not meet the case. For the declaration is, that the Canaanites, at 'the time the author of Joshua was writing, were living with the Ephraimites and serving under tribute. But the declaration in Kings is, that in the time of Solomon Pharaoh burned the city and slew the Canaanites. They certainly did not pay tribute, nor even live in Gezer, after Pharaoh had killed them. The two facts then remain: the Canaanites were living in Gezer in the time of the author of Joshua, but they ceased to live there during the early part of Solomon's reign. Hence the author of Joshua lived and wrote before the time of Solomon.

4. Joshua was written before the time of King David, for at the time it was written the Jebusites held and inhabited Jerusalem; but in David's time they were conquered. "As for the Jebusites, the inhabitants of Jerusalem, the children of Judah could not drive them out: but the Jebusites dwell with the children of Judah at Jerusalem unto this day."[2] Their subjugation by David is related both in Samuel[3] and in Chronicles.[4] The plain and legitimate conclusion is, that the above declaration was made by the author of Joshua before the conquest of Jerusalem, which took place in the earlier part of the reign of David.

Kuenen's way of meeting this argument is as follows: He affirms that this passage in Joshua points to the time after David, "for till then Jerusalem was still completely in the power of the Jebusites, but after its capture by David they remained there side by side with the Israelites."[5] Reuss favors this interpretation by his rendering of the passage, as follows: "The

[1] *Hexateuch*, p. 36. [2] Josh. 15:63. [3] II. Sam. 5:6-9.
[4] I. Chr. 11:4-8. [5] *Hexateuch*, p. 36.

Jebusites have inhabited Jerusalem conjointly with those of Judah until this day."[1] To all this it may be replied, (1) that if the Jebusites dwelt in Jerusalem and the Israelites in the surrounding country and towns, the conditions of the declaration would be fulfilled, so far as the dwelling together of the two races is concerned. (2) The passage in question refers to a time when the Israelites "*could* not drive the Jebusites out of Jerusalem." If the Israelites did not expel the Jebusites in David's time, it was not for the want of power. The passage, then, refers to a state of things before David's time. For he conquered and captured Jerusalem.[2]

5. There are several passages in Joshua which point to a time not long after the conquest. The writer states that Joshua placed in Jordan twelve stones as a memorial of the miraculous crossing of the children of Israel, and he adds that at the time he was writing these stones were still remaining in the midst of Jordan, where Joshua had placed them: "And they are there unto this day."[3] But it is not probable that these stones would remain in the Jordan a very long time. Freshets would wash them away. The rushing waters of the rapid river would wear them away, in accordance with the old adage that the constant drop will wear the stone. About four hundred years intervened between the crossing of the Jordan and the reign of King David. It is preposterous to suppose that those memorial stones remained in the swift current of the Jordan during one-half of that time, or even one-fourth. But the author of Joshua says, "They are there unto this day." If they remained there only fifty years, the Book of Joshua was written within fifty years after the crossing of the Jordan. If they remained only twenty-five years, the book must have been written within that period after the crossing.

There are other and similar indications of time. The writer says that the pile of stones placed over the dead body of Achan was still to be seen in his day: "And they raised over him a great heap of stones unto this day."[4] How long would that pile of stones probably remain? Would it be likely to remain five hundred, four hundred, or three hundred years? Would it be likely to remain a century even, exposed to frost, and flood, and fire, and earthquake, and whirlwind, and the doings of men and beasts?

Again, the writer employs the formula "unto this day" in

---

[1] *L'Histoire Sainte*, Vol. II., p. 398. [2] II. Sam. 5: 6-9; I. Chr. 11: 4-8.
[3] Josh. 4: 9.   [4] Josh. 7: 26.

regard to the stones which were placed in the mouth of the cave of Makkedah, in which the five kings were buried. It is not probable that these stones would remain five hundred years, or even a century. Curiosity, if nothing else, would induce some one to remove the stones and enter the cave.

Once more, the declaration concerning the Gibeonites points to a time before Samuel and Saul: "And Joshua made them that day hewers of wood and drawers of water for the congregation, and for the altar of the Lord, even unto this day, in the place which he should choose."[1] There are two notes of time in this declaration: (1) The words "should choose," being the words of the historian, not of Joshua, indicate that at the time of writing the choice of a place for the altar and worship of God had not yet been made. The time, therefore, was at least before the building of the temple. (2) The other indication of time is by the phrase "unto this day." Evidently the author means that in his day the Gibeonites were in the condition in which they were placed by Joshua. But they were not in this condition in the time of Saul, David, or Solomon, or in succeeding times. The Nethinim were not mere wood-cutters and water-drawers. Clearly, then, the writer of Joshua 9: 27 lived at least before the time of Samuel.

Kuenen makes two remarks about this passage. One is that Saul did not kill all the Gibeonites,[2] which is true. The other remark is, that in this verse we have a double representation put together in defiance of consistency and grammar. This is not criticism, but mere skeptical dogmatism.

6. The date of the Book of Joshua is fixed by the declaration made concerning Rahab: "And Joshua saved Rahab the harlot alive, and her father's household, and all that she had; and she dwelleth in Israel even unto this day; because she hid the messengers which Joshua sent to spy out Jericho."[3] The obvious meaning of this passage is that Rahab was still living at the time it was written. And this clearly proves that this passage, and presumptively the whole Book of Joshua, were written not later than the generation immediately succeeding Joshua and the conquest.

The critics, of course, make an effort to set aside this testimony so damaging to their theories. Kuenen asserts, and in this case does nothing more than assert, that Joshua 6: 25 "does not

[1] Josh. 9: 27.   [2] *Hexateuch*, p. 36.   [3] Josh. 6: 25.

refer to Rahab, but to her descendants."[1] We ask the reader's attention to the absurdity of this construction. It makes the name of Rahab change from a personal to a figurative meaning, and back again from a figurative to a personal meaning in one short verse. "And Joshua saved *Rahab* the harlot alive and *her* father's household and all that *she* had; and *she* dwelleth in Israel even unto this day, because *she* hid the messengers, which Joshua sent to spy out Jericho." To say that the pronoun "she" in the middle clause does not mean Rahab, though it does so mean immediately before and after, is an illustration of the shifts to which some critics will resort in order to refute an unanswerable argument. Reuss also tries his hand on the passage, and his effort is to get rid of the reference to present time. Avoiding the present tense of the English version and the present-perfect of the French, he translates as follows: "Josué la laissa vivre, et elle demeura parmi les Israelites jusqu'a ce jour"[2] ("Joshua saved her life, and she lived among the Israelites until this day"). But, after all, the words "until this day" signify *present time*, and even if in Reuss's translation the death of Rahab is implied, it is further implied that she had lived on up to the time in which the author lived and wrote, and that she had died only a short time previous. The critic seems to have been aware of this, and in a marginal note says, "S'il est dit que Rahab demeure *encore* in Israel, il s'agit naturellement de ses descendants"[2] ("If it is said that Rahab *lives* still in Israel, it naturally applies to her descendants"). This is as much as to say that "Rahab" does not naturally mean Rahab, but her descendants. Evidently the critic felt the necessity of holding this construction, as it were, in reserve, to be resorted to in case of failure of his other expedient. But Reuss has completely spoiled this construction by his translation. For the expression, "She lived until this day," implies that she was dead at the time of writing. But as her *posterity* did not cease to exist, this clause cannot apply to them, and must refer to Rahab personally.

We are not aware that Wellhausen deals specially with this passage. He recognized the necessity of getting rid entirely of the testimony of the Book of Joshua to the early existence of the Pentateuch, and hence denies its historical character. This delivers him from the necessity of petty shifts and unnatural constructions.

[1] *Hexateuch*, p. 36. [2] *L'Histoire Sainte*, Vol. II., p. 373.

7. Another passage bearing on the question in hand is as follows: "And Israel served the Lord all the days of Joshua, and all the days of the elders that overlived Joshua."[1] It is to be observed that the writer in this declaration does not go beyond the time covered by the life of Joshua and the lives of his contemporaries that survived him, and that he is entirely silent in regard to the course of the Israelites after that time. Why this silence? The hypothesis that the writer was one of those contemporaries that outlived Joshua, and wrote in the age immediately succeeding, accounts for this silence. Nothing else accounts for it, or at least so well. There is, then, a strong presumption in favor of this hypothesis. This presumption is strengthened by what the author of the Book of Judges says concerning the subsequent course of the Israelites. He first repeats the declaration made in Joshua that "the people served the Lord all the days of Joshua, and all the days of the elders that outlived Joshua, who had seen all the great works of the Lord that he did for Israel"; then, after mentioning the death of Joshua, he adds: "And also all that generation were gathered unto their fathers. And there arose another generation after them, which knew not the Lord, nor yet the works which he had done for Israel. And the children of Israel did evil in the sight of the Lord, and served Baalim."[2] The author of the Book of Judges, living after Joshua and his surviving contemporaries, is a competent witness to testify as to what took place in the succeeding generation as well as to the course of Israel in Joshua's time. But, to use the phrase of the critics, the author of Joshua "knows nothing" of what took place in Israel in the generation after Moses and his contemporaries. There is a marked difference between the two writers in this respect.

8. Finally, the author of Joshua speaks of himself as taking part in the conquest of Canaan. In speaking of the crossing of the Jordan by the Israelites, under the command of Joshua, to attack Jericho, he employs the pronoun *we*,—"until *we* were passed over."[3] According to the plain meaning of these words, the writer of this declaration was one of those who crossed the Jordan under the leadership of Joshua. It is by just such evidence that it is proved that the author of the Acts was the contemporary and companion of Paul.[4] The analytic critics do not agree as to the mode of getting rid of the testimony of this

[1] Josh. 24:31.   [2] Judg. 2:7-11.   [3] Josh. 5:1.   [4] Acts 16:10.

passage. Kuenen claims that the text is erroneous, and that the true reading gives us "they" instead of "we." He thinks he knows how the error originated, namely, by the eye of the transcriber resting on the twenty-third verse of the preceding chapter and by his copying therefrom the word "we."[1] This is mere assertion based on conjecture. There is, however, a various reading which gives the pronoun in the third person. The Revised Version places this reading in the margin. The accepted reading is, however, sustained by the manuscripts, and is probably correct. The argument is therefore entitled to consideration. De Wette, without questioning the correctness of the reading, maintains that the writer, though living long afterward, identified himself in thought with the Israelites as they crossed the Jordan, and therefore said "we." He refers to Psalm 66:6, which is not a parallel case. Our passage in Joshua is a historical statement and is to be understood in a literal way. Reuss's way of getting rid of the pronoun in the first person is certainly the most convenient, if not the most successful. He omits it from his translation and says nothing about it. He is by no means singular in this, but such a procedure was not to be expected in a famous critical work gotten up to overthrow traditional beliefs.

Such are the evidences of the early date of the Book of Joshua. To plead that these marks of antiquity are the work of revisers is of no avail unless that plea is accompanied with the proved charge of dishonesty. For the book revised must precede the revision, and the original writer be more ancient than the reviser. The hypothesis, then, of revision only makes matters worse for the analysts, unless it can be shown that the revisers inserted marks of antiquity for the purpose of deceiving. Our critics, however, are not very forward to make, at least in a direct way, the charge of fraud against the biblical writers. Kuenen does indeed indulge pretty freely in charges of this kind, in his work entitled, "The Bible for Learners," but when he assumes to write with the dignity of a critic he suppresses pretty thoroughly out-givings of that sort, being led, perhaps, by a sense of decency.

Now the antiquity of the Book of Joshua demonstrates the mistakes of our critics. The existence of this book soon after the death of Moses plays havoc with their hypotheses and arguments.

[1] *Hexateuch*, p. 36.

1. The Book of Joshua presupposes the Mosaic laws. It makes express mention of them. "Only be thou strong and very courageous, that thou mayest observe to do according to all the law which Moses my servant commanded thee."[1] "This book of the law shall not depart out of thy mouth; but thou shalt meditate therein day and night, that thou mayest observe to do according to all that is written therein."[2] "As Moses the servant of the Lord commanded the children of Israel, as it is written in the book of the law of Moses, an altar of whole stones, over which no man hath lift up any iron."[3] "There was not a word of all that Moses commanded, which Joshua read not before all the congregation of Israel, with the women, and the little ones, and the strangers that were conversant among them."[4] "Be ye therefore very courageous to keep and to do all that is written in the book of the law of Moses, that ye turn not aside therefrom to the right hand or to the left."[5]

These and other passages set forth the following facts: (1) that in the time of Joshua the Israelites had a body of laws for their guidance as a nation and as individuals; (2) that these laws were written; (3) that Moses was their recognized author; (4) that they were recorded in a book, called the "book of the law" and the "book of the law of Moses"; (5) that the law and the book of the law were distinguished from one another. Joshua *wrote* a copy of the law of Moses on the stones of the altar, in the presence of the Israelites; but he *read* to the people all the words of the law, according to all that was written in the book of the law.[6]

These facts are an additional proof, if any were needed, of the utter inadmissibility of the hypothesis of the analysts that the so-called "Mosaic code" originated by development after the time of Moses.

2. The Book of Joshua recognizes the existence of the ark and the tabernacle. The ark was prominent in the crossing of the Jordan and in the capture of Jericho. The first mention of it indicates its prior and well-known existence.[7] This is true also of the tabernacle. The first mention of it presupposes its previous institution and history: "And the whole congregation of the children of Israel assembled together at Shiloh, and set up the tabernacle of the congregation there."[8] Aside from the

[1] Josh. 1:7. [2] Josh. 1:8. [3] Josh. 8:31. [4] Josh. 8:35.
[5] Josh. 23:6. [6] Josh. 8:32, 34. [7] Josh. 3:3. [8] Josh. 18:1.

time of the writing of the Book of Joshua, the historical statement just quoted must be pronounced false by every one who follows our critics in holding that the Mosaic tabernacle existed only in the imagination and fictions of later writers. But in view of the antiquity of the book, he who agrees with these critics in this matter must conclude that its author was guilty of known and willful falsehood; for a writer who was partly contemporary with Joshua must have known whether any Mosaic tabernacle then existed. The antiquity of this book, then, proves the existence of the ark and the tabernacle in the time of Joshua, unless we assume that the writer of Joshua affirmed what he knew to be false. On the other hand, the existence of the tabernacle and the ark presupposes a Levitical code and service, in opposition to the evolutionary hypothesis of the analysts.

3. Accordingly, in this book Levitical ideas and customs are set forth very prominently. We have an example of this in the account of the destruction of Jericho. The ark borne by the priests, preceded by seven priests bearing seven trumpets, proceeded around the beleaguered city once a day for six days, the seven priests blowing their seven trumpets; but on the seventh day they thus marched around the walls seven times: "And seven priests bearing seven trumpets of rams' horns before the ark of the Lord went on continually, and blew with the trumpets: and the armed men went before them; but the rearward came after the ark of the Lord, the priests going on, and blowing with the trumpets." [1] Here are brought to view the Levitical priests and their service. To use Reuss's expression, we have here "Leviticism in full view." [2] The account, merely as history, is a blow to the hypothesis of the origin of the Levitical code by development, and greater force is imparted to it by the antiquity of the book.

4. The Book of Joshua reveals the fact that in Joshua's time it was recognized as an existing law that there should be but one central place of worship. When the two and a half tribes east of the Jordan erected an altar, their brethren charged them with trespass and rebellion, and were restrained from going to war only by the assurance that the new altar was not intended for sacrifice and worship, but merely as a memorial. They of the east side said, "God forbid that we should rebel against the

---

[1] Josh. 6: 13.　　　　　[2] "En pleine Leviticism."

Lord, and turn this day from following the Lord, to build an altar for burnt-offerings, for meat-offerings, or for sacrifices, besides the altar of the Lord our God that is before his tabernacle."[1] Thus both the parties accepted the law as requiring the centralization of worship, and recognized the offering of sacrifices elsewhere than at the altar before the tabernacle as disobedience and rebellion. This is the statement of the author of Joshua. Who has a right to contradict this statement and pronounce it a mistake or a lie? But, in addition to this, the accuracy and truthfulness of the account are guaranteed by the fact that it was written in the time of Joshua.

5. The Book of Joshua presupposes the books of the Pentateuch. It more especially presupposes Deuteronomy, and through it the preceding books. As an example, let us take the first chapter of Joshua. Almost every verse contains a quotation from, or a reference to, some passage found in the Pentateuch; more generally in the last book. In the first and second verses the words, "Now after the death of Moses the servant of the Lord," and "Moses my servant is dead," clearly point to Deuteronomy 34:5. The words, "Joshua the son of Nun, Moses' minister," in the first verse, point to Exodus 24:13; 33:11. Verses 3, 4, and 5 are a repetition of Deuteronomy 11:24, 25. Verses 6 and 7 are taken from Deuteronomy 31:6, 7. The eighth verse refers to Deuteronomy 31:9, 26; 5:32, 33. Verses 14 and 15 refer to Numbers 32:28-33.

The twenty-third chapter also abounds in references to the preceding books. To be convinced that Joshua makes almost continual reference to the books of the Pentateuch the reader needs only to hunt up the references in an ordinary polyglot Bible.

[1] Josh. 22:29.

CHAPTER II

HISTORICAL BOOKS AFTER JOSHUA

1. In the Book of Judges the Pentateuchal laws and history are repeatedly and variously recognized.

God's covenant with Israel, the prohibition of leagues with the nations of Canaan [1] and of intermarriages [2] with them, the separation of the Levites to the priestly office, [3] the law of the Nazarite, [4] circumcision, [5] a central place of worship, [6] and many other laws and institutions are mentioned just as they are set forth in Deuteronomy and other books of the Pentateuch.

The message which Jephthah sent to the king of the Ammonites, and much else that is contained in the eleventh chapter of Judges, have all the marks of quotations from the twentieth and twenty-first chapters of Numbers. That they really are such, and that Jephthah quoted the very language of that book, is not likely to be denied by any, except by those who have an hypothesis to maintain.

2. The books of Samuel, in like manner, presuppose the Pentateuchal laws and institutions.

In them Shiloh appears as the one place of central worship. Here were the tabernacle of the congregation, the ark of the covenant, the altar, the show-bread, and the Levitical priests, clothed with the ephod. To Shiloh the Israelites came yearly to eat and to drink before the Lord, to worship and to offer sacrifices. There were various services and sacrifices—the yearly sacrifice and special sacrifices, burnt-offerings and whole burnt-offerings, peace-offerings, trespass-offerings, vows, incense, offerings of meal and wine, the burning of the fat upon the altar, and a portion for the priests. [7] Besides these incidental allusions, there is a more distinct recognition of many of the Mosaic laws—the divine appointment of the Levitical priesthood; [8] the festival of the new moon; [9] ceremonial cleanness and unclean-

---

[1] Judg. 2:2; Deut. 7:2,3. [2] Judg. 3:6. [3] Judg. 17:7-13; Num. 3:5-10.
[4] Judg. 13:4,5; Num. 6:2-12. [5] Judg. 14:3. [6] Judg. 19:18.
[7] I. Sam. 1:3, 9, 11, 25; 2:15. [8] I. Sam. 2:27-29. [9] I. Sam. 20:5, 18.

ness;[1] the regulations in regard to the slaughtering of animals for food and the prohibition of the eating of blood;[2] the capital punishment of wizards and witches;[3] the Lord's purpose and command to exterminate the Amalekites;[4] and many other allusions to laws, institutions, and customs which are known to us only in the Pentateuchal books.

The analytic critics endeavor to set aside the testimony of the books of Samuel to the early existence of the Mosaic laws and institutions and of the Pentateuch by their convenient hypothesis of revisions and interpolations. They claim that some of the statements are Deuteronomic insertions, and that others are even of post-exilic origin. Besides this, they claim that these books are not trustworthy, anyhow. Wellhausen says of one portion, "Es genügt den Inhalt dieser Geschichte zu referiren, um ihre geistliche Mache und ihre innere Unmöglichkeit sofort zur Empfindung zu bringen"[5] ("It is sufficient to refer to the contents of this history in order to make us at once perceive its ghostly make-up and its inherent impossibility"). Again he exclaims, "An der ganzen Erzählung kann kein wahres Wort sein"[6] ("In the whole narrative there is not a truthful word"). Of course, there are many of the analytic school who would not go so far as Wellhausen in denying and making void the Holy Scriptures. Less logical, as well as less daring, than he, they do not so fully realize what must be done in order to defend the analytic hypothesis.

3. The books of Kings and Chronicles.

These books unmistakably refer to the Mosaic laws and the Pentateuch. David charged Solomon, saying, "And keep the charge of the Lord thy God, to walk in his ways, to keep his statutes, and his commandments, and his judgments, and his testimonies, as it is written in the law of Moses."[7] Here the written laws, statutes, commandments, and judgments are mentioned. Again, "And it came to pass, as soon as the kingdom was confirmed in his hand, that he slew his servants which had slain the king his father. But the children of the murderers he slew not: according unto that which is written in the book of the law of Moses, wherein the Lord commanded, saying, The fathers shall not be put to death for the children, nor the children be put to death

---

[1] I. Sam. 20: 26; 21: 4, 5. [2] I. Sam. 14: 33-35; Lev. 20: 27.
[3] I. Sam. 28: 10, with Ex. 22: 18; Lev. 20: 2.
[4] I. Sam. 15: 1-3, with Ex. 17: 16; Deut. 25: 19.
[5] *Prolegomena*, p. 257.   [6] *Idem*, p. 258.   [7] I. Kings 2: 3.

for the fathers; but every man shall be put to death for his own sin."[1] Here we have a quotation from "the book of the law of Moses," as contained in Deuteronomy.[2] There are various other passages in which the book and the law of Moses are either expressly or impliedly mentioned.[3] So strong, indeed, is the testimony to the existence of the Mosaic institutions and books in the time of the kings that the analysts are compelled to apply their india-rubber hypothesis of interpolations by later writers, and to deny the historical character of these two books.

That the books of Chronicles refer to and mention the book and the law of Moses, goes without saying. Thus are mentioned "the statutes and judgments which the Lord charged Moses with concerning Israel."[4] Of King Jehoshaphat it is recorded that "also in the third year of his reign he sent to his princes [five are named] . . . to teach in the cities of Judah. And with them he sent Levites [nine are named] . . . ; and with them Elishama and Jehoram, priests. And they taught in Judah, and had the book of the law of the Lord with them, and went about throughout all the cities of Judah, and taught the people."[5] It is not necessary to quote the many other passages in which reference is made to Mosaic institutions and writings.[6]

In order to nullify the testimony of Chronicles to the early existence of the Pentateuch, the analytics represent them as a late production, and deny their historical character. Wellhausen maintains that they were written three hundred years after the exile, and, besides, charges their author with invention, fiction, discrepancy, contradiction, mutilation, deliberate mutilation, and with nearly everything else that is improper and discreditable in a historical writer. He sneers at what he calls "the law-blessed (crazed) fancy of the chronicler."[7]

Though these critics endeavor to set aside the testimony of the books of Kings by the hypothesis of interpolations, and that of Chronicles by the charge of historical untrustworthiness, they are more than willing to avail themselves of any statements contained in one or the other that seem in any way favorable to the analytic hypothesis. Hence they accept, at least in part, the account of the finding of the book of the law

---

[1] II. Kings 14:5,6. [2] Deut. 24:16. [3] II. Kings 10:31; 17:13,34,37; 23:21,24,25.
[4] I. Chr. 22:13. [5] II. Chr. 17:7-9.
[6] I. Chr. 16:40; 22:12,13; II. Chr. 5:10; 6:16; 12:1; 33:8; 34:14,15,19; 35:12,26. [7] "Gesetzesseligen Phantasie."—*Prolegomena*, p. 201.

in the temple, by Hilkiah, in the time of King Josiah.¹ The most of the analysts claim that Deuteronomy was the book that was thus found. But on this point they are far from unanimous. Voltaire flitted between the hypothesis that the book thus found was the entire Pentateuch and that other hypothesis which assigns its origin to the exilic period. Graf maintains that the newly-found book was Deuteronomy.² Wellhausen dogmatically affirms that the book, when found, was purely a law-book, and embraced only chapters 12-26 of Deuteronomy.³ Kuenen is quite confident that it contained only "the laws and exhortations that make up the kernel of the Book of Deuteronomy,"⁴ and he suggests that it may have been "a still smaller collection."⁵ Reuss goes still further and says, "Que le code publié du temps du roi Josiyah n'était autre que ce que nous lisons anjourd'hui dans le Deuteronome chap. v. à xxvi. and chap. xxviii."⁶ ("That the code published in the time of King Josiah is what we now read in Deuteronomy, chapters 5-26 and chapter 28"). Though this critic concedes that much that is contained in Deuteronomy was not new, being a reproduction of former laws and the teaching of the prophets, he yet seems to hold that the book contains no writing of earlier origin than the times of Josiah or the age immediately preceding. He also brings in the hypothesis of additions and interpolations by later writers.

Such are the disagreements of the leaders of the analytic school in their efforts to keep out of the book found in the temple by Hilkiah everything that does not fall in with their views and theories. They cannot allow the lost and found book to be either the Pentateuch or even Deuteronomy without endangering the whole analytic hypothesis; hence their labors and difficulties. Of these critics Reuss is about the only one who thinks it proper to argue the points connected with this particular subject. The others seem to think it sufficient that they should imperiously inform mankind how, in their judgment, matters stand.

One of the contentions of Reuss is, that the book found in the temple was read twice in one day, and therefore could not have been the Pentateuch. "On nous dit que le prêtre en fit lecture au secrétaire, et que celui-ci alla incontinent en faire lecture au

---

¹ II. Kings 22 : 8-13 ; II. Chr. 34 : 14-19.
² *Die Geschichtlichen Bücher des Alten Testaments*, pp. 2-5.
³ "Ein reines Gesetzbuch."— *Prolegomena*, p. 360.
⁴ *Hexateuch*, p. 214.   ⁵ *Idem*, p. 215.   ⁶ *L'Histoire Sainte*, Int., p. 160.

roi. Deux fois en un seul jour, lecture du Pentateuque entier!"[1] ("They tell us that the priest read it to the secretary, and that the latter went immediately to read it to the king. The reading of the entire Pentateuch twice in a single day!") We have here both inaccuracy and assumption. The record does not say that Hilkiah read the book to Shaphan, but that Hilkiah *gave* the book to Shaphan and that *he* read it.[2] But the chief error of Reuss and other critics is the groundless assumption that the reading of the book by Shaphan and his reading of it to the king necessarily took place on the same day. For anything that is contained in the narrative, these readings may have taken place, each at several sittings, on different days. As well might our critic include the assembling of the people and the reading of the book to them, and, indeed, all the events recorded in the two chapters, for there is no break in the narrative, and nearly all the verses are connected by the copulative "and" (Hebrew, *waw*). Reuss and his fellow-critics ignore the obvious fact that in Bible history the time intervening between one event and another is often passed over in silence. Perhaps some critic, in the advocacy of his favorite notion, will maintain that according to the Bible narrative Noah built the ark, gathered in all the animals, and stowed away all the necessary food in a single day.

Again, it is a groundless assumption that the *whole* book was read, either by Shaphan for himself, or to the king. The sacred narrative neither says nor implies it. The statement is, indeed, that the book was read, but there is a difference between reading a book or newspaper and reading it *through*. We have an illustration of this in the account of the reading of Jeremiah's roll to King Jehoiakim. "And Jehudi read it in the ears of the king, and in the ears of all the princes which stood beside the king." But not *all* the roll was read, for it is immediately added, "That when Jehudi had read three or four leaves, he [the king] cut it with the penknife, and cast it into the fire that was on the hearth."[3]

The further plea of Reuss that the Pentateuch is not adapted to produce the profound impression that is ascribed to the book found in the temple is altogether futile, since it is not maintained that the book contained anything that is contradicted in the Pentateuch. Surely, the other books of the Pentateuch would not neutralize the influence of Deuteronomy, or whatever portion

---

[1] *L'Histoire Sainte*, Int., p. 159. [2] II. Kings 22:8. [3] Jer. 36:21, 23.

of it our critics are willing to admit was contained in the book found in the temple. Besides, Hilkiah and Shaphan, who were favorable to the reformation, would be sure to call the attention of Josiah to those portions of the Pentateuch that demanded the changes they desired.

The proof that the book found in the temple, whether the whole of the Pentateuch or only a part of it, was of Mosaic origin, is as follows:

(1) The direct testimony of both Kings and Chronicles. The book is called expressly the "book of the law" and the "book of the covenant."[1] It is idle to say that this language does not describe the book as an ancient one, and as one that had originated in Mosaic times. Besides this, it is expressly stated that Josiah in his reformation proceeded "according to all the law of Moses."[2] Still further, it is declared that this reformation was carried on "according to the word of the Lord by the hand of Moses," and "as it is written in the book of Moses."[3] It is clearly in evidence, then, that what was found in the temple by Hilkiah and became the guide to Josiah and the people in their reformatory acts was the book and the law of Moses. If this testimony is not to be accepted, we may as well treat the whole account as a fiction and deny that any book at all was found in the temple. The course of Reuss and his fellow-critics in this affair, as in many others, is entirely arbitrary, inconsistent, and illogical. They introduce witnesses to prove that Deuteronomy was first published and became known in the time of King Josiah, and was written not earlier than the reign of Manasseh. But when their own witnesses testify that the newly-found book was a very old one and of Mosaic origin, they turn against them and declare them to be untruthful and untrustworthy. In a civil court an attorney is not allowed to assail witnesses that he has himself introduced.

(2) Evidently Hilkiah, Shaphan, the king, and all who saw the newly-found book must have known whether it was a new or an old one. Hilkiah and Shaphan certainly were intelligent enough to distinguish between a book written in the time of Moses and one written in the time of Manasseh or Josiah. Reuss asks "how the priest and the scribe could read so fluently and readily a writing eight centuries old." Our critic is still proceeding on the mistaken and absurd notion that all the events

---

[1] II. Kings 22: 8; 23: 2.   [2] II. Kings 23: 25.   [3] II. Chr. 35: 6, 12.

connected with this affair took place in a single day. But scholars in our own day can readily read manuscripts even one thousand five hundred years old, though written in a dead and foreign language. Surely these scholarly Jews might readily read in their mother-tongue a book not more than eight hundred years old. And, besides, if the newly-found book was a production of their own age, they were not such ignoramuses as to mistake it for an ancient book, written in Mosaic times, eight centuries before. But they call it *the book of the law* and *the book of the covenant*. If, then, it was not an ancient book, the old book of the law and of the covenant which had been known and reverenced in former times, these men must have been guilty of willful and deliberate misrepresentation and lying. If they were not, the analytic theory in regard to the origin of Deuteronomy is false.

(3) The book itself purported to be ancient. It enjoined old laws and commandments. The very first reading of it aroused apprehension in Josiah of divine displeasure and punishment. He was alarmed because, as he said, "our fathers have not hearkened unto the words of this book."[1] It certainly was not the promulgation of new laws, but the neglect and violation of laws enacted long before, that caused the king to rend his clothes and to fear the wrath of the Lord.

(4) Deuteronomy itself speaks of a book of the law again and again.[2] When Moses had finished "writing the words of this law in a book," he commanded the Levites, saying, "Take this book of the law, and put it in the side of the ark of the covenant of the Lord your God."[3] The only way to avoid the conclusion that this book of the law, written by Moses, and placed by Moses' command in the ark, was the book of the law found afterward in the temple, is simply to deny the truthfulness of the history.

(5) Josiah and his people, in order to avert the wrath of God on account of their own and their fathers' neglect and violations of God's laws as contained in the newly-found book, prosecuted the already-begun reformation more vigorously than before. The facts stated in regard to this reformation indicate that the laws which guided the reformers are contained, not in Deuteronomy alone, but at least partly in other books of the Pentateuch.

(*a*) Josiah and the people engaged "to perform the words of

---

[1] II. Kings 22 : 13.   [2] Deut. 28 : 58 ; 29 : 21 ; 30 : 10.   [3] Deut. 31 : 24-26.

this covenant that were written in this book."[1] This points to Exodus 24: 7, 8.

(*b*) One of the prevalent sins at that time was idolatry, and this caused apprehensions of divine wrath and punishment. The reformers burned the vessels of Baal, stamped the images to powder, and put down the idolatrous priests.[2] The warrant for these proceedings is found in Exodus 23: 24; 34: 13; Numbers 33: 52.

(*c*) The sodomites were suppressed.[3] The Levitical law provided capital punishment for such transgressors. Leviticus 18: 22, 29; 20: 13.

(*d*) Josiah defiled Topheth, so that the offerings of children to Molech might cease.[4] See Leviticus 18: 21; 20: 1-5.

(*e*) The priests of the high places were destroyed.[5] Leviticus 26: 30.

(*f*) The wizards and witches were destroyed.[6] Exodus 22: 18; Leviticus 19: 31; 20: 27.

(*g*) The Passover was observed with unusual solemnity.[7] The institution of the Passover and directions for its observance are recorded in the three middle books of the Pentateuch: Exodus 12: 3-28; 13: 3-10; 23: 15; 34: 18; Leviticus 23: 5; Numbers 9: 2-14; 28: 16, 17. It is indeed true that the Passover is mentioned in Deuteronomy;[8] but the day of the month on which this feast was to be celebrated is not there specified, nor what kind of animal the victim should be, nor is anything said about the sprinkling of its blood, the cooking and eating of its flesh, nor about many other things pertaining to the manner of observing this ordinance. If left to the guidance of Deuteronomy alone in the observance of this feast, Josiah and his people would not have known how to proceed. The same is true, in a large measure, in regard to other reforms introduced in Josiah's time. Some of the laws and regulations which were then resuscitated and enforced are indeed mentioned in Deuteronomy, but mainly for the purpose of supplement or modification. For a full knowledge of them we must refer to the preceding books. The reformation of Josiah's time was therefore based, not on Deuteronomy, but on the laws and regulations contained in Exodus, Leviticus, and Numbers; hence, these books were known in Josiah's time, or at least the laws and regulations contained in them. Either conclusion is fatal to the analytic hypothesis.

[1] II. Kings 23: 3.
[2] II. Kings 23: 4-6.
[3] II. Kings 23: 7.
[4] II. Kings 23: 10.
[5] II. Kings 23: 20.
[6] II. Kings 23: 24.
[7] II. Kings 23: 21, 22; II. Chr. 35: 1-19.
[8] Deut. 16: 1-8.

4. Ezra and Nehemiah.

It is not necessary to prove that the Pentateuch was in use among the Jews immediately after their return from Babylon. The hypothesis of the analysts is, that the first four books and the priestly code are of exilic origin. The foremost champion of the analytic school, in his usual oracular style, says, "Gleichwie bezeugt wird, dass das Deuteronomium im Jahr 621 bekannt geworden, bis dahin unbekannt gewesen ist, geradeso wird bezeugt, dass die anderweitige Thora des Pentateuchs — denn das Gesetz Ezra's der ganze Pentateuch gewesen ist, unterliegt keinem Zweifel — im Jahre 444 bekannt geworden, bis dahin unbekannt gewesen ist"[1] ("As it is in evidence that Deuteronomy became known in the year 621, until which time it was unknown, so also it is in evidence that the further torah of the Pentateuch — for that the law of Ezra was the whole Pentateuch does not admit of a doubt — became known in the year 444, until which time it was unknown").

Our critics, then, hold that Ezra introduced the Pentateuch after the exile, though they may not be entirely agreed as to whether he was the writer or only the chief redactor of it; and their belief is founded mainly on the testimony of the books of Ezra and Nehemiah. It is admitted, then, that Ezra introduced the Pentateuch. It was, of course, written before it was introduced. But who wrote it, and when was it written? Wellhausen expresses the opinion that Ezra was only "the real and chief redactor of the Pentateuch." Be it so. It, of course, was in existence before he began to work upon it. Whence came it into his hands? May not the Pentateuch be the book which was found in the temple in Josiah's time, and which was recognized as ancient, and as being the law-book of Moses?

(1) The law-book which Ezra introduced was declared by him impliedly, if not expressly, to be the production of Moses. "This Ezra went up from Babylon; and he was a ready scribe in the law of Moses, which the Lord God of Israel had given."[2] "And all the people gathered themselves together as one man into the street that was before the water-gate; and they spake unto Ezra the scribe to bring the book of the law of Moses, which the Lord had commanded to Israel."[3] It is thus shown that Ezra represented the book and law which he introduced to be the book and the law of Moses. It is further shown that

---

[1] Wellhausen, *Prolegomena*, p. 427   [2] Ezra 7: 6.   [3] Neh. 8: 1, 2.

Nehemiah joined with him in this representation.[1] Now, if the Pentateuch was a production of their age, they must have known it, and their representing and declaring it to be of Mosaic origin must have involved willful, deliberate, and long-continued deception and falsehood. It is of no avail to attempt to soften this charge of deception and falsehood by the use of the terms *legal fiction* and *pious fraud*. Lying does not lose its criminality, though practiced in the name of God and professedly for a holy purpose.

(2) The analysts, in dealing with Ezra and Nehemiah, pursue, as is of frequent occurrence with them, an arbitrary, inconsistent, and illogical course. They accept the testimony of these books just so far as it harmonizes with their preconceived views, but so far as it does not they discredit it and cast it aside. All that they believe or know in regard to the introduction of the Pentateuch and the Pentateuchal laws after the exile they obtain from Ezra and Nehemiah and accept on their testimony alone; but they accuse these same witnesses of misrepresentation and falsehood, when they testify that these books and laws did not originate in their own, but in former times. The statements in the books of Ezra and Nehemiah in regard to the improper observance of the Feast of Tabernacles from the time of Joshua on down to the return from Babylon, and other such matters, are accepted as true and trustworthy, but the statement that the book of the law came from Moses is treated as incorrect and false. Nor may our critics plead that the testimony of these witnesses on this point is rejected on the ground that, living long after Moses, they were incompetent to testify in regard to his authorship of the Pentateuch and its laws; for their testimony that these did not originate in their times, a point in regard to which they were competent witnesses, is rejected also. Evidently the principle on which the critics proceed is this, that all testimony *which conflicts with their preconceived views is to be rejected as false.*

(3) According to the hypothesis that the first four books of the Pentateuch and the laws contained in them were gotten up during the exile, Ezra and Nehemiah certainly engaged in a stupendous undertaking in endeavoring to palm off these books and laws as the work of Moses. But how admirably they succeeded! They completely deceived their own countrymen, and

[1] Neh. 8:9.

nearly the entire intelligent world besides. The fraud has lasted for more than two thousand years, and has not yet fully run its course. To undo the deception and expose the fraud has cost "the higher critics" immense and long-continued labor and has tasked their learning, ingenuity, and skill to the utmost; and, withal, their success is only partial. What adepts in the art of deception Ezra and his coadjutors must have been!

(4) Yet on the hypothesis that Ezra intended to deceive mankind in regard to the authorship of the Pentateuch, it is unaccountable that he omitted to do some things that he might have done in furtherance of this design. The analysts maintain that the Pentateuch itself does not claim to be the production of Moses. This is one of their trusted arguments. They proceed upon the idea that if there were only a declaration in the Pentateuch itself, expressly affirming its Mosaic origin, the question would be forever and completely settled. Why, then, did not Ezra and his shrewd and skillful coöperators insert such a declaration? Wellhausen is of the opinion that Ezra went from Babylon to Jerusalem carrying in his hand the Pentateuch ready to be fastened on the returned Jews as the work of Moses, and he can only conjecture why he waited fourteen years before proceeding to promulgate it as such.[1] Reuss affirms that it is indubitably proved that he "did not bring it all redacted from Babylon, and that it required him to labor thirteen years, if not to make out a fair copy, at least to secure its acceptance."[2] While engaged in working over and correcting the Pentateuch and getting it ready for promulgation as the book of Moses, why did he not, in the beginning of each book, insert some such declaration as this: "The words (or the writing) of Moses, the man of God"? This would have been the probable procedure of a man who was intending to publish a book in another's name, and he thus would have conformed to the prevalent style in Ezra's own time, as shown by the writings of the prophets.

(5) The style of the Pentateuch is adverse to the hypothesis that it, or a large portion of it, was written by Ezra, or in Ezra's time, or that it was much changed by Ezra or by any redactor in Ezra's time. Doubtless many a modern critic considers himself a competent judge of Hebrew style. Even Thomas Paine argues from the style of Deuteronomy against the Mosaic authorship. Yet style in general is a matter largely of taste, and most assur-

---

[1] *Prolegomena*, p. 424 *sqq.*   [2] *L'Histoire Sainte*, Int., p. 233.

edly there are very few competent judges of the peculiarities of style in Hebrew. But we certainly risk nothing in saying that all the books of the Pentateuch, and these books in all their parts, even those parts that are said by critics to have been supplied by editors, redactors, or interpolators, are written in pure Hebrew. Professor Green, of Princeton, who is certainly one of the most accomplished Hebrew scholars of our age, says, "The language of the Pentateuch is, throughout, the Hebrew of the purest period, with no trace of later words, or forms, or constructions, or of the Chaldaisms of the exile."[1] Testimony to the same effect has been given by many other distinguished scholars and critics. The purity of the language of the Pentateuch is by no means a favorite idea with the analytic critics. It would suit them much better to find in the Pentateuch many of the later Hebrew words, Aramaisms, and other characteristics of the post-exilic style. But even they are compelled expressly or impliedly to confess the purity of the Pentateuchal Hebrew. Reuss says, "La langue du Pentateuque est à peu près la même que celle de la presque totalité des livres de l'Ancien Testament"[2] ("The language of the Pentateuch is almost the same with that of nearly all of the books of the Old Testament"). There are some of the Old Testament books, then, that differ much in style from the Pentateuch. These confessedly are Chronicles, Daniel, Ezra, and Nehemiah, all of which were written after the transportation to Babylon, and contain words, sentences, and whole passages in Aramaic. On this point the testimony of Professor Driver is, that in Ezra, Nehemiah, and Chronicles "many new words appear, often of Aramaic origin, occasionally Persian, and frequently such as continued in use afterwards in the 'New Hebrew' of the Mishna."[3]

Now the problem for the analytic critics to solve is this: How came it to pass that men who had such a mixed and mongrel style after all wrote the purest Hebrew, as it is found in the Pentateuch? Why did not Ezra and his colaborers put some of their Aramaic idioms, new words, or words with a new meaning into the five books which they either wrote or redacted? It is in vain to plead that Ezra was not the author, but only one of the redactors, of the Pentateuch. For in that case there ought to be many passages marked by the impurities of the exilic style of

---

[1] *Religious Encyclopedia*, Schaff-Herzog, Vol. III., p. 1799.

[2] *L'Histoire Sainte*, Int., p. 135.

[3] *Introduction to the Literature of the Old Testament*, pp. 473, 519.

the redactors. Besides, the analytic hypothesis is, that the first four books of the Pentateuch were gotten up in exilic times, and hence must have been composed by an author or authors whose style was equally impure with that of Ezra, Nehemiah, Daniel, and the author of Chronicles.

(6) Another difficulty presents itself. If the Pentateuch was originated by Ezra or near his time, how comes it that it contains no allusion to the temple, nor to its worship, nor to Jerusalem, nor to David, Solomon, or any of the kings, nor to any historical event after the time of Moses? It is, perhaps, not altogether inconceivable that a set of writers in exilic or post-exilic times, intent on fastening a priestly code of their own devising on their people, manufactured four or five books of history and law, partly out of preëxisting documents, and partly out of their own compositions, mingling together the original documents with their own interpolations, substitutions, additions, and emendations; and that all these writers, compilers, interpolators, and emendators, either with or without formal agreement, not only repressed their own linguistic peculiarities and weeded out those of others, imitating to perfection the older Hebrew style which prevailed many centuries before their time, but also, with wonderful self-restraint and caution, avoided making any statement, allusion, or suggestion in regard to any occurrence in all the Jewish history after the death and funeral of Moses, and succeeded in saying absolutely nothing in all their writings to indicate that they did not live in Mosaic times. All this is perhaps conceivable, but is certainly very improbable. How exceedingly shrewd and skillful those exilic writers, compilers, interpolators, and redactors who got up the Pentateuch must have been! Here is a very weak point in the analytic hypothesis. Its advocates have much to say about the silence of succeeding writers concerning the Pentateuch, a claim which the traditionalists deny. But here is absolute silence in regard to the whole Jewish history from the crossing of the Jordan to the Babylonian exile.[1]

[1] See Part III., ch. x.

CHAPTER III

THE PSALMS

The testimony of the Psalms to the early existence of the Pentateuch depends largely on their authorship and date. The opponents of the Mosaic authorship are disposed, and for an obvious reason, to maintain that nearly all the psalms are of post-exilic origin. Our discussion of this point must be brief.

That many of the psalms were composed before the exile is shown by several considerations. The exiles had been accustomed to sing the Psalms in their own beloved land.[1] David is expressly called "the sweet psalmist of Israel," which implies that he wrote more psalms than any one else.[2] Some of the psalms are ascribed to David and a few to Asaph—seventy-three to one and twelve to the other. It is recorded that Hezekiah commanded the Levites to sing praise in "the words of David, and of Asaph the seer."[3] Whether these twelve psalms are ascribed to Asaph as author or as leader of the song service matters not, so far as the question of date is concerned; for in either case the psalms belong to the age of Asaph, who was the contemporary of David.

The psalms are at least as old as their superscriptions, and when the Septuagint translation was made the superscriptions were so old that they had become obscure in meaning. This obscurity is accounted for by the fact that the musical arrangements of the first temple ceased with its destruction. Gesenius, speaking of the words "To the Chief Musician," says, "This inscription is wholly wanting in all the psalms of a later age, composed after the destruction of the temple and its worship, and its signification was already lost in the time of the LXX."[4]

These considerations, with others that might be mentioned, indicate that some of the psalms are as ancient as the time of David.

Taking the Seventy-eighth as an example, we find both exter-

[1] Ps. 137 : 3, 4.   [2] II. Sam. 23 : 1.   [3] II. Chr. 29 : 30.   [4] *Lexicon*, p. 688.

nal and internal evidence of its antiquity. (1) It is ascribed to Asaph. (2) It deals with Israelitish history from the exodus to the reign of King David. That the writer did not refer to events after David's time is accounted for only by the fact that he lived in David's time. This psalm could have been written only by an author who was familiar with the history contained in the Pentateuch. It is an epitome of Pentateuchal history. It treats of the plagues of Egypt, the exodus, the crossing of the Red Sea, the water from the rock, the miracle of the quails and of the manna, the temptation, the wandering in the wilderness, the cloud by day and the fire by night, the settlement in Canaan, God's abandonment of Shiloh in the time of the judges, and the elevation of David to the throne of Israel. Nearly this whole history—all, indeed, except the reference to the time of the judges—is contained in the Pentateuch, and is contained nowhere else. There is, besides, express mention of the law. "For he established a testimony in Jacob, and appointed a law in Israel, which he commanded our fathers, that they should make them known to their children."[1] The reference here is obviously to a written law, and points to certain portions of the Pentateuch.[2]

The One Hundred and Fifth Psalm. A part of this psalm (the first fifteen verses) is given in Chronicles, and is expressly ascribed to David. The internal evidence points to Davidic times. Like the Seventy-eighth Psalm, it is a summary of Pentateuchal history from the call of Abraham to the settlement in Canaan. It mentions the covenant with Abraham, the sojourning of the patriarchs, the sale and elevation of Joseph, the famine, the emigration into Egypt, the increase of the people, the bondage and oppression, the mission of Moses and Aaron, the plagues, the exodus, the cloud and fire, the miraculous supply of flesh and the bread from heaven, the water from the rock, and the taking of the lands of the heathen. Undoubtedly the author of this psalm was acquainted with Jewish history, just as we have it in the Pentateuch. There are also express references to a code of laws as existing in Mosaic times. For example, the last verse: "That they might observe his statutes, and keep his laws."

The One Hundred and Sixth Psalm is in style, construction, and contents like the One Hundred and Fifth, and may, there-

---

[1] Ps. 78 : 5.   [2] Deut. 33 : 4 ; 6 : 7, 8.

fore, be presumed to be of the same age and authorship. It deals with the national history previous to the establishment of the monarchy. The idolatry at Horeb, the rebellion of Dathan and Abiram, and all the events treated of are related in the Pentateuch, and are related nowhere else.

The Fifteenth Psalm is declared by the inscription to be Davidic, and is admitted to be such by some of the more prominent analytic critics. It refers to the law of usury, which is found only in the Pentateuch.[1]

The Eighteenth Psalm is shown by several considerations to be one of David's. (1) In the title it is ascribed to him. (2) The occasion of his writing it is stated. (3) This psalm is recorded in the Second Book of Samuel as the production of David, and the time and occasion of his writing it are there mentioned.[2] In this psalm there is reference made to the law, obviously a written code. "For all his judgments were before me, and I did not put away his statutes from me."[3]

The Nineteenth Psalm is ascribed to David in the title and also inscribed to the chief musician. It is generally admitted to be the production of the chief psalmist. That it refers to a written code of laws enjoining moral duties, can scarcely be doubted. The terms and language employed—"law," "testimony," "statutes," "commandment," "judgments of the Lord," "more to be desired . . . than gold," "sweeter . . . than honey," "converting the soul," "making wise the simple," "rejoicing the heart," "enlightening the eyes," "true and righteous altogether"—seem to be not only written precepts, but those contained in the Pentateuch, and doubtless would be admitted to be such, provided this did not logically necessitate the abandonment of a favorite hypothesis.

The Fortieth Psalm has the double title, "To the Chief Musician. A Psalm of David." The Fifty-first Psalm has the same title, and, besides, the occasion of David's writing it is stated. The Sixty-sixth Psalm is inscribed "To the Chief Musician."

1. These psalms indicate acquaintance with the Pentateuchal ritual. The different kinds of sacrifices and services are clearly distinguished — prayer, songs of praise, vows, hyssop, burnt-offerings, whole burnt-offerings, sin-offerings, burnt sacrifices of fatlings, of incense, of rams, bullocks, and goats.

---

[1] Ex. 22 : 25 ; Lev. 25 : 25 ; Deut. 23 : 19.   [2] II. Sam. 22 : 1-51.   [3] V. 22.

2. In the Fortieth Psalm the written law is undoubtedly referred to in these words: "In the volume of the book it is written of me"; and, "Yea, thy law is within my heart."[1] Gesenius, who was not overcharged with traditional ideas, says that herein is meant *the book of the law.*[2]

[1] Vs. 7, 8. [2] *Lexicon,* p. 732.

CHAPTER IV

THE PROPHECIES

1. ISAIAH, who prophesied about one hundred and fifty years before the exile and more than one hundred before the time of Josiah, recognizes the prevalence of Pentateuchal ideas, customs, and regulations. He speaks of sacrifices and offerings — burnt-offerings, meat-offerings (מִנְחָה); offerings of bullocks, rams, lambs, and he-goats; incense, prayers, sabbaths, appointed feasts, fasts, new moons, and calling of assemblies.[1] Evidently Isaiah was familiar with the entire round of the Pentateuchal ritual. Further, he was familiar with it in full operation in his time. It is true, he severely reprimanded the people, but not because they engaged in the services above mentioned. It was their impiety and wickedness in these services that the prophet denounced. Even their Sabbath observance and their prayers came in for a share of the prophet's reprobation; not, however, because prayer and the keeping of the Sabbath are not according to the law and will of God, but because their hands were full of blood.[2] Just here Cheyne, who reproves Driver for his timidity and conservatism, makes some very remarkable admissions. He remarks as follows: "Not that Isaiah intends to condemn ritual altogether, any more than St. James does." He is further willing to admit that the burnt-offerings may be the guilt-offerings as provided for in Leviticus; that the calling of assemblies points to Leviticus 23:4; the new moons to Numbers 10:10; 28:11-16; and that Isaiah 4:5 is "the first of a long series of references to the exodus" (see Ex. 13:21, 22).[3] Were not, then, Leviticus and Exodus in existence in the time of Isaiah?

2. Hosea, who prophesied about two hundred years before the exile, often alludes to laws and events as recorded in the Pentateuch. We give references as follows: Hos. 4:6 and 8:1; Hos. 5:10 with Deut. 19:14 and 27:17; Hos. 8:11 and 12:11 with

---

[1] Isa. 1:11-15; 57:6; 58:3-7. [2] Isa. 1:15.
[3] Cheyne on *Isaiah*, pp. 6, 7, 29.

Deut. 12: 11-14; Hos. 9: 4 with Num. 19: 11, 14, 22 and Deut. 26: 14; Hos. 9: 10 with Num. 25: 3-9; Hos. 11: 8 with Gen. 19: 24, 25; Hos. 12: 3-5 with Gen. 25: 26 and 32: 24 and 28: 30 and 35: 15; Hos. 12: 9 with Lev. 23: 34, 41-44 and Neh. 8: 17; Hos. 12: 12 with Gen. 29, 30.

We call special attention to one passage, as follows: "I have written to him the great things of my law, but they were counted as a strange thing."[1] This is a very troublesome passage to the critics, who maintain that the Pentateuchal law was not formulated before the exile. The word translated "the great things" (רִבֵּי) properly means *ten thousand* or *multitudes*. Hence the passage at least seems to indicate that there was a large body of laws in the time of Hosea, two hundred years before the destruction of the first temple. This is fatal to the analytic hypothesis. Hence, of course, the advocates of this hypothesis have much to say about this passage. Their struggles with it are amusing. Kuenen (1) admits "that the existence of written 'torah' also is expressly asserted in one passage (Hos. 8: 12) and rendered highly probable by the context in others." He translates as follows: "I write (or, if I write) for him (Israel) ten thousand of my torahs, they are accounted as those of a stranger." But (3) he pronounces the text itself doubtful, not justified by the context, and "militated against by the displeasing hyperbole of ten thousand." (4) Next he is forced to the alternative of thinking that "perhaps we must make up our minds simply to read, 'If I write for him the words of my torah'"—a hypothetical utterance. (5) But, as a last resort, our critic, though compelled to admit that in the time of Hosea there was a written torah, yet says, "In case of need, 'torah' may be taken to refer to the oral teaching of priests and prophets."[2] Such criticism needs neither answer nor comment. Wellhausen deals with the passage, not in a more masterly, but certainly in a more magisterial way. He endeavors to silence our passage as a witness against his views by adopting a various reading and also by changing the translation, *i. e.*, by substituting "instruction" for "law" (in German, "Weisungen" for "Gesetz"). Having settled things to his own satisfaction in this way, he expresses his sympathy for the text as having experienced "the undeserved misfortune" of being cited in support of traditional views. Professor W. R. Smith claims that the passage ought to be translated

[1] Hos. 8: 12. [2] *Hexateuch*, pp. 175-178.

as follows: "Though I wrote to him my torah in ten thousand precepts, they would be esteemed as a strange thing." He admits the torah or law here spoken of to be Mosaic, but claims that it was *unwritten*.[1] Professor Briggs would translate, "Though I write for him my law in ten thousand precepts, they are accounted as a strange thing," but admits that in the passage there is "a general reference to the fact that divine laws were recorded."[2]

In regard to this passage, we remark as follows:

(1) About the only point of agreement concerning it, among these critics, is that it must be construed so as not to favor the traditional belief. The difficulty of this undertaking is demonstrated by their antagonistic efforts and discordant interpretations.

(2) In one sense, Kuenen and Wellhausen are right; for if Hosea here speaks of a divine law in ten thousand precepts as already existing, the analytic theory of the gradual formation of the Torah by evolution is certainly in danger. Hence the necessity of getting rid of the passage by impeaching its genuineness and introducing a various reading.

(3) We suggest that the analysts might get rid of this troublesome passage by their much-used expedient of supposing that it was not written by Hosea, but was inserted by some redactor in the time of Ezra.

(4) As to the employment, in this passage, of the imperfect tense of the Hebrew verb, this is not inconsistent with the usual interpretation, since in Hebrew, as in English, the past is often represented as present.

3. Amos, who prophesied about two centuries before the exile, makes many allusions to Pentateuchal laws, customs, and ideas. "Also I brought you up from the land of Egypt, and led you forty years through the wilderness, to possess the land of the Amorite."[3] This very language is found in Deuteronomy 8:2 and in other places in the Pentateuch. "And I raised up of your sons for prophets, and of your young men for Nazarites. . . . But ye gave the Nazarites wine to drink."[4] Compare with Numbers 6:2, 3. "Bring your sacrifices every morning, and your tithes after three years."[5] See Exodus 29:30; Numbers 28:4; Deuteronomy 14:28; 26:12. "And offer a sacrifice of thanksgiving with leaven, and proclaim and publish the free offerings."[6] See Leviticus 7:13; 23:17; 22:19-21; Deuteron-

[1] *Old Testament in the Jewish Church*, p. 297.
[2] *Higher Criticism of the Pentateuch*, p. 14.
[3] Amos 2:10.   [4] Amos 2:11, 12.   [5] Amos 4:4.   [6] Amos 4:5.

omy 12 : 6. "I hate, I despise your feast days, and I will not smell in your solemn assemblies. Though ye offer me burnt-offerings and your meat-offerings, I will not accept them; neither will I regard the peace-offerings of your fat beasts."[1] See the regulations in Leviticus 23 : 2-36; 1 : 3-14; 2 : 1; 3 : 1. "When will the new moon be gone?"[2] See Numbers 10 : 10. Thus Amos alludes to the tithes, the three-year tithes, the feasts, the convocations, the Nazarites and their abstinence from wine, the daily sacrifices, the burnt-offerings, the meat-offerings, the peace-offerings, the free-will offerings, the new moons, the Sabbaths, and nearly all the Levitical institutions. Had there been in the writings of this prophet an *express* reference to the laws and books of Moses, the advocates of the analytic hypothesis would, of course, have claimed an interpolation by a later hand, or that Hosea lived after the exile.

4. Joel also mentions the meat-offering and the drink-offering, the priests and the altar, sanctifying the fast, calling an assembly, and sanctifying the assembly, and he makes other allusions to Pentateuchal laws and institutions.[3] That his prophecy presupposes the Pentateuch seems to be admitted, as is evinced by the fact that the analytic critics have finally found it necessary to assign to it a post-exilic date in order to maintain their hypothesis of the late origin of the Pentateuch.

[1] Amos 5 : 21, 22. [2] Amos 8 : 5. [3] Joel 1 : 9, 13; 2 : 17; 1 : 14; 2 : 16.

CHAPTER V

THE HISTORICAL ARGUMENT, INCLUDING THE QUESTION OF THE CENTRALIZATION OF WORSHIP

Our proposition is, that the history demonstrates that the Levitical and Deuteronomic laws were in operation long before the times in which, according to the analytic theories, the Pentateuchal books came into existence.

The opponents of the Mosaic authorship of the Pentateuchal laws and books claim the evidence of history to be in their favor. They contest every inch of ground in maintaining that according to biblical narratives the practices of the Israelites in general, even the best and most intelligent among them, on down to the time of King Josiah, were such as to indicate that they knew nothing of these books and laws. They reason as follows: If Joshua, Gideon, Manoah, Samuel, and David, and other good and intelligent Israelites who were their contemporaries, had known the Pentateuchal laws, they would have obeyed them. But they did not obey them; therefore, they did not know them. If the laws had been in existence, these men would have known them. Hence the laws were not in existence.

This argument, as employed by the analytic critics, contains two incorrect assumptions. Many good people remain ignorant of some laws all their lives, and some good people violate known laws all their lives. It is very unsafe to infer that because good people do certain things, therefore these things are lawful. Prevalent violations of a law do not prove its non-existence. Paul says, "Where no law is, there is no transgression." But it does not follow that where there is transgression there is no law. In order, then, to determine whether the practices of the Israelites at any time prove their ignorance of Pentateuchal laws, and whether this ignorance, if proved, would further prove the non-existence of these laws, we must know thoroughly the facts in the case.

Many of the critics, in treating of these matters, commit the same error which so often appears in their argumentation elsewhere—that of taking silence for denial, and inferring that a law was not observed because in the history of particular times nothing is said about it. They do worse even than this in their presentation of the historical argument. They set aside the biblical history as untrue and set up a history of their own invention. When they speak of the biblical history, they mean the history as they think it ought to be, and as they manufacture it to support their theories. We intend to verify these charges as we proceed.

1. We begin with the unity of worship.

The fact that the Pentateuchal laws required the Israelites to offer sacrifices in one chosen place has already been mentioned.[1] A passage in Exodus has been construed as favoring a plurality of places of worship.[2] The traditionalists, however, maintain that the expression, "in all places where I record my name," in this passage does not mean several places at the same time, but many places in succession, the places at which the altar and the tabernacle were from time to time set up; and they point, in support of this construction, to the fact that but *one* altar is mentioned. How could there be more than one place of sacrifice, when there was but one altar?

It is maintained, however, that as a matter of fact there were many altars and many places of worship; that pious and law-abiding Israelites offered sacrifice on private altars; and that up to the later times of the monarchy there could have been no law requiring unity of worship, as otherwise the ignorance and disregard of it would be incredible. The analysts reason as follows: If there was a law requiring unity of worship, it was almost continually disobeyed by pious and law-abiding Israelites; but such disobedience is incredible; therefore, there was no such law down to the time of Josiah. The objectors in this case appeal to the history, that is, *in spots*. They take the history so far as it presents facts that seem favorable to their views. The rest of the history they either ignore or decry as untrustworthy.

Let us ascertain, then, what the facts are as brought to view in the history.

(1) The history shows that for about forty years at least, during the time of Moses, the law requiring unity of worship was fully obeyed. During the wandering in the wilderness there

---

[1] See Part III., ch. ix.   [2] Ex. 20 : 24.

was but one altar, one tabernacle, and one central place of worship. Neither the pillar of cloud by day, nor the pillar of fire by night, ever divided itself. This symbol of God's presence moved on from time to time, and from place to place, and wherever it rested, there the tabernacle and the altar were erected, and the tribes of God encamped around them. Thither Moses, and Aaron, and the godly Israelites came to sacrifice and to worship. During the entire wandering in the desert, the whole time covered by the historical parts of the last four books of the Pentateuch, there is not a single instance of sacrifice being offered elsewhere than at the door of the tabernacle of the congregation. The Israelites repeatedly rebelled in the desert. Some of the laws were, in a certain sense, held in abeyance. Circumcision was neglected or withheld for forty years.[1] The Passover during that time was probably not observed, at least generally, as circumcision was a prerequisite for the performance of that duty;[2] but there is not a particle of evidence that there was, before the death of Moses, a single infraction of the law requiring all sacrifices to be offered at one divinely-chosen place.

(2) There is historical evidence that this law was operative after the death of Moses, and during the lifetime of Joshua.

After the crossing of the Jordan and the defeat at Ai, Joshua and the elders of Israel prostrated themselves before the ark of the Lord.[3] The ark, of course, was in the tabernacle. After the destruction of Ai, Joshua built an altar to the Lord on Mount Ebal, "as it is written in the book of the law of Moses." On the stones of this altar a copy of the law of Moses was written. On this altar they sacrificed burnt-offerings and peace-offerings. Here all Israel, and their officers, elders, and judges, surrounded the ark, and, in the presence of the priests the Levites, listened to the reading of all the words of the law.[4] Here, then, for the present was the central place of worship.

The account given of the Gibeonites plainly implies that there was but one altar and one place of assembling for worship. Joshua declared to them, "There shall none of you be freed from being bondmen, and hewers of wood and drawers of water for the house of my God." It is accordingly declared that Joshua "made them that day hewers of wood and drawers of water for the congregation, and for the altar of the Lord."[5] Here we have

[1] Josh. 5: 2-9. [2] Josh. 5: 10. [3] Josh. 7: 6. [4] Josh. 8: 31-35. [5] Josh. 9: 23, 27.

one house of God and *one* altar of God spoken of, which certainly implies *one* place of worship for all Israel.

After the conquest, the whole congregation of Israel assembled at Shiloh and set up the tabernacle of the congregation (or tent of meeting). Shiloh was thus recognized as the place of God's presence and the place of sacrifice and worship.[1] Men went to Shiloh to appear *before the Lord*.[2]

We do, indeed, read of the erection of a second altar in the time of Joshua. The two and a half tribes beyond Jordan built an altar, "a great altar to see to." But this alarmed their brethren in western Canaan, who assembled for war, and sent messengers to remonstrate with the supposed transgressors. The builders of this second altar informed the messengers that it was intended, not for sacrifice or worship, but merely as a witness that the inhabitants of eastern Canaan had a right to worship the God of Israel. The answer was satisfactory.[3] The negotiations clearly reveal the fact that the law of the unity of worship was fully recognized by both parties.[4] The remonstrants said, "Notwithstanding, if the land of your possession be unclean, then pass ye over unto the land of the possession of the Lord, wherein the Lord's tabernacle dwelleth, and take possession among us; but rebel not against the Lord, nor rebel against us, in building you an altar besides the altar of the Lord our God." The builders of the second altar replied, "God forbid that we should rebel against the Lord, and turn this day from following the Lord, to build an altar for burnt-offerings, for meat-offerings, or for sacrifices, besides the altar of the Lord our God that is before his tabernacle."[5] These facts make it evident that in Joshua's time the Israelites fully recognized the unlawfulness and sinfulness of offering sacrifices elsewhere than at the one tabernacle and on the one altar of the Lord.

It is thus shown that according to the history the Israelites understood and obeyed this law for about forty years during the time of Moses, and for about a quarter of a century during the leadership of Joshua. So far, the testimony of the history clearly points to the existence of the law of centralized worship; and we might here rest our case. For since the law existed as a matter of history in the times of Moses and Joshua, it must have existed in subsequent times, however much it may have

---

[1] Josh. 18:1.   [2] Josh. 18:6, 8, 10; 19:51.   [3] Josh. 22:9-34.
[4] See p. 207.   [5] Josh. 22:19, 29.

been ignored and disobeyed, unless, indeed, it was *repealed*. But of this there is no evidence; and, besides, repeal would be the very reverse of the analytic hypothesis; it would be evolution going backwards.

(3) Antecedently, we should expect to find this law, to some extent, ignored and disobeyed in the time of the judges; for during this time religion and morality were often at a low ebb, and anarchy and lawlessness prevailed. The people were obedient as long as Joshua lived, and for a short time after his death. "And Israel served the Lord all the days of Joshua, and all the days of the elders that overlived Joshua."[1] But declension and idolatry had partially begun even during the last days of Joshua. He referred to this fact in his final address: "Put away the gods which your fathers served on the other side of the flood, and in Egypt." And again: "Now therefore put away . . . the strange gods which are among you."[2] After his death apostasy soon set in. "And also all that generation were gathered unto their fathers. And there arose another generation after them, which knew not the Lord, nor yet the works which he had done for Israel. And the children of Israel did evil in the sight of the Lord, and served Baalim: and they forsook the Lord God of their fathers, which brought them out of the land of Egypt, and followed other gods, of the gods of the people that were round about them, and bowed themselves unto them."[3] The Israelites "knew not the Lord" at this time. Of course they knew not his laws. The record further relates that the Lord raised up judges, and that the people "would not hearken unto their judges, but they went a whoring after other gods"; and that, though "the Lord was with the judge," yet, when the judge was dead, "they returned, and corrupted themselves more than their fathers, in following other gods to serve them, and to bow down unto them; they ceased not from their own doings, nor from their stubborn way."[4] In such times of apostasy, rebellion, and disobedience, of course the law requiring sacrifices to be offered to the God of Israel at his one tabernacle and one altar was forgotten or disregarded.

Our critics ignore these facts. They ignore also the fact that the Israelites were in a chronic state of alienation and rebellion during almost their entire history from the exodus to the exile —that the commonwealth established by the Lord and Moses

---

[1] Josh. 24:31.   [2] Josh. 24:14, 23.   [3] Judg. 2:10-12.   [4] Judg. 2:16-19.

was a failure almost from the beginning and was displaced by the monarchy; that the chosen people were a failure, proving to be stiff-necked and rebellious, and had to be cast off, scattered, and riddled, in order that, as after the exile, a new start might be made with the better and chosen few; and that previous to this second experiment many of the laws were inoperative through the weakness and perverseness of the people and their rulers. We speak of failure, but really it was neither of God, nor of his law. It was through no failure of God or Christianity that the only copy of the Bible to which Luther had access was locked up and chained in a convent. It was through no failure of God and Christianity that the Christians engaged in the business of man-stealing and the slave trade. It is through no fault of the ten commandments that "every mere man doth daily break them in thought, word, and deed." The golden rule of Christ is no failure, though everybody fails to obey it. These failures and all this disobedience do not prove the moral law of God either to be entirely unknown, or to be an absolute nullity. Nor does disobedience to any particular law among the Israelites, whether that disobedience was conscious or unconscious, whether through ignorance or perverseness, prove that the law was either unknown or non-existent.

Antecedently, then, we would expect the law in regard to the centralization of worship to be ignored and disobeyed, like many other laws in the time of the judges, a time in which idolatry, violence, and other forms of sin and immorality frequently prevailed, and in which frequently there was no central or settled government to repress lawlessness and transgression—a state of things brought to view in the history by the repeated use of the formula, "In those days there was no king in Israel."[1] It is evident that this state existed only at particular times during the period of the judges.

After all, there is satisfactory evidence that the law requiring unity of worship was not unknown, nor altogether a dead letter, during the period of the judges, notwithstanding the degeneracy and perverseness of the times. Shiloh was recognized still as the place of God's presence and worship. It is expressly declared that "the house of God was in Shiloh."[2] This, of course, refers to the tabernacle as God's dwelling-place, which had been set up in Shiloh, in the time of Joshua.[3] Here was an

---

[1] Judg. 17:6; 18:1; 19:1; 21:25.   [2] Judg. 18:31.   [3] Josh. 18:1.

annual feast of the Lord — whether the feast of unleavened bread or of tabernacles matters not, so far as the present argument is concerned.[1] Let it be observed that but *one* house of the Lord is mentioned, not the *houses*, nor *a* house, but *the* house of the Lord. While Micah's graven image was worshiped by the Danites, the house of God was in Shiloh. Though they had a descendant of Moses for their priest, their place of worship was neither *the* house nor *a* house of God.[2] The Levite whose wife's shocking death led to a destructive civil war, said in Gibeah, "I am now going to the house of the Lord."[3] The reference was doubtless to the tabernacle at Shiloh, which lay in the direction in which he was going.[4] At this time the Israelites went repeatedly to the house of God (or to Bethel, as in the Revised Version) to ask counsel in regard to the war against Benjamin.[5] They went for divine counsel to the place (whether Bethel or Shiloh) where the ark of the covenant of God was, and where Phinehas, a descendant of Aaron, was the ministering priest.[6] The building of an altar on the morrow after the defeat of the Benjamites seems to indicate that the tabernacle and the ark had been brought from Shiloh to be near the battlefield (perhaps to Bethel), and that hence an altar was needed.

(4) Shiloh appears still as the central place of worship in the time of Samuel. Samuel's pious father and mother went "yearly to worship and sacrifice unto the Lord of hosts" in Shiloh. Here were the tabernacle, and the ark of God, and an Aaronic priesthood, as in the time of Joshua. The people of Israel came here to sacrifice and worship. A law of sacrifice was recognized, which the sons of Eli, the high priest, violated. The right of the priests to certain parts of the sacrifice was admitted. The wicked sons of Eli gave offense to the pious worshipers by unlawful proceedings in taking their lawful perquisites.[7] It thus appears that Shiloh continued to be the home of the tabernacle, and the ark, and the altar, and the place of sacrifice and worship for all Israel, from Joshua to Samuel. We do not say that the tabernacle and the ark were never absent during all this time from Shiloh. The tabernacle, with its sacred furniture, was removed from place to place in the wilderness, and it may not have been entirely stationary after the conquest. We think, indeed, that it was not. But the history shows that

[1] Judg. 21 : 19. [2] Judg. 18 : 31. [3] Judg. 19 : 18. [4] Judg. 19 : 1.
[5] Judg. 20 : 18, 23, 26. [6] Judg. 20 : 27, 28. [7] 1. Sam. 1 : 1-3 ; 2 : 12-17, 22-26 ; 3 : 3.

Shiloh became the abiding-place of the tabernacle and the ark, and the place of sacrifice and worship, soon after the death of Moses, and continued such until, in the time of Samuel, the Lord forsook the place, and laid it waste because of the wickedness of Eli's house and of the people of Israel.[1] Thus Shiloh, chosen to be the place for recording God's name at the first, continued century after century to be honored as the place of his presence and the place of sacrifice and worship. Such is the testimony of the history—the history as presented in the Bible, and not mutilated and mangled to suit the theories of the analysts. These facts alone are sufficient to show that there was a restriction of sacrifices in general to the one tabernacle and one altar. There were exceptions, doubtless, but these serve to show that the law was generally obeyed.

(5) Moses erected an altar immediately after the defeat of the Amalekites. But this was a memorial altar—not for sacrifice. No sacrifice was offered upon it.[2] So, too, as we have shown, the altar erected by the two and a half tribes east of the Jordan was merely monumental in design, and was not intended for sacrifice. All parties united in declaring the erection of an altar for sacrifice besides the altar before the tabernacle to be rebellion against God and a grievous sin. The account of these exceptional altars confirms the existence of the law against a plurality of altars for sacrifice and worship.

Another exceptional case is presented, at least apparently, in the fact that the children of Israel sacrificed to the Lord in Bochim.[3] We speak of this as an *apparent* exception; for the tabernacle and the ark may have been brought to Bochim, and the place may thus have become, for the time, the central place of worship, or Bochim may have been Shiloh. But an angel of the Lord appeared at Bochim, and this angel, as his words show, was Jehovah himself. Thus the place, at least temporarily, came within the law. God had chosen it for the time to *put his name there;*[4] hence, it became the duty of the Israelites to erect an altar there (if the tabernacle and altar were not there already), and to offer sacrifices upon it. But Jehovah's appearing at Bochim, if it was not Shiloh, was temporary. He put or recorded his name there but once, and then withdrew. Accordingly, the history records but the one sacrifice at Bochim, and

---

[1] Ps. 78: 60; Jer. 7: 12, 14, 15; 26: 6, 9.   [2] Ex. 17: 15, 16.
[3] Judg. 2: 1-5.   [4] Deut. 12: 5.

while sacrificing there the Israelites, so far as the history relates, sacrificed nowhere else. This, then, is only an apparent exception, and does not indicate a plurality of altars.

Another apparently exceptional case is found in the present offered by Gideon to the angel of the Lord. But so far as Gideon was concerned this present was not a sacrifice at all. It consisted of the flesh of a kid, unleavened cakes, and a pot of broth, which were intended as food for the man whom Gideon thought the angel to be. The angel burned these articles of food and disappeared. It appears that in this case the angel was Jehovah.[1] But, at all events, Gideon did not offer sacrifice on this occasion. However, immediately after this Gideon built an altar in Ophrah to the Lord. In regard to this altar several things are to be observed. (1) There is no account of any sacrifice being offered upon it. (2) It appears to have been a memorial altar, like to the one erected by Moses to commemorate the victory over the Amalekites,[2] and the one erected by the two and a half tribes beyond Jordan.[3] (3) The altar for sacrifice was the one built at God's command on the top of the rock or stronghold.[4]

The offering of sacrifice on this second altar was not in violation of the law which forbade separate and private altars and sacrifices, for the Lord had made himself known at this place—had "recorded his name" there. So, too, when Manoah offered his sacrifice upon a rock, the Lord was visibly present; for though the heavenly visitant is called an angel of the Lord, yet when he ascended in the flame of the sacrifice Manoah recognized him as God. God appeared to Manoah no more, and he offered not another sacrifice.[5] There are, indeed, some other cases of irregular sacrifices mentioned in the Book of Judges, but they are condemned as unlawful and idolatrous. During forty years spent in the desert, and the quarter of a century of Joshua's leadership, and the whole time of the judges, four hundred years or more, there are recorded only three instances of lawful and acceptable sacrifice offered elsewhere than at the central place of worship; and at all these three places, Bochim, Ophrah, and Manoah's field, where the irregular sacrifice was offered, the Lord himself was present, "recording his name" there.

In the time of Samuel the circumstances were peculiar. The

---

[1] Judg. 6: 11-23.　　[2] Ex. 17: 15, 16.　　[3] Josh. 22: 21-29.
[4] Judg. 6: 25-32.　　[5] Judg. 13: 1-23.

priesthood was corrupt; the people were in a state of rebellion and alienation. For the prevalent wickedness the Lord slew the priests, delivered the ark and the people into the hands of the Philistines, forsook the tabernacle, and laid Shiloh waste. The ark was brought back to Israel, but it was now an object of fear, and it was placed in the house of Abinadab, where it remained twenty years. The ark and the tabernacle were separated, and the central altar seems to have gone out of sight, if not out of mind. Israel was in a state of apostasy. Samuel called on the people to repent. "Put away [said he] the strange gods and Ashtaroth from among you, and prepare your hearts unto the Lord."[1] His exhortations had temporary effect, but the reformation was not effectual, and the alienation between God and Israel continued, the ark and the tabernacle remained apart, and the services of the sanctuary were not restored. There was altogether an anomalous state of things when the priests had been slain or set aside for their wickedness, and the sanctuary was broken up and suspended. There was no recognized place of central worship, because there was no place where God "recorded his name" by special manifestation of his presence. In these circumstances Samuel and other pious Israelites doubtless did many things which they would not have done, had the regular services of the sanctuary not been interrupted.

The desire of David to have the ark in Jerusalem, his building a tabernacle for it, the account of the removal of it from the house of Abinadab, and David's offering burnt-offerings and peace-offerings before the Lord at the time of his placing it in the tabernacle, all indicate that the neglect of the ark for twenty years was not in accordance with the law and former custom. The death of Uzzah, in consequence of his having touched the ark of God, points to a law that must be rigidly observed, and even the unconscious violation of which must be punished.[2] When David fled from Jerusalem because of Absalom, Zadok and the Levites accompanied him, "bearing the ark of the covenant of God." Though David directed them to return with it to Jerusalem, the facts show that where the ark was, God's habitation was.[3] The hallowed bread at Nob suggests that the tabernacle and its service had been established at that place, only to be abolished by King Saul's slaughter of the priests and the destruction of the city.[4]

[1] I. Sam. 7:3.   [2] II. Sam. 6:1-18.   [3] II. Sam. 15:24-29.   [4] I. Sam. 21:1-6; 22:9-19.

From this time on to the erection of the temple on the spot where the angel of the Lord had stood in the time of David, God had no chosen place in Israel. Indeed, from the time that God forsook Shiloh and laid it waste, because of the sins of Israel, until the building of the temple, there was no place in all the land which could be regarded by the intelligent and pious Jews as possessing the grand characteristic of the central place of worship, according to the Pentateuchal formula, "The place which the Lord your God shall choose out of all your tribes to put his name there."[1]

In this anomalous state of things, resulting from the apostasy of the chosen people and God's withdrawal from them as a community, the law of the unity of worship was necessarily held in abeyance, like circumcision and the Passover in the wilderness, while God was waiting until the rebellious generation should pass away. The appeal of the analysts to the history of these anomalous times and to the examples of irregular sacrifices which it furnishes, in order to prove that as yet there was no legal requirement for the centralization of worship, involves a discreditable ignoring of historical facts and an audacious disregard of logical consistency. Wellhausen says, "Desgleichen wird durch I. Reg. 3 : 2 die Vorstellung eines vorsalomonischen Centralheiligtums ausgeschlossen"[2] ("The representation of a pre-Solomonic central sanctuary is precluded by I. Kings 3 : 2").

The passage which Wellhausen thus imperiously claims settles the question in regard to the existence of the Mosaic tabernacle is as follows: "Only the people sacrificed in high places, because there was no house built unto the name of the Lord, until those days." This is a favorite text with our critic; he refers to it again and again. But his reliance on it is, on his part, a self-contradiction; for he denounces the Book of Kings as untrustworthy and false in its every statement that contravenes his views. We refer, as a specimen, to his declaration that "the thirteenth chapter of I. Kings is one of the coarsest examples of historical worthlessness, comparable with Judges 19–21, or I. Samuel 7 *sqq.*, or occupying a still lower grade."[3] But now, when he finds a passage that seems helpful to his argument, he quotes it as trustworthy and conclusive.

But the critic injects into the passage his notion that there never was a Mosaic tabernacle or tabernacle service. He ignores

---

[1] Deut. 12 : 5. [2] *Prolegomena*, p. 292. [3] *Idem*, p. 297.

the fact that it refers to the time in which the Israelites were in an abnormal state. From the time that God forsook and destroyed Shiloh on account of prevailing wickedness, until the building of the temple, there was no centralized worship, and could be none, because no place was divinely chosen for it; but by the building of the temple in the place chosen of God, and by the bringing of the ark, and the tabernacle, and the holy vessels into it,[1] the central worship was restored as in the days of Moses, Joshua, and the judges.

The analytic critics, some of them at least, rely confidently on II. Samuel 8: 18, last clause, "David's sons were chief rulers," as proving that the law of the Levitical priesthood was not in force in David's time. The word in the original (*cohenim*) here rendered "chief rulers" or "princes," generally means *priests*. If David's sons were priests, the Levitical law must have been disregarded, or was not in force. The argument depends on the translation of the word *cohenim*. May it be translated here "chief rulers" or "princes," as in our Authorized Version? Wellhausen, of course, is quite certain that the passage means that the sons of David were literal priests, and is more than willing to accept the statement on the authority of an author whose historical veracity he repeatedly impugns. His declaration is, "So durfen diese Worte nicht dem Pentateuch zu liebe anders gedreht werden als wie sie lauten"[2] ("These words must not, out of love for the Pentateuch, be twisted out of their proper meaning"). Wellhausen's faithful follower, Professor W. R. Smith, affirms that "the Hebrew word means priests, and can mean nothing else."[3]

Notwithstanding the dogmatical assumption of these critics, there is something to be said on the other side.

(*a*) The author of the Book of Kings includes priests (*cohenim*) among the princes and officers of Solomon. His words are, "And these were the princes which he had," and among these he classes Zadok and Abiathar.[4] Aside from the question of divine inspiration and also the question of historical accuracy, the author of Kings undoubtedly knew the meaning of the Hebrew word *cohen*, and here we find him calling priests *princes*, classing them with civil and military officers.

(*b*) The chronicler also evidently understood the word in the

---

[1] I. Kings 8: 1-6. [2] *Prolegomena*, p. 133.
[3] *The Old Testament in the Jewish Church*, p. 265. [4] I. Kings 4: 2-6.

same way. He interprets this very passage as follows: "And the sons of David were chief about the king."[1] The analytic leaders impeach the historical character of the chronicler; but he at least understood the Hebrew language.

(c) The Septuagint Version translates thus: "The sons of David were *aularchai*" (chamberlains or rulers of the palace).

(d) Gesenius says that it is the opinion of the Hebrew interpreters that *cohen* signifies *prince* as well as priest, and that the Chaldee translators have rendered it in several places by the former word.[2]

Other authorities might be given, but we deem the above a sufficient, and more than a sufficient, answer to the unsupported assertions of our analytic critics.

There is no necessity, then, for understanding that King David made his sons *priests* in the common acceptation of that word.

We conclude that the history, on the whole, is favorable to the centralization of worship in Mosaic times. When the history is taken in its entirety; when it is recollected that in the whole Pentateuchal history and during the times of Moses and Joshua there is not mentioned a single instance of sacrifice offered elsewhere than at the altar before the tabernacle; when it is further recollected that all the irregular sacrifices during the time of the judges are condemned as idolatrous and sinful except in three cases, and that in these three cases the sacrifices were offered where Jehovah was visibly present; and when it is still further recollected that the instances of irregular sacrifice on which the critics mainly rely occurred at a time when the sanctuary services had been interrupted, and there was no place where God was "recording his name," and hence there could be no place of central worship,—when these and all the other facts are taken into consideration, it must be seen that the history, instead of militating against the traditional view, in reality confirms and vindicates it.

2. Another point at which the analytic criticism comes into conflict with the history is the existence of the Mosaic tabernacle. Some of the analysts, yes, many of them, admit its existence, but they do so at the expense of logical consistency. The analytic hypothesis of the origin of the Pentateuchal books and of the Levitical code in post-Mosaic times logically necessitates the rejection of the account of the tabernacle in the wilder-

[1] I. Chr. 18: 17.   [2] *Lexicon*, p. 450.

ness as fictitious and false. With it are connected the ark and the altar. Where it stood was the place of sacrifice. Admit the tabernacle in the wilderness, and you are forced to admit the centralization of worship. The idea of one tabernacle, one holy ark, and one altar, and many places of worship, is absurd. Besides, minute directions were given to Moses concerning the construction of the tabernacle and all its furniture. All the instruments, even the tongs and the snuff-dishes, were made according to the pattern shown to Moses in the mount.[1] Of course, then, divine directions were given to Moses concerning the tabernacle service. It is absurd to suppose that God would give minute prescriptions in regard to the material structure and its furniture, and yet establish no code for sacrifice and worship for priests and priestly service. It is unreasonable to suppose that Moses, even without divine guidance, would pursue such a course. If he constructed the tabernacle, with its sacrificial altar and altar of incense, its lamps, and lights, and show-bread, and all its instruments of service, then also is he the author of its code and ritual. Those, therefore, who deny the Mosaic origin of the Levitical code and service must deny the reality of the Mosaic tabernacle. No doubt Voltaire, with his quick vision, recognized this truth when, anticipating the leaders of the modern analytic school, he declared the Mosaic tabernacle to be a fiction. Those leaders, Reuss, Graf, Kuenen, and Wellhausen, knew what they were about when, in rounding out and completing the analytic system, they took up and carried out Voltaire's idea by maintaining that the tabernacle in the wilderness is but Solomon's temple in miniature projected, by the Jewish imagination, back into the past.

Perhaps there are some analytic critics who repudiate the opinions of these leaders on this subject, and accept the account of the Mosaic tabernacle as entirely true. We impeach neither the truthfulness nor the honesty of such men, but suggest that they must and will either recede or advance from their present position; for, according to the history as given in Exodus, Moses, in accordance with the divine command, gave minute directions not only in regard to the construction of the tabernacle, the altar, and the ark, in regard to the altar of incense, the table, the candlestick, and oil for the light, but also in regard to the consecration of Aaron and his sons, their regalia for the taber-

[1] Ex. 25: 9, 40.

nacle,—breastplate, ephod, robe, broidered coat, miter, and girdle; gold, blue, purple, scarlet, and fine linen,—and in regard to the daily service,—a bullock for a sin-offering every day, two lambs of the first year day by day continually. Even the very day in which the tabernacle was to be set up and Aaron and his sons were to be consecrated, was specified. And, according to the history, the tabernacle and all its vessels and furniture were constructed precisely as Moses directed, and were consecrated on the day appointed. Aaron was set apart to the office of chief priest, with his sons as assistants, and the daily service of the sanctuary according to the prescribed ritual was inaugurated. All this and much more is related in the history, and related *as history*.[1] Now, if all this be true, we have a Levitical priesthood, Levitical ritual, and Levitical code established and inaugurated by Moses in the wilderness. But in case a man will not accept this Leviticism and ritualism as inaugurated by Moses, he must join the more advanced analytic critics in declaring the history to be false. Nor is the history thus set aside confined to one book. The Mosaic tabernacle figures largely in Exodus, Leviticus, and Numbers; it is mentioned in Deuteronomy;[2] it is mentioned also in Joshua, Judges, Samuel, Kings, and Chronicles. Thus the analysts are under the necessity of contradicting nearly every historical book of the Old Testament; and yet they try to array the biblical history against traditional views.

3. The analytic critics reject also the historical account of the Passover. Reuss claims that it was instituted in the time of King Josiah.[3] Graf maintains that it belongs to the time of the exile.[4] Wellhausen, of course, maintains its evolutionary and post-Mosaic origin.[5] This position is taken in accordance with the logical requirements of the analytic theories. The passover lamb was to be killed at the door of the tabernacle. If the Passover originated in Mosaic times, then must the tabernacle also date back to Mosaic times. But priests and a priestly ritual are connected with the tabernacle. Hence the priestly ritual would be shown to be Mosaic. But this is contrary to the analytic theories. Hence the analysts, who have thoroughly thought out their hypothesis to its necessary conclusions, maintain the post-Mosaic origin of the Passover. They take this

[1] Ex. 40: 17-38.   [2] Deut. 31: 14, 15.   [3] *L'Histoire Sainte*, Int., pp. 148, 164.
[4] *Die Geschichtlichen Bücher des Alten Testaments*, pp. 84, 72.
[5] *Prolegomena*, p. 91.

position, however, in defiance of the history. They virtually give the lie to the twelfth chapter of Exodus, which records the origin and first celebration of the Passover under Moses in Egypt. They disregard the references to it in Leviticus.[1] They reject and trample under foot the account of the second observance of it by Moses and the Israelites in the wilderness, as given in Numbers.[2] They account the record concerning it in Deuteronomy worthless.[3] They in some way get rid of the account of the keeping of the Passover by the Israelites after crossing the Jordan, as given in Joshua.[4] The chronicler's account of the celebration of this feast in the time of King Hezekiah gives them but little trouble, since they decry the historical veracity of that writer even more than that of most of the other sacred narrators.

Our critics thus reject not only the testimony of the historical books, but also that of the authors who are supposed to have lived and written at different times. According to Kautzsch-Socin, the account of the institution of the Passover in Exodus 12: 1-20 is by P, who is supposed to have lived and written about 450 B.C.; the reference to the Passover in Exodus 34: 25, by J, about 800 B.C.; that in Deuteronomy 16: 1-8, by D, 600 B.C.; that in Numbers 28: 16, 17, by R, and that in Numbers 33: 3, by P (R).[5] Kautzsch-Socin mark Exodus 12: 21-27 (which refers to the Passover) with an interrogation point (?), but Driver[6] ascribes the passage to JE, 800 to 750 B.C.

Some of these supposed authors, as J and E, are claimed to have lived and written many years before the time in which, according to our critics, the Passover became known. The absurdity and self-contradiction of ascribing statements concerning the Passover to such authors, and yet maintaining that that institution had no existence before the exile or the time of Josiah, is quite obvious. How illogical it is in these critics, after setting aside as untrustworthy the testimony of Exodus, Leviticus, Numbers, Deuteronomy, Joshua, and Chronicles; of D, E, J, P, and R, who, perhaps, owe their entire existence to the critics who thus abuse them, then to turn round and argue that the biblical history is opposed to the traditional belief!

4. Logical and consistent analysts are under the necessity of referring the origin of the Sabbath to a comparatively late

---

[1] Lev. 23: 4-8. [2] Num. 9: 1-14. [3] Deut. 16: 1-8. [4] Josh. 5: 10.
[5] *Heilige Schrift des Alten Testaments.*
[6] *Introduction to the Literature of the Old Testament,* p. 25.

period. According to the analytic hypothesis the reference to the institution of the Sabbath in Genesis 2: 2, 3 originated with the supposed author P, 450 B.C., nearly a thousand years after the time of Moses. Driver ascribes the reference to the Sabbath in Exodus 16: 22-30 partly to J, 900 B.C.,[1] but Kautzsch-Socin refer no part of this passage to J, but divide it between P and R. The various references to the Sabbath elsewhere in the Pentateuch are ascribed to exilic or other late authors. The twentieth chapter of Exodus (1-21), which contains the decalogue, gives trouble to the analysts. Driver ascribes the passage to E, 750 B.C., many centuries after Moses, but he affirms that "the decalogue was of course derived by E from a preëxisting source."[2] This remark of Driver's indicates a desire to trace the ten commandments back to Moses. Kautzsch-Socin ascribe the passage to E in brackets, thus [E][3] Reuss says the passage is "the result of a compilation much later than the time generally assigned to it."[4] Wellhausen denies the Mosaic origin of the decalogue. He even affirms that we have two decalogues and that we have no real or certain knowledge as to what the stone tables placed in the ark contained.[5] Kuenen declares that the decalogue has been redacted and interpolated, and that its original form is uncertain and its date doubtful. He refers it to 800 or 700 B.C.[6] Graf's views are about the same.

Thus these critics view the ten commandments. The fourth, of course, fares no better at their hands than any of the others. They nullify the divine authority for the Sabbath, as contained in the decalogue. Reasoning as they do about other matters, they must hold that the fourth commandment was ignored and disobeyed by the people of God in ancient times. There is no reference either to the law or to its observance from Adam to Moses. There is nothing to indicate that the ancient saints of God, Adam, Seth, Enoch, Noah, Abraham, Isaac, Jacob, and Joseph, and their godly contemporaries, either obeyed the fourth commandment or knew anything about it. The Sabbath is not mentioned, nor even alluded to (unless in the references to the seven days in the account of the flood),[7] from the creation to the exodus. To use the current style of the analytic school, the Bible history knows nothing about Sabbath observance among the people of God from the creation on down to the giving of the

[1] *Introduction to the Literature of the Old Testament*, p. 28. [2] *Idem*, p. 30.
[3] *Heilige Schrift des Alten Testaments*. [4] *L'Histoire Sainte*, Int., p. 66.
[5] *Prolegomena*, p. 411. [6] *Hexateuch*, p. 244. [7] Gen. 7: 4, 10; 8: 10, 12.

manna—a period of more than two thousand six hundred years. Then, again, the Bible history knows nothing about obedience to the fourth commandment among the Israelites from Moses to Isaiah; and even in Isaiah's time Sabbath desecration was a prevalent sin.[1] Though the Sabbath is mentioned in the books of Kings and Chronicles, there is not a word about the observance of it as a day of rest.[2]

Yet all this silence in regard to the Sabbath, silence lasting for centuries, and even for thousands of years, and this neglect of it, though general, persistent, and long-continued, do not prove that the law requiring men to rest one day in seven was not in force from the earliest times, or was at any period altogether unknown. The analytic critic, in drawing such conclusion, does it in defiance of the biblical history. That history states that God instituted the Sabbath at man's creation.[3] That history further states that the Israelites had a knowledge of this primitive institution and observed it when they came out of Egypt and before the giving of the decalogue at Sinai.[4] Still further, the history states that at the giving of the law Jehovah issued no new command in regard to the Sabbath, but reminded the Israelites of the commandment already given, "Remember the Sabbath day to keep it holy." And still further, the history states that Moses incorporated this command among the civil laws of his people. The only way the analytic critics can, with any show of consistency or reason, maintain the non-primitive and non-Mosaic character of the fourth commandment and of the institution of the Sabbath, is to impeach and set aside the biblical history. This is what the most logical and boldest of the analysts have done.

5. The argument from silence and neglect has been applied to the institution of the Day of Atonement. This institution is referred to in each of the three middle books, but is set forth most particularly in Leviticus.[5] But what must be admitted as strange and scarcely accountable is, that outside of the Pentateuch there is no reference to the Day of Atonement in the Old Testament—at least no certain reference. But in this case the argument from silence cuts both ways. If the analytic critic should say that, as there is no mention of the observance of the law in regard to

---

[1] Isa. 56:2; 58:13.
[2] II. Kings 4:23; 11:5; 7:9; 16:18; I. Chr. 9:32; 23:31; II. Chr. 2:4; 8:13; 23:4, 8; 31:3; 36:21.   [3] Gen. 2:2, 3.   [4] Ex. 16:22-30.
[5] Ex. 30:10; Lev. 16:1-34; 23:26-32; Num. 29:7-11.

the Day of Atonement previous to the exile, there was no such observance, and hence there was no such law, the answer is easy and obvious; for there is no mention of the observance of the law even in post-exilic times. Indeed, there is no reference to the law at all after the exile until the first century. There is a supposed reference to it in Josephus[1] and another in the Acts of the Apostles,[2] and there is a clear reference to it in the Epistle to the Hebrews.[3] Hence, according to the *argumentum e silentio*, which our analytic critics are so fond of using, the law establishing the Day of Atonement and the books which refer to it had no existence until the first century of the Christian era. The argument which involves such a conclusion is worthless. Reuss makes an effort, though not a very vigorous one, to show from the silence of the record that the restored exiles did not observe the Day of Atonement until the arrival of Ezra among them.[4] The critic seems oblivious of the fact that his reasoning involves the absurd conclusion mentioned above.

Graf accepts the argument from silence as proving that the Day of Atonement was not observed until long after the exile. According to his view, the law was in the Pentateuchal books from the time of Ezra, but was neglected and disobeyed for hundreds of years. By parity of reasoning, the law may have been in the Pentateuchal books *before* the time of Ezra, though neglected and disobeyed.

We conclude, then, that the laws in regard to the Day of Atonement, the Sabbath, the Passover, and the unity of worship were in force in the time of Moses and afterward. This not only refutes the argument of the analysts drawn from the neglect and violation of these laws, but also constitutes presumptive proof that the books containing these laws were in existence in the time of Moses.

[1] *Antiquities*, 14 : 16 : 4.   [2] Acts 27 : 9.   [3] Heb. 9 : 7.
[4] *L'Histoire Sainte*, pp. 260, 261.

CHAPTER VI

TESTIMONY OF CHRIST AND THE APOSTLES

THAT the testimony of the New Testament is in favor of the Mosaic authorship of the Pentateuch needs scarcely to be proved. The most of the analytic critics admit that the authority of Christ and the apostles is against them. So fully convinced are they of this fact that they have been trying to push the doctrine of the kenosis far enough to include the fallibility and errancy of Christ. A few of the analysts, not willing to believe that our Lord and Saviour erred in biblical matters, have refused to admit that he recognized Moses as the author of the Pentateuchal books. Such critics are doubtless in a strait betwixt two, unwilling to believe that the great Teacher erred in his didactic utterances, and yet unwilling to give up their anti-Mosaic theories. Such men have our commiseration.

Christ distinctly recognized Moses as the author of both the Pentateuchal laws and books.

1. The laws.

"And the Pharisees came to him, and asked him, Is it lawful for a man to put away his wife? tempting him. And he answered and said unto them, What did Moses command you? And they said, Moses suffered to write a bill of divorcement, and to put her away. And Jesus answered and said unto them, For the hardness of your heart he wrote you this precept."[1] The law or the part of the law here mentioned is found in Deuteronomy 24:1-4.

"Offer the gift that Moses commanded, for a testimony unto them."[2] The law of leprosy here mentioned is contained in the thirteenth and fourteenth chapters of Leviticus.

"Moses said, Honor thy father and thy mother."[3] Moses is here recognized as the author of the fifth commandment, and impliedly of the whole decalogue.

"These are the words which I spake unto you, while I was yet with you, that all things must be fulfilled which were written

[1] Mark 10:2-5.   [2] Matt. 8:4.   [3] Mark 7:10.

in the law of Moses, and in the Prophets, and in the Psalms, concerning me."[1] In this declaration "the law of Moses" is undoubtedly the law contained in the Pentateuch; but the Pentateuch, as containing the law, is also meant, and is distinguished from the two other parts of the Old Testament—the prophecies and Psalms. Moses is thus designated as the author both of the Pentateuch as containing the law, and of the law itself.

Again, "Moses therefore gave unto you circumcision; (not because it is of Moses, but of the fathers;) and ye on the Sabbath day circumcise a man; . . . that the law of Moses should not be broken."[2] Our Lord in this declaration states that circumcision did not originate with Moses, but with his predecessors; that Moses had transmitted this rite to the Israelites, and that he was the author of the law which enjoined it upon them.

2. In regard to Moses as the author of the Pentateuchal writings, our Saviour spoke as follows: "And as touching the dead, that they rise; have ye not read in the book of Moses, how in the bush God spake unto him, saying, I am the God of Abraham, and the God of Isaac, and the God of Jacob?"[3] The passage here referred to is contained in Exodus.[4] But so far as the question of Pentateuchal authorship is concerned, it makes little difference, whether by "the book of Moses" is meant the whole Pentateuch or only the Book of Exodus. For if Moses wrote this, he certainly wrote also the other books of the Pentateuch. To every reverent and logical mind who believes in Christ, the Son of God, as an infallible and inerrant Teacher, this one declaration is a complete refutation of all the analytic theories.

"Do not think that I will accuse you to the Father: there is one that accuseth you, even Moses, in whom ye trust. For had ye believed Moses, ye would have believed me: for he wrote of me. But if ye believe not his writings, how shall ye believe my words."[5] Our divine Lord thus spoke of compositions of Moses that were accessible to those whom he addressed. He speaks of these writings as being known to his hearers. They had read them, but did not believe them. He addresses them as having these well-known writings of Moses in their possession. But where? Undoubtedly in the Pentateuch, which they had in their Hebrew Bibles and the Septuagint Version. The only writings ascribed to Moses are found there, and are found nowhere else. The hearers of Christ would naturally and inevitably

---

[1] Luke 24:44. [2] John 7:22, 23. [3] Mark 12:26. [4] Ex. 3:6. [5] John 5:45-47.

understand him as referring to the writings of Moses in the Pentateuch, and undoubtedly he intended that they should so understand him.

"He wrote of me." How and where did Moses write of Christ? He wrote of him as the seed of the woman;[1] as the seed of Abraham;[2] as the coming Shiloh;[3] as the Star out of Jacob;[4] as the Scepter rising out of Israel;[4] as the Passover Lamb, not a bone of which was to be broken;[5] as the goat for separation, bearing away the sins of Israel;[6] as represented in the types and shadows of the tabernacle and of the tabernacle service, and as the great Prophet.[7]

"They have Moses and the Prophets; let them hear them. . . . If they hear not Moses and the Prophets, neither will they be persuaded though one rose from the dead."[8] In this passage the Prophets are put for what the prophets wrote, and Moses is put for what Moses wrote. And our Lord speaks of the writings of Moses, as well as of the prophets, as being known and accessible to the people whom he addressed. It is clearly implied that there were writings in the Old Testament that were understood to be Mosaic, and our Saviour here refers to them as such.

In one of the passages quoted above we have a threefold division of the Old Testament—the law of Moses, the Prophets, and the Psalms.[9] The first division, called the Law, is undoubtedly the Pentateuch.

It is thus shown that the authorship of the Pentateuchal books is ascribed by our Saviour to Moses, in almost every possible form of expression—"the law of Moses," "book of Moses," "writings of Moses," "Moses wrote," "Moses said," "Moses commanded," "Moses gave"; and in every case he was necessarily understood as referring to books, writings, and laws that are contained in the Pentateuch, and that his hearers ascribed to Moses. And further, he was necessarily understood by his hearers as himself acknowledging these books, writings, and laws as the productions of Moses.

The testimony of the apostles and New Testament writers in regard to the authorship of the Pentateuch of course harmonizes with that of Christ. "For the Law was given by Moses."[10] "We have found him of whom Moses in the Law, and the Prophets, did write."[11] "And when the days of her purification

---

[1] Gen. 3:15. [2] Gen. 22:18. [3] Gen. 49:10. [4] Num. 24:17.
[5] Ex. 12:46. [6] Lev. 16:20-22. [7] Deut. 18:18. [8] Luke 16:29,31.
[9] Luke 24:44. [10] John 1:17. [11] John 1:45.

according to the law of Moses were accomplished."[1] "Both out of the law of Moses, and out of the Prophets."[2] "Moses describeth the righteousness which is of the law."[3] "It is written in the law of Moses."[4] "When Moses is read."[5] "He that despised Moses' law."[6] Thus we have the testimony of the apostles and New Testament writers in harmony with that of Christ in regard to the Mosaic authorship of the Pentateuchal laws and writings.

The validity of this testimony, the validity of the testimony even of the Lord Jesus Christ, has been called in question by some of his professed friends and followers. Many of that class of analytic critics who profess the evangelical faith, rather than give up their theories take the position that our Lord and Saviour was fallible and errant, and that he was mistaken in regard to the authorship of the Pentateuch. Some of these critics seem to think that it devolves upon them to point out errors in the public and biblical instructions of Christ, the Son of God. Such men, under the Old Testament dispensation, according to the Mosaic law, would have been stoned to death for blasphemy.

In regard to Christ's inerrancy, we remark as follows:

1. We expect such men as Reuss, Graf, Kuenen, and Wellhausen—rationalists, skeptics, veritable infidels—to reject the testimony of Christ in regard to the authorship of the Pentateuch and in every other case in which it is opposed to their views and theories. These leaders of the analytic school were and are disbelievers in the Bible, in divine inspiration, and the deity of Christ. Their writings indicate that they consider Christ a mere human being, much inferior to themselves in biblical knowledge. That such men should charge our Lord with error creates no scandal.

2. The Scripture doctrine of Christ's *kenosis*[7] does not imply that he was fallible and errant. Truly he *emptied* himself[7] when he became man. Christ as man was doubtless subject to limitations. His knowledge, it appears, was not absolutely infinite. For there is one thing he did not know—*the time of the end.*[8] But this is the only thing which our Saviour is said not to have known. The language employed concerning him implies that he knew everything else. Peter said to him, "Thou knowest all

---

[1] Luke 2:22. [2] Acts 28:23. [3] Rom. 10:5. [4] I. Cor. 9:9.
[5] II. Cor. 3:15. [6] Heb. 10:28. [7] Phil. 2:7. [8] Mark 13:32.

things."[1] He knew the hearts of men, reading their thoughts, though secret and concealed.[2] The future was known to him.[3] Things absent and distant were to him as things present. It was Christ's omniscience as indicated by the declaration, "Before that Philip called thee, when thou wast under the fig tree, I saw thee," which drew from Nathanael the confession, "Thou art the Son of God; thou art the King of Israel."[4] The woman of Samaria proclaimed Christ's omniscience, in saying, "Come, see a man which told me all things that ever I did: is not this the Christ?"[5] The talk of the Jews concerning Christ's learning and knowledge is very significant: "And the Jews marveled, saying, How knoweth this man letters, having never learned?"[6] Yet our analytic critics will have it that he did not know who wrote the Pentateuch. The examples we have given of Christ's extraordinary and superhuman knowledge, we may indeed say, of his omniscience, all relate to him as beset by human conditions in this life. There is but one exception stated as to the universality of his knowledge, namely, his not knowing the time of the end. This exceptional case is mysterious and strange. Reverent minds, that have no theories to support, are not disposed to draw conclusions from it. The reasoning of some of our analysts in regard to it is preposterous, as follows: Christ did not know the time of the end; therefore, he was mistaken in regard to the authorship of the Pentateuch. There is a wide chasm between the premises and the conclusion.

3. The analytic critics, in endeavoring to get rid of Christ's testimony against their theories of Pentateuchal authorship, charge him not with ignorance merely, but with thinking that he knew, when he did not; with such ignorance as led him to make an untrue declaration. Christ knew that he did not know the time of the end, and he made no declaration concerning it. According to the analytic theory, Christ overrated his own knowledge. He thought he knew who wrote the Pentateuch, but did not, and hence made a mistaken declaration in regard to it. Here again the logic of the analyst is exceedingly bad. It proceeds thus: Christ knew that he did not know the time of the end, and was silent in regard to it; therefore, he might in some case overrate his knowledge, thinking he knew, when he did not, and thus be led to make a mistaken declaration.

[1] John 21:17. [2] Luke 6:8. [3] John 1:48. [4] John 1:48, 49.
[5] John 4:29. [6] John 7:15.

4. Many of the declarations of Christ concerning the Mosaic authorship of the Pentateuch were made by him after the transfiguration, and one of them was made after his resurrection.[1] Indeed, after these events it is evident that he held the same views in regard to this subject as before, for he took back nothing that he had said, but, on the other hand, virtually reiterated after his resurrection all his previous declarations in regard to it. "These are the words which I spake unto you, while I was yet with you, that all things must be fulfilled which were written in the law of Moses, and in the Prophets, and in the Psalms, concerning me."[1] According to the analytic criticism, our blessed Lord held and taught error up to the very time of his departure from the earth. According to the analytic criticism, he did not learn his error in regard to the authorship of the Pentateuch, though he talked with Moses on the mount of transfiguration; nor were his views on this subject clarified and corrected by his death and resurrection. To us the spectacle of men, professors of the Christian faith, however learned and able they may be, assuming that the Lord of life and glory was fallible and errant, and undertaking to tell how and why he erred, would be supremely absurd and ridiculous, were it not so sad and repulsive. All this, of course, is lost upon such leaders of the analytic school as Reuss and Wellhausen, who have no more faith in the incarnation, transfiguration, resurrection, or ascension of Christ, or in any other supernatural event, than Paine and Voltaire. But there are analytic critics, not leaders, who ought not to be impervious to the foregoing considerations.

5. The smooth phrases that are sometimes employed by analytic critics to express their notion of Christ's fallibility are deceptive. That "Christ condescended *not to know*," like most other euphemisms, is misleading. These critics would express their notion of our Lord's fallibility more fully and fairly by saying that he condescended to *err;* that he condescended to make untrue declarations; and that he condescended to keep on making untrue declarations after his resurrection from the dead, even up to the time of his ascension. They, of course, give him credit for uttering only what he believed to be strictly true, and for aiming to tell nothing but the truth. Yet they hold that, in fact, he deviated from the truth in regard to the authorship of the Pentateuch, and also in some other matters.

[1] Luke 24:44.

Even the smooth-speaking Driver says that Christ was mistaken in regard to the Davidic authorship of the One Hundred and Tenth Psalm.[1] Are such mistakes and errors to be proved and accounted for by Christ's *condescension?* The next thing for our analysts to do is to maintain that the Holy One of God condescended to commit sin.

6. Aside from the divine nature in Christ's person, there is an antecedent probability, or rather certainty, that the gift and influence of the Holy Spirit would secure truth and accuracy in all his biblical instructions and didactic utterances. Christ assured his apostles that the Holy Spirit would teach them all things, and bring to their remembrance whatsoever he had spoken to them.[2] He promised that the Spirit of truth should guide them into all truth, and also show them things to come.[3] He informed them that the Holy Spirit should so enter into them, possess and actuate them, that their speaking would be the Holy Spirit speaking in them.[4] Accordingly, on the day of Pentecost "they were all filled with the Holy Ghost, and began to speak with other tongues, as the Spirit gave them utterance."[5] Men thus filled, influenced, and guided by the Spirit were certainly inerrant. We do not enter upon the discussion of plenary inspiration. We are not now maintaining that the apostles were inerrant as teachers at all times, though we believe they were. But when they were filled and guided by the Spirit; when they were speaking as the Spirit gave them utterance; when they were so much under the influence of the Spirit that the Spirit spake in them; when this state of things existed and as long as it existed, the apostles would no more mistake and err than a child would fall when guided and held by its parent's hand. Now Christ's humanity was sustained and guided not only by the deity within him, but also by the Holy Spirit. After his baptism at Jordan the Holy Spirit descended upon him.[6] Next we read that he was full of the Holy Spirit, and was led or driven by the Spirit into the wilderness to be tempted of the devil.[7] Again, we read that "God giveth not the Spirit by measure unto him."[8] These declarations show that he had more of the Spirit and more of the Spirit's influence than the apostles. Since the Spirit guided them and spoke in them so that they spoke as the Spirit gave them utterance, much more

---

[1] *Introduction to the Literature of the Old Testament,* Preface, p. xiv ; also, p. 302
[2] John 14 : 26.   [3] John 16 : 13.   [4] Mark 13 : 11.   [5] Acts 2 : 4.
[6] Luke 3 : 22   [7] Luke 4 : 1 ; Mark 1 : 12 ; Matt. 4 : 1.   [8] John 3 : 34

were Christ's sayings in accordance with the mind of the Spirit.

Besides this, the relation between Christ and the Father was such as to make the acts and sayings of the former the acts and sayings of the latter. Of this there are many proofs. Christ himself said: "I am in the Father, and the Father in me. The words that I speak unto you I speak not of myself: but the Father, that dwelleth in me, he doeth the works."[1] And again: "For I have not spoken of myself; but the Father which sent me, he gave me a commandment, what I should say, and what I should speak. And I know that his commandment is life everlasting: whatsoever I speak therefore, even as the Father said unto me, so I speak."[2] Once more, "I do nothing of myself; but as my Father hath taught me, I speak these things."[3] Thus Christ taught that the Father concurred and coöperated with him in all that he said and did. Still further, Christ was in constant communion with the Father. He spent whole nights in prayer. His prayers were always effectual. At the tomb of Lazarus Christ said, "I knew that thou hearest me always."[4] Now Christ certainly prayed for all that was desirable for himself. It was certainly desirable that he should be kept from all errors in regard to biblical matters. The order and connection of these ideas are as follows: It was desirable that our Saviour should be exempt from all errors in teaching, including those charged upon him by the analytic critics in regard to the authorship of the Pentateuch; he, therefore, prayed for exemption from such errors; he never prayed to the Father in vain; therefore, in all his didactic utterances and in all his declarations concerning the Scriptures he was infallible and inerrant.

It is not likely that the analysts will take the position that it was not desirable that our Lord should avoid all mistakes in his teaching. They will scarcely apply to the supposed errors of Christ the doctrine that evil, even sin, is overruled for good. They have been at work for a hundred years, trying to overthrow the opinion which Christ sanctioned, namely, that Moses wrote the Pentateuch; and that he sanctioned it is one of the obstacles in the way of success. According to their theories, most assuredly it was desirable that Christ should have been kept from this error, which is certainly not to be accounted for on the principle of doing evil that good may come.

[1] John 14:10.   [2] John 12:49, 50.   [3] John 8:28.   [4] John 11:42.

It has been urged that on the question of the authorship of the Pentateuch there should be no appeal to the teachings of Christ. This seems to us a strange and narrow view. Critics are accustomed to quote anything they can find in Josephus or any other author bearing on any biblical question under discussion. Critics do not hesitate to test the accuracy of Genesis by the discoveries of modern science. It is entirely proper to employ the discoveries of Egyptologists and other archæologists in discussing the accuracy and authorship of the Pentateuch, though, indeed, the testimony derived from such sources is pretty much all in favor of one side. It is, perhaps, because of the one-sidedness of this testimony that the analysts are by no means fond of it, and that Wellhausen uttered his famous sneer that "Jehovah has nothing in common with the God-forsaken dreariness of certain Egyptologists."[1] It is, of course, good policy on the part of the opponents of the Mosaic authorship of the Pentateuch to exclude, if possible, the declarations of Christ and the apostles from consideration in the decision of the question. The attorney in court may be counted on to keep out, if he can, all testimony that would prove damaging to his case.

[1] *Israel*, p. 440.

CHAPTER VII

CONSEQUENCES

WE propose in this closing chapter to speak of the tendencies and effects of the analytic system, the hypotheses and ideas embraced in it, and the arguments by which they are supported.

It may be said,—indeed, it has been said,—that at most not much harm can result from the acceptance of the hypothesis of the non-Mosaic origin of the Pentateuch, or the acceptance of analytic views of the authorship of any of the anonymous books of the Bible. It is indeed true that the human authorship of a divinely inspired book is in itself of little importance. Nor is the question whether such a book was produced through the instrumentality of one author or many of much importance in itself. We recognize the fact that the great question concerning the Pentateuch, as well as concerning every other book of the Bible, is whether it is divinely inspired. If God is its author, it is to be believed, reverenced, and obeyed, no matter by whom or in what age it was written. But in the case of the Pentateuch the question of its authorship, as discussed by the analysts, is intimately connected with the question of its divine inspiration, and of that of the whole Bible. We are of the opinion that the Pentateuch can neither be the word, nor contain the word, of God, nor have any divine authority, if it is such a book as the analytic school represents it to be. We think that the analytic view of its authorship, as now set forth and defended, must, in the end, result in thoroughgoing skepticism. We believe, indeed, that the outcome of the hypotheses and argumentation necessary to defend that view must logically and inevitably be downright rationalism and infidelity. Such will not be the immediate result in most, or perhaps in many, cases. Generally, those who construct or adopt a new theory do not carry it out to its legitimate consequences. In many cases a generation or two must pass before the character and tendencies of a new theory can be tested by its practical results. The foremost thinkers, the men of logic and intellectual intrepidity, are the first to carry new views and ideas to their ultimate conclusions. Already the leaders of the analytic school, the men who have filled out and completed the system, and who best know what positions must be taken in order to defend it, have become rationalists, which is another name for infidels. Many of their followers—men possibly of equal learning, but of feebler intellectual grasp—are lagging at a distance behind them, but moving on in the same direction. Some of these may stop in their course and stand doggedly still; some may turn round and retrace their steps; but a logical mind once adopting analytic views can scarcely avoid moving on towards skepticism and infidelity.

1. In the first place, as shown in the preceding chapter, the analytic hypothesis in regard to the authorship and date of the Pentateuchal books involves the conclusion that the Lord Jesus Christ, while on earth, was fallible and errant, adopting erroneous opinions current among the Jews and giving them out in his public instructions. The analytic hypothesis charges our divine Lord with more serious error than incorrect teaching in regard to the authorship of the Pentateuch and the Psalms. It virtually charges him with false teaching in regard to the infallibility and authority of the Scriptures. He declared that "the Scripture cannot be broken."[1] Again, having spoken of "the Law and the Prophets," he said, "Till heaven and earth pass, one jot or one tittle shall in no wise pass from the Law, till all be fulfilled."[2] Again, having spoken of "the Law and the Prophets," he added, "And it is easier for heaven and earth to pass, than one tittle of the Law to fail."[3] All these declarations were necessarily understood by Christ's hearers as referring to Scripture and law as contained in the Pentateuch, as well as to the other Scriptures, and he undoubtedly intended them to be so understood. But our analytics, in opposition to our Lord's teachings, maintain that much of the Pentateuchal Scripture is broken and marred by contradictions, misstatements, and other errors, and that much of the Pentateuchal law is nullified and fails in the same way. Thus our Saviour is declared to be fallible and errant even in his public declarations concerning the Scriptures. Now what must be the effect of such an opinion, when fully accepted? What effect must it have upon little children and upon larger boys and girls to inform them that Jesus, the Lord from heaven, was a fallible teacher and made

[1] John 10 : 35.   [2] Matt. 5 : 18.   [3] Luke 16 : 17.

mistakes even in speaking of the Scriptures? And what effect must all this have on men in general? Had Nathanael found Christ mistaken in his declaration as to having seen him under the fig tree, the Israelite without guile would have rejected his claims to the Messiahship. Had the woman of Samaria found him mistaken in any of his declarations in regard to her former life, instead of proclaiming, "Come, see a man which told me all things that ever I did," she would have pronounced him an impostor. And just let mankind in general become convinced that Jesus made mistakes in his teachings and uttered incorrect declarations about the Scriptures, and the conclusion will eventually be reached that he is not the Son of God and Lord from heaven. The logic and common sense of the human mind will advance from belief in the fallibility and errancy of Christ to the skepticism of Reuss, Graf, Kuenen, and Wellhausen, Paine and Voltaire.

Some of the analytic critics of the less advanced class seem themselves to consider the doctrine of Christ's fallibility dangerous. Their cautious and euphemistic way of speaking of it indicates this, or else, like the ancient enemies of Christ, they "fear the people." These critics, of course, represent the errors which they charge on him as *trivial*. Yet they themselves, after a century of effort, continue to write essays, reviews, and books, and to employ all the resources of learning and logic, to convince the world that the Mosaic authorship of the Pentateuch, though recognized by Christ, is an error. Besides, the analytic criticism virtually charges it as an error on Christ and the apostles that they refer to and quote the Pentateuch as divinely inspired and authoritative.

2. The analytic system tends and leads to the rejection of the doctrine of divine inspiration.

No portion of the Old Testament is more distinctly and authoritatively recognized in the New than the Pentateuch. It is referred to by Christ and the apostles as trustworthy and authoritative. It is quoted as divinely inspired. The laws and writings are appealed to, indeed, as those of Moses, but they are appealed to as being at the same time the laws and writings of God. In all the references to it and the quotations from it its declarations are treated as unquestionably true, trustworthy, divinely inspired, authoritative, proceeding indeed from Moses, but proceeding also from God. Thus was the Pentateuch regarded and treated by Christ, the apostles, and the writers of the New Testament. But the views given of it by the analytics are totally different, and are incompatible with its divine inspiration and authority. They claim that the Pentateuch, except possibly a few scraps of it, was not written by Moses, but was gotten up by a crowd of utterly unknown authors, compilers, redactors, and interpolators, who worked on original documents, combining, selecting, omitting, arranging, inserting, altering, and adding, each one according to his own judgment and taste, the result being a conglomerate patchwork, characterized by inaccuracy, contradiction, and error. To claim divine authorship, inspiration, and authority for such a production looks like an attempt to burlesque the doctrine of divine inspiration. Doubtless some relics of this old-fashioned doctrine still linger in the minds of many of the less advanced analytic critics. These will manage in some way, though at the expense of logic and self-consistency, to believe the Pentateuch to be in some sense a book from God. But even analysts of the evangelical class argue that the Pentateuch is too inaccurate and self-contradictory, abounds too much in legends and fictions, and is altogether too untrustworthy to have been written by Moses. Men who reason thus, and who have as much respect for the Almighty as for Moses, will be very likely to conclude that the Pentateuch is not to be attributed in any sense or in any degree to supernatural authorship; and they further will be likely to apply their idea of inspiration, or rather of non-inspiration, to all other parts of the Bible. Thus is evinced the utter incompatibility between the analytic view of the Pentateuch and any respectable doctrine of divine inspiration. In the meantime, the chiefs and leaders of the analytic school, who repudiate the doctrine of the divine inspiration of the Scriptures, can well afford to be silent in regard to their infidel views, expecting, and rightly expecting, that the expulsive power of the analytic criticism will in time do its perfect work in the minds of their disciples.

3. The analytic criticism discredits and dishonors nearly all the historical books of the Old Testament. The essence of history is *truthfulness*. Take this away and the history is destroyed. It is not enough that the historian be truthful as an individual. It is not enough that he desires and endeavors to tell the truth; he must actually do so. He must present facts,

and present them as they occurred. If, even unconsciously, he deals in fiction, legend, and falsehood, he forfeits the confidence and esteem of mankind. A book of legends and fictions may be in itself well enough. But a book which claims to be historical, and yet is made up largely of myths, tales, and doubtful narratives, does not command the respect of mankind. Now this is the character assigned by the analytic criticism to the Pentateuch. Divine inspiration is of course discarded or left out of view. The individual veracity of the historian counts for nothing. The narratives are constantly spoken of as traditions. Almost every narrative is declared to be made up of two or more stories which contradict one another. Legends and myths are said to constitute a considerable portion of the history. In short, the history embraced in the Pentateuch is declared by the analysts to be largely legendary, fictitious, and untrue, and therefore untrustworthy. Thus is treated not only the history embraced in the Pentateuch, but nearly the entire history from Adam to Ezra. Thus a large portion of the Old Testament is discredited and dishonored—nearly all of Genesis, Exodus, and Numbers, a part of Deuteronomy, all of Joshua, Judges, Samuel, Kings, and Chronicles. If mankind shall ever be taught to suspect, doubt, and disbelieve these historical books, it will be useless to insist on the inspiration and authority of the remaining portions of the Scriptures. One wonders what impression a critic who is not altogether an unbeliever expects to make on the minds of his fellow-men, and what outcome he expects from that impression, who maintains that the Pentateuchal history is so untrue and untrustworthy that it is incredible that Moses should be the author of it, and that the most of the succeeding Old Testament history is of like character. A phrase often in the mouths of such critics is that the doctrine of inspiration must be recast. They would more consistently say cast out. For if their theories and argumentation prevail, the doctrine of divine inspiration will be eliminated from the minds of men.

4. One of the conclusions involved in the analytic hypothesis is that we have in the Pentateuch one of the most stupendous and audacious falsifications known in literary history. We have already stated that the analysts, in maintaining their hypothesis of the post-Mosaic origin of the Levitical ritual, are under the logical necessity of denying the existence of the Mosaic tabernacle. According to the account given in Exodus, God gave

minute directions to Moses concerning the tabernacle—its size, form, covering, furniture, and the materials to be employed. Now, it is absurd to suppose that God would give minute directions concerning the tabernacle and altar, and concerning their furniture and instruments, including even the dishes, spoons, and bowls,[1] and no directions be given in regard to sacrifice and worship. Accordingly, in Exodus we have a record of directions for the consecration of Aaron and his sons[2] and the daily morning and evening sacrifice.[3] In Leviticus is given the code in full for the tabernacle service. The tabernacle and the altar without the code are meaningless. If we admit the existence of the tabernacle, we must admit also the service and the ritual. The leading and ablest men of the analytic school, denying as they do the ritual, find it necessary to deny the existence of the tabernacle also. Their hypothesis is that the Mosaic tabernacle is the projection of Solomon's temple back into the past by Jewish romancers. This implies that the Pentateuchal account of the Mosaic tabernacle is a pure falsification, and if so it is one of most stupendous proportions.

According to Exodus,[4] and Numbers[5] also, God showed to Moses in the mount a pattern of the tabernacle. In all this, according to the analytic hypothesis, there is not a word of truth. In Exodus we have the statement that God called the people to contribute materials for the construction of the tabernacle—blue, purple, scarlet, fine linen, goats' hair, rams' skins, badgers' skins, oil for the light, and many other articles. In another place we have an account of the way the people responded to this call, and the articles contributed by them are mentioned.[6] The analytic hypothesis declares this whole account to be untrue. Exodus relates that God instructed Moses in regard to the boards for the construction of the tabernacle—their number, length, breadth, tenons, and sockets; in regard to the candlestick—the number of its branches, bowls, and flowers; in regard to all the instruments of service, even to the tongs and snuff-dishes; in regard to the priestly garments for Aaron; in regard to the ark, the mercy-seat, the cherubim of glory, the altar, the table, and the bread of exposition. In regard to all these, minute directions were given. There is an account of the erection of the tabernacle on the day appointed, and of

[1] Ex. 37: 16.   [2] Ex. 29: 1-37.   [3] Ex. 29: 38-44.   [4] Ex. 25: 9, 40.
[5] Num. 8: 4.   [6] Ex. 25: 1-8; 35: 5-29.

the resting of the cloud upon it by day and the fire by night. In Numbers we have an account of the princes of Israel providing six wagons and twelve oxen for the transportation of the tabernacle and its furniture, and of the assignment of two wagons and four oxen to the sons of Gershon, and four wagons and eight oxen to the sons of Merari.[1] In the first and tenth chapters of Numbers we have directions in regard to the position of the tabernacle in the camp and on the march. But according to the analytic criticism all these accounts are purely fictitious. Assuming the account of the tabernacle itself to be a fabrication, it impliedly assumes that the pattern shown to Moses in the mount is also a fabrication; that the account of contributions of materials for the construction of the tabernacle is a fabrication; that the transportation of it by six wagons and twelve oxen is a fabrication; that the camping of the tribes around it is a fabrication; that the hovering of the cloud over it by day and of the fire by night is a fabrication; that this account, as a whole and in all its parts, is a fabrication.

We speak of this supposed falsification of Jewish history as stupendous. It is in advance, we think, of every other known in history in two respects—minuteness of detail, and extent and permanence of success. This gigantic fiction, as claimed by the leading analytics, spreads itself over nearly all the Old Testament history. It is set forth in Exodus; it is continued in Leviticus and Numbers; it appears in Deuteronomy; it runs through Joshua; it crops out frequently in Judges; it shows itself in Samuel; it is brought to view in Kings and Chronicles, and it is reproduced in the New Testament.[2] We do not mention this matter in order to point out the impossibility of the success of a historical falsification on so grand a scale, but to call attention to the legitimate effect of this hypothesis, if accepted as proved and true. In the judgment of logical and reflective minds, what claims can books which contain a huge falsification of history have to be considered in any sense the word of God, who loves the truth and hates a lie?

Some of the analysts may say that they accept the account of the Mosaic tabernacle in the wilderness and that we err in representing the analytic hypothesis as involving the rejection of it. To this we reply, (1) that we regard Voltaire, Colenso, Reuss, Kuenen, Graf, and Wellhausen as the best exponents of

---

[1] Num. 7: 3-9.   [2] Heb. 9: 1-10.

the analytic criticism, and the best judges of what is necessary to its logical defense; (2) to accept the historical account of the Mosaic tabernacle up to the record of the ritual and to reject that, is justified by no law either of logic or common sense; (3) to accept the ritual as of Mosaic origin is to punch a hole in the bottom of the analytic ship that will soon cause it to founder; (4) the lagging analytics may about as well go the whole figure with their leaders, and declare the whole account of the Mosaic tabernacle an enormous falsification, so far as views touching the Pentateuch and inspiration are concerned. The charge of small lying and small thieving effect reputation nearly as much as charges of larger criminality. God is not more disposed to make little liars or little thieves his special agents than big ones. If falsification is to be charged on any part of the Scriptures, it may as well be on a grand scale.

5. The doctrine of evolution as set forth and applied by the analysts to the Pentateuchal books is incompatible with the divine inspiration and authority of the Scriptures. We admit that there is a doctrine of scientific evolution that is consistent with theism, and that there are many Christian evolutionists. But evolution is merely a natural process, not creation. The evolutionist may believe that God created something, and that then the process of evolution began in that something. Evolution which accounts for the origin of things, such as the unscientific dogma of "spontaneous generation," is atheistic. Whatever is evolved existed previously, as the chick from the egg, and the germ from the seed. After the evolution, not a particle of matter exists that did not exist before. Hence evolution as accounting for the origin of things, that is, evolution out of nothing, is a contradiction and an absurdity. The only real evolution is not an absolute beginning, is not a creation, involves nothing supernatural, but is a development, by a perfectly natural process, of what previously existed.

If, then, the Pentateuchal laws and books are to be accounted for on the principle of evolution, they are merely human productions. In that case, the often-repeated formula, "God spake to Moses," is untrue; the account of the giving of the law on Mount Sinai, a fiction; the pattern of the tabernacle and its furniture, showed beforehand to Moses, a fabrication, and the whole Pentateuch the outcome of the Jewish intellect and imagination. The hypothesis of the origin of these books and laws by evolution is thus opposed to their origin by divine revelation or inspiration. And if the hypothesis of evolution is applied to the Pentateuch, it will in the end be applied to all other parts of the Bible. At present many of the analysts shrink from doing this. But some of these will get rid of their scruples and more fully carry out their views; and, at all events, their successors, being more fully delivered from former views and beliefs, will be more ready to carry the analytic premises to their legitimate conclusions. The divine inspiration and authority of the Pentateuchal laws and books are as fully recognized by Christ and the apostles as any other portion of the Scripture. This testimony is necessarily set aside and denied by those who maintain that the Pentateuch originated by evolution. How long will it be until such men will attempt to explode the doctrine of divine inspiration altogether? The Apostle Paul speaks of "Scripture given by inspiration of God"—theopneustic.[1] The Apostle Peter says, speaking of "the prophecy of the Scripture," that "holy men of God spake as they were moved by the Holy Ghost."[2] But since the testimony of Christ in regard to the authorship of the Pentateuch is counted for nothing by the analysts, that of Paul and Peter is not likely to deter them from finally concluding that the entire Scriptures, as well as the Pentateuch, were given, not by inspiration, but by evolution.

6. The practical treatment which the Pentateuch and other parts of the Bible receive at the hands of the analysts, not only proceeds from unbelief and irreverence in the writers, but inevitably tends to produce the same unbelief and irreverence in others. We speak now, not of all the analytic school, but of the *leaders*. These ignore the divine element in the sacred Scriptures. With them divine inspiration counts for nothing. They are mostly silent in regard to it. There is more said in the writings of Voltaire about the inspiration of the Scriptures than by all the other analytic leaders together. The argument from silence is conclusive in some cases, and this is one of them. The silence is evidently studied and intentional. Clearly, these men reject the supernatural altogether, and their own doubts, unbelief, and irreverence they are more than willing to infuse into the minds of their readers. They treat the Pentateuch and other books of the Bible as merely human, and as fallible and erroneous. Nor do they restrict themselves to charges of slight

[1] II. Tim. 3 : 16.   [2] II. Pet. 1 : 20, 21.

degrees of fallibility and erroneousness. They go much farther than the rejection of verbal and plenary inspiration. They impeach the historical character of the Pentateuch and of many other books of the Bible. They declare the historical books — more than half the Bible—to be untrustworthy. They virtually teach that these books are more contradictory, inaccurate, erroneous, and untrustworthy than Herodotus and Livy. They do not hesitate to set aside as untrue any passage that contravenes their theories. They dispose of every such passage as a redaction, an interpolation, or a false reading, or by endeavoring in some other way to throw doubt or suspicion on the integrity of the text. The practical effect of such a course is to produce uncertainty, suspicion, and skepticism. Even if the reader retains belief in the Scriptures as given by divine inspiration, he is taught that they are patched over with interpolations, false readings, contradictory statements, and other errors. Thus the reader who accepts the guidance of the analytic critics must be in doubt as to whether he can find the word of the Lord anywhere in the Bible. Thus, too, the analytic school, as represented by its most distinguished champions, is doing more to paralyze Christian faith than did the outspoken infidels of the last century. We have, however, neither doubt nor fear as to the final result. We have full faith in the Bible as the inspired word of God, and an assured confidence that, through the overruling providence of God, all assaults upon it by concealed as well as by avowed enemies, together with the errors of mistaken friends, will in the end contribute to the vindication of its divine inspiration and authority.

INDEX OF SUBJECTS

AARON, 170, 171.
Aben-Ezra, 13.
Abraham, 12, 149, 158.
Abydenus, 156.
Acquaintance with Egypt, 136.
Adaptation, 119.
Allotopisms, claimed, 57.
Amos, 227.
Anachronisms, claimed, 35.
Analytic criticism founded by Voltaire, 18-24.
Analytic views, 9.
Ants, intelligence of, 148.
Aramaisms, 130, 131, 219.
Argumentum e silentio, 19.
Ark, 155, 156.
Arming of the Israelites, 101.
Asa's burial, 139.
Assyrian sculptures, 154.
Astruc, 13, 14, 103.
Asurbanipal, 150.
Atonement, Day of, 246, 247.
Authors, plurality of, 103.

BABEL, 156, 157.
Babylonian tradition, 150, 154.
Bacon, B. W., 9, 10.
Bacon, Lord, 108.
Bancroft, 23.
Bashan, 159.
Beer-sheba, origin of the name, 66.
Berosus, 155.
"Beyond Jordan," 57-60.
Bleek, 27, 38.
Bolingbroke, 16.
Book of the wars of the Lord, 18, 43-45.
Book found in Josiah's time, 210.
Brick-making, 140.
Briggs, Professor, 31, 227.
Brugsch-Bey, 38, 159, 162, 193.

Burckhardt, 159.
Burke, 109.
Burns, 110.
Byron, 109.

CÆSAR, Julius, 31.
Carlyle, quoted, 95.
Cattle and sheep in the wilderness, 89.
Cave, his hypothesis, 104, 116.
Centralization of worship, 230.
Chaldean account of Genesis, 154-156.
Chedorlaomer, 157.
Cheyne, referred to, 21, 111, 130.
  on Isaiah, 198, 225.
  on style, 111.
"Childe Harold," 109, 112.
Christ and the apostles, testimony of, 248.
Chronicles, books of, 209.
Chronology, 164.
Cities and places in Egypt, 140-142.
Cities and places in Palestine, 141, 142.
Clericus (Le Clerc), 13, 15.
Colenso, 73, 79, 80, 91, 100.
Coleridge, 109.
Consequences, 257.
Contradictions, claimed, 63.
Cory's "Ancient Fragments," 155, 157.
"Cosmos," 176.
Cowper, 31, 109.
Creation, account of, 63, 143.
Cromwell, 95.
Cyrus, 20.

"D," 9, 10, 244.
Dan, 18, 39.
Daniel, 20.
Darwinism, 146-148, 153.
David as Psalmist, 221-224.
Decalogue, 245.

Deluge, 154-156, 164.
De Wette, 13, 14.
"Dictionnaire Philosophique," 16, 43, 49, 55, 57, 79.
Difficulties, claimed, 72.
Dinah, 74, 76.
Diodorus Siculus, 163, 175.
Discussion, history of, 13.
Diseases of Egypt, 139.
Divine names in Genesis, 113.
Documentary hypothesis, 9, 103.
Driver, referred to, 21, 130, 219.
    his list of phrases, 111, 112.
    his egotism, 34.
"Dt," 34.

"E," 9, 10, 108, 111, 115, 191.
Ebedtob, 158.
Edda, 154.
Eden, 153.
Edom, kings of, 39-42.
Egotism of Moses, 31-34.
Egypt, acquaintance with, 136.
Egyptian words and names, 193.
Embalming, 139, 175.
Errors in the Pentateuch, 12, 15.
Esau's wives, 69.
Etham, 132, 141, 175.
Eusebius, 156.
Evolution, 9, 146-149, 206, 227.
Exactness, 161.
External evidence, 197.
Ezekiel, 30.
Ezra, 11, 76.
Ezra and Nehemiah, books of, 216-220.

FALL of man, 153.
First-born, number of, 85.

GARFIELD, 66.
Genealogies, 72-79.
George, 13.
Gesenius, 221, 224, 241.
Gibeonites, 231.
Goshen, 140.
Graf, 99, 197, 211.
Green, Professor W. H., 101, 219.

HAECKEL, 143, 147, 148, 153.
Har-el, 43.
Hebron, 37, 38, 141.
Hengstenberg, 175.

Henriade, 109.
Herodotus, 137, 162, 163, 175.
Historical integrity of the Pentateuch, 152.
History, argument from, 229.
History of the discussion, 13.
Hobbes, 13.
Hosea, 225.
Humboldt, 176.
Hume, 31.
Hyksos, 158.

IMAGININGS, arguments from, 93.
Improprieties, claimed, 30.
Increase in Egypt, 79-85.
Interest or usury laws, 126.
Internal evidence, 119.
Isaiah, 30, 225.

"J," 9, 10, 105, 107, 111, 115, 191.
Jacob-el, 158.
Jasher, Book of, 45.
"JE," 34, 112, 113, 244.
Jebel Musa—Sinai, 177.
Jefferson and Washington, 34.
Jeremiah, 30, 130.
Jethro, 12, 69.
Joel, 228.
John, 30.
Joseph-el, 158.
Josephus, 30, 39, 83, 101.
Joshua presupposes Pentateuch, 205-207.
Journalistic form and theory, 132.
Judges, Book of, 208.

KAUTZSCH-SOCIN, 34, 81, 108, 182, 244.
Kenosis, 251.
Kenrick, 162, 164.
Kirk White, 31.
Ktesias, 163.
Kuenen, 47, 49, 51, 63, 65, 81, 111, 121, 124, 134, 178, 199, 204, 226.
    his egotism, 34.

LAMECH, 164, 165.
Landmarks, law of, 56, 185.
Layard, 154.
Legislation, argument from, 178.
Lemuria, 153.
Lenormant, 153, 154.
Leprosy, law of, 127, 185.
Lepsius, 90, 164, 177.

INDEX OF SUBJECTS

Letters of some Jews to Voltaire, 22.
Leviticism — Reuss, 206.
Lincoln, 66.
Linguistic argument, 108-113.
Lubbock, Sir John, 148.

MACAULAY, 108.
Manna, cessation of, 45-47.
Marah, 132, 133.
Maspero, 164.
Matthew, 30.
Max Müller, 147.
Megiddo, 38.
Melchizedec, 158.
Menephtah II., 158.
Methuselah, 149.
Midianites were Ishmaelites, 67.
Migdol, 132, 133, 141.
Milton, 109.
Miracles, 92, 161.
Mivart, 147.
Mixed multitude, 159.
Moriah, 42.
Moses, 11, 12, 32, 40, 96, 103, 129, 132, 133, 171, 193.
Mt. Serbal, 90.

NAVILLE, 159, 164, 176.
Negeb, 60, 62.
Nehemiah, 30.
Nehemiah and Ezra, books of, 216-220.

OBJECTIONS, 27.
Og, 18, 48.
On, 140.

"P," 9, 10, 244.
Paine, Thomas, 30, 39, 49, 218.
Palestine, 141, 142.
Palmer, Professor, 90, 176, 177.
Pandora, 154.
Passover, 126, 243.
Paul, 33, 83.
"PC," 134.
Peyrere, 13.
Pharaoh of the exodus, 158.
Pharaoh of the oppression, 158.
Pi-hahiroth, 175, 176.
Pithom, 140, 158, 159, 175, 176.
Place of man's origin, 152, 153.
Plenary inspiration, 12, 31.
Plurality of authors, 103.

Plutarch, 163.
Points in dispute, 9.
Preliminary, 9.
Presupposition, 123.
Primitive condition of man, 153.
Prophecies, 225.
Proverbs, 20, 190.
Pucelle, 109.

"Q," 9.

"R," 136.
Rameses, 132, 140, 193.
Rameses II., 38, 158.
Rameses III., 38.
"Religious Encyclopedia," 219.
Renan, 33.
Rephidim, 176.
Reuss, 13, 36, 39, 40, 41, 43, 45, 47, 49, 50, 53, 54, 63, 65, 67, 68, 70, 72, 81, 93, 97, 98, 133, 199, 204, 211.
Ritter, 90.
Robinson, Dr., 159.

SABBATH, institution of, 244, 245.
Sale of Joseph, 67.
Samuel, books of, 208.
Sayce, 38, 43, 60, 61, 157, 160, 163, 177.
Scientific accuracy, 143.
Scott, Sir Walter, 109.
Self-commendation by Moses, 31.
Septuagint, 80, 82, 165, 174, 241.
Serah, 74, 76.
Shaving in Egypt, 137.
Shiloh, 232, 234-236, 239.
Silence, argument from, 189, 190, 220.
Sinai, 90, 176.
Sixty cities, 18.
Smith, George, 150, 155.
Smith, Professor W. R., 30, 31, 130, 176, 226.
Sojourn in Egypt, 79-84, 169.
Spinoza, 13.
Spontaneous generation, 146, 147.
Strabo, 163.
Style, 108-113, 129, 218, 219.
Succoth, 132, 140, 141, 159.

TABERNACLE, 14, 99, 241, 243.
Tables of stone, 97.
Tabular view of the analytic hypothesis, 9.
Terah, 80, 167.

Third person employed by Moses, 30, 31.
Thothmes III., 43.
Thucydides, 31.
Traditional view, 11.
"Traité sur Tolérance," 15, 16, 18.

UNITY of the human race, 151.
Unity of worship, 230-247.
"Unto this day," 49-53.
Ur of the Chaldees, 149, 158.

VATKE, 13.
Virchow, 147.
Vitringa, 103.
Voltaire, 13, 14-23, 109, 211.

WALLACE, ALFRED R., 147.
Wars of the Lord, book of, 18, 43, 45.
Washington, 34.
Webster, 33.
Wellhausen, 13, 101, 102, 111, 134, 209, 210, 216, 226, 239.
Wilkinson, 61, 137, 162, 164.

XENOPHON, 31.
Xisuthrus, 155.

YAM for west, 60-62.

ZEND-AVESTA, 154.
Zipporah, 95, 97.

SCRIPTURE INDEX

GENESIS—	Page
1 : 1-31	113
2 : 2, 3	246
2 : 7	148
2 : 7-25	64
2 : 8, 14	153
3 : 15	250
5 : 32	166
7 : 1-8 : 7	105, 106
7 : 4, 10	245
7 : 9, 17	114
7 : 11	165, 166
8 : 6	96
8 : 10, 12	245
9 : 28, 29	166
10 : 21	167
11 : 3	157
11 : 10-32	166
11 : 26	167
11 : 31	65
11 : 32	167
12 : 4	167, 168
12 : 6	35, 141
12 : 8	141
13 : 3	141
13 : 7	35
13 : 18	36, 141
14 : 14	39
14 : 18	158
15 : 1	114
15 : 13	79, 83
15 : 16	79, 82
16 : 3	168
16 : 16	168
17 : 24, 25	168
20 : 1-18	65, 187
21 : 5	168
21 : 14	93
21 : 25-31	66
22 : 2	42
22 : 14	43

GENESIS, Continued—	Page
23 : 2	37, 38, 141
23 : 4	78
23 : 19	37
24 : 4	78
25 : 17	167, 168
25 : 20	168
26 : 15, 18	66, 67
26 : 34	69
28 : 9	69
32 : 3	70
32 : 28	68
35 : 10	68
35 : 16, 26	70
35 : 16-19	69
35 : 21-26	70
35 : 27	37, 141
36 : 24	90
36 : 31	39, 42
36 : 39	41
37 : 13-35	107
37 : 18-36	67
39 : 1	67
40 : 15	53, 68
40 : 16	175
41 : 2-6	175
41 : 14	137
41 : 56 – 42 : 38	107
42 : 1-8	108
42 : 27	96
44 : 1	99
45 : 4	68
46 : 1-3	83
46 : 8	74, 76, 173
46 : 8-27	173
46 : 15	74, 76, 173
46 : 17, 18	74
46 : 21	75
46 : 26	72
46 : 27	75, 76, 173, 174
46 : 28, 29	140

GENESIS, Continued—

	Page
49 : 10	250
49 : 18	114
50 : 2	139
50 : 3	175
50 : 26	139, 175

EXODUS—

	Page
1 : 8	158
1 : 11	158
2 : 1, 2	95
2 : 15-22	96
3 : 1	90
3 : 6	249
4 : 25	96
5 : 6-19	140, 158
6 : 16-18	76, 82, 83
7 : 7	171
9 : 18-26	137
9 : 25	137
9 : 28, 29	138
12 : 1-28	125
12 : 2, 42	170
12 : 37	79, 140
12 : 38	79, 89
12 : 40	80
13 : 1-16	88
13 : 18	100
13 : 20	141
14 : 2	141
14 : 21	92
14 : 30	101
15 : 3	43
15 : 21	44
15 : 23-25	91
15 : 26	140
16 : 35	45, 46
17 : 1-6	91
17 : 3	89
17 : 6	92
17 : 14	44, 129, 133
17 : 8-13	44, 101
18 : 3	94
20 : 1 – 23 : 33	129
20 : 24	178, 186, 230
21 : 13, 14	125
22 : 25	126, 223
23 : 14-17	179
24 : 3, 4	133
25 : 9, 40	242, 262
32 : 15	98
33 : 7	100
34 : 1	102

EXODUS, Continued—

	Page
34 : 3	90
34 : 18-24	179
40 : 17-38	243

LEVITICUS—

	Page
13, 14	127
13 : 2	127
14 : 34	185, 186
14 : 33-53	184
16 : 20-22	250
17 : 3, 4	126
17 : 3-9	186
19 : 23	186
23 : 4-8	125, 244
25 : 2	186
25 : 35-37	126
27 : 5, 6	89

NUMBERS—

	Page
1 : 1	88, 170
1 : 46	86
3 : 40	87
3 : 43	85, 87, 88
3 : 46, 47	89
7 : 3-9	263
8 : 10-16	180
9 : 1	126, 170
10 : 11	170
12 : 1	69, 97
13 : 22	37, 141
20 : 8	92
21 : 1-3	44
21 : 14	43
21 : 16	92
21 : 21-31	44
21 : 33-35	44, 48
24 : 17	250
31 : 1-47	44
32 : 19	59
32 : 41	55
33 : 1-49	132
34 : 15	59
35 : 11-29	125
35 : 30	127

DEUTERONOMY—

	Page
1 : 1	57, 58
1 : 3	170
1 : 5	58
2 : 12	47
3 : 8	58, 59
3 : 14	51, 55

DEUTERONOMY, Continued—

Reference	Page
3 : 20	58, 59
3 : 25	58
4 : 41, 46, 47, 49	58
4 : 41-43	125
7 : 2, 3	208
7 : 15	139
10 : 2, 4	102
10 : 8	51
11 : 10, 11	138
11 : 30	58
12 : 5	186, 236, 239
16 : 1-8	126, 215, 244
16 : 16	180
17 : 1-13	189
17 : 6, 7	127
17 : 14	186
18 : 18	250
19 : 1-13	125
19 : 14	185
23 : 19, 20	126, 223
24 : 7	68
24 : 8	127
28 : 27	139
28 : 58	214
28 : 60	139
29 : 21	214
30 : 10	214
31 : 9	133
31 : 19	133
31 : 24-26	133, 214
33 : 4, 5	40, 222
34 : 6	51

JOSHUA—

Reference	Page
1 : 1, 2	207
1 : 7, 8	205
1 : 15	59
3 : 3	205
4 : 9	200
5 : 1	59, 203
5 : 2-9	231
5 : 10	231, 244
5 : 12	45
6 : 13	206
6 : 25	201
7 : 6	231
7 : 26	200
8 : 28	198
8 : 31, 35	205, 231
8 : 32, 34	205
9 : 1	59, 60
9 : 1-27	60

JOSHUA, Continued—

Reference	Page
9 : 27	201
10 : 13	45
12 : 1, 7	59
14 : 15	37
15 : 63	199
16 : 10	198
18 : 1	205, 232, 234
18 : 7	59
18 : 6, 8, 10	232
19 : 51	232
20 : 8	59
22 : 7	59
22 : 9-34	232
22 : 29	207, 232, 237
23 : 6	205
24 : 14, 23	233
24 : 31	203, 233

JUDGES—

Reference	Page
2 : 1-5	236
2 : 2	208
2 : 7-11	203
2 : 10-12	233
2 : 16-19	233
3 : 3, 5	36
3 : 6	208
6 : 11-23	237
6 : 25-32	237
8 : 2	67
9 : 6, 22	40
10 : 3, 4	55
13 : 1-23	208, 237
14 : 3	208
17 : 6	234
18 : 1	234
18 : 31	234, 235
19 : 18	208, 235
20 : 27, 28	235

I. SAMUEL—

Reference	Page
1 : 1-3	235
1 : 3, 9, 11, 25	208
2 : 15, 27-29	208
7 : 3	238
20 : 5, 18	208
21 : 1-6	238
22 : 9-19	238
27 : 7	51
30 : 11-20	188

II. SAMUEL—

Reference	Page
1 : 17-27	45

II. SAMUEL, Continued—

5 : 6-9	199, 200
6 : 1-18	238
15 : 24-29	238
23 : 1	221

I. KINGS—

4 : 2-6	240
8 : 1-6	240
9 : 16, 17	198

II. KINGS—

14 : 5, 6	210
22 : 8-13	211, 212, 214
23 : 3	215
23 : 10	215

I. CHRONICLES—

7 : 6-12	75
7 : 22-27	76, 82
11 : 4-8	199, 200
18 : 17	241
22 : 13	210
23 : 27	182
24 : 4	77

II. CHRONICLES—

2 : 4	246
5 : 10	210
16 : 14	139
17 : 7-9	210
29 : 30	221
33 : 8	210
34 : 14-19	211
35 : 1-19	215
35 : 6, 12	213

EZRA—

2 : 28	198
7 : 3	76
7 : 6	216

NEHEMIAH—

5 : 14-19	33
7 : 32	198
8 : 1, 2	216
11 : 31	198

PSALMS—

15	223
18	223
18 : 22	223
19	223

PSALMS, Continued—

40	223
51	223
78	221
78 : 5	222
78 : 60	236
105	222
105 : 45	222
106	222

ISAIAH—

1 : 11-15	225
1 : 15	225
10 : 28	198
57 : 6	225
58 : 3-7	225

JEREMIAH—

10 : 11	130

DANIEL—

9 : 23	32
10 : 11	32

HOSEA—

4 : 6	225
5 : 10	225
8 : 11	225
8 : 12	226
9 : 4	226
11 : 8	226
12 : 3-5	226
12 : 12	226

JOEL—

1 : 9, 13	228
2 : 17	228

AMOS—

2 : 10	227
2 : 11, 12	227
4 : 4, 5	227
5 : 21, 22	228

MATTHEW—

1 : 1	119
1 : 8	77
1 : 11	77
4 : 1	254
5 : 18	258
8 : 4	248
12 : 13	92
14 : 15	90

SCRIPTURE INDEX

MARK—
	Page
7 : 10	248
10 : 2-5	248
12 : 26	249
13 : 11	254
13 : 32	251

LUKE—
2 : 22	251
3 : 22	254
4 : 1	254
16 : 17	258
16 : 29, 31	250
24 : 44	249, 250, 253

JOHN—
1 : 17	250
1 : 45	250
1 : 48, 49	252
3 : 34	254
4 : 29	252
5 : 45-47	249
6 : 10	90
7 : 15	252
7 : 22, 23	249
8 : 28	255
10 : 35	258
11 : 42	255
12 : 49, 50	255
14 : 10	255
14 : 26	254
16 : 13	254
21 : 17	252

ACTS—
	Page
2 : 4	254
7 : 6	80
7 : 14	173
16 : 10	203
27 : 9	247
28 : 23	251

ROMANS—
10 : 5	251

I. CORINTHIANS—
9 : 9	251
11 : 8, 9	121
15 : 10	33

II. CORINTHIANS—
3 : 15	251

GALATIANS—
3 : 17	83

PHILIPPIANS—
2 : 7	251

II. TIMOTHY—
3 : 16	265

HEBREWS—
7 : 9, 10	77
9 : 1-10	263
9 : 7	247
10 : 28	251

www.ingramcontent.com/pod-product-compliance
Lightning Source LLC
Chambersburg PA
CBHW031940230426

43672CB00010B/1997